D. H. Lawrence

D. H. Lawrence

Self and Sexuality

James C. Cowan

The Ohio State University Press
Columbus

Library of Congress Cataloging-in-Publication Data

Cowan, James C., 1927–
    D. H. Lawrence : self and sexuality / James Cowan.
        p. cm.
Includes bibliographical references (p.) and index.
    ISBN 0-8142-0914-9 (cloth: alk. paper)
1. Lawrence, D. H. (David Herbert), 1885–1930—Knowledge—Psychology.
2. Psychoanalysis and literature—England—History—20th century. 3. Psychological fiction, English—History and criticism. 4. Sex (Psychology) in
literature. 5. Psychology in literature. 6. Self in literature. 7. Sex in literature.
I. Title.

        PR6023.A93 Z62319 2002
        823'.912—DC21

                                        2002007614

Cover design by Melissa Ryan
Type set in Adobe Garamond
Printed by Thomson-Shore Inc.

The paper used in this publication meets the minimum requirements of the
American National Standard for Information Sciences—Permanence of
Paper for Printed Library Materials. ANSI Z39.48-1992.

                9   8   7   6   5   4   3   2   1

To my wife Judy
for the best years of our life
and for the years to come

Contents

Acknowledgments

I am grateful to Keith Cushman, Howard Harper, Dennis Jackson, Judith Ruderman, and Michael Squires for many years of mutual affirmation in Lawrence studies. I am indebted to two friends, David Werman, M.D., a psychoanalyst, and the late Philip M. Griffith, a professor of English literature, for their helpful comments on various sections of the manuscript as it was being written; and to Barbara Ann Schapiro and Elizabeth Fox for their cogent critiques of the manuscript.

I want to acknowledge also the benefit of my four years as an academic candidate in the University of North Carolina–Duke University Psychoanalytic Education Program, a training institute of the American Psychoanalytic Association. I am indebted to the psychoanalysts who served as instructors in this program. In particular, I wish to thank David F. Freeman, M.D., who at that time was director of the institute and with whom I was privileged to work. His wise knowledge of psychoanalysis, his empathy, and his generous humanity were invariably helpful to me. The greatest influence on my thinking and my personal understanding of the critical issues that emerge in this book is that of my wife, Judith R. Cowan, M.D., a psychiatrist, who after more than four decades of marriage still makes a place in our home for D. H. Lawrence.

Finally, I wish to thank Gerald Pollinger of Laurence Pollinger, Ltd. and the Estate of Mrs. Frieda Lawrence Ravagli for permission to quote from the works of D. H. Lawrence in the editions cited. I also acknowledge the editors and publishers of the following publications for permission to reprint in revised form work of mine that appeared elsewhere in an earlier form: Borealis Press for material in chapter 2 from *D. H. Lawrence: The Cosmic Adventure*, ed. Lawrence Gamache with Phyllis Sternberg Parrakis; *Annual of Psychoanalysis*, for material in chapter 4; *Journal of the History of Sexuality*, for material in chapter 6; *Mosaic*, for material in chapter 7; and *Literature and Medicine*, for material in chapter 9.

Introduction

In this study, I explore some of the psychoanalytic and human sexuality issues in D. H. Lawrence and his work—psychoanalytically from the perspective of the self psychology of Heinz Kohut as well as the object relational theories of Stephen A. Mitchell and D. W. Winnicott; and in sexual terms, from the perspective of authoritative research in human sexuality by William H. Masters and Virginia E. Johnson; by Alfred C. Kinsey, Wardell B. Pomeroy, and Clyde E. Martin; by more recent medical researchers such as psychiatrist Helen Kaplan; by urologists Hunter Wessells, Tom F. Lue, Culley C. Carson III, and their associates; by nurse researcher Beverly Whipple and psychologist Barry Komisaruk; and by psychologist Joseph Sparling.

The first chapter, "Lawrence Criticism and the Four Psychologies of Psychoanalysis," surveys previous psychoanalytic criticism of Lawrence, which parallels the history of psychoanalysis from its beginnings in an early Freudian psychology of instinctive drives and oedipal conflicts, followed by the ego psychology of Anna Freud, Heinz Hartmann, and Erik Erikson, and then by the object relations theories of W. R. D. Fairbairn, Melanie Klein, D. W. Winnicott, and others. The widening scope of mainstream psychoanalysis today includes a psychology of the self rooted in the preoedipal experience of very early childhood, elaborated in Margaret Mahler's concept of separation-individuation, Michael Balint's concept of the "basic fault," and Heinz Kohut's self psychology, as well as relational concepts of Stephen A. Mitchell, Jessica Benjamin, and others. It is this widening scope of psychoanalysis, especially as represented in Mahler, Kohut, and Winnicott that I will turn to in an effort to further our understanding of Lawrence's personal psychological issues.

Chapter 2, "The Two Analyses of D. H. Lawrence," focusing on *Sons and Lovers,* examines the major issues set forth in traditional Freudian studies of Lawrence and his work, then proposes a reanalysis of this material in terms of Kohut's psychoanalytic self psychology. It points out the differences in theoretical approach and the concurrent changes in emphasis and therapeutic considerations.

Chapter 3, "Lawrence and the Sensitive Man," discusses Lawrence's construct of the "sensitive man" in light of his own narcissistic injuries in early childhood. In an early manuscript of the fourth part of "The Crown," Lawrence postulates a basic split in masculine consciousness between "coarseness" and "sensitivity," neither of which promotes wholeness and integration of the self. From this split springs Lawrence's fictional and personal efforts to find and describe those "transmuting experiences" through which men can be both "coarse" and "sensitive," and women both "coarse" and "spiritual." Lawrence recognized in himself the "wound to the soul" that had left a painful deficit. His next works explore the quest for a male figure, first a blood brother, then a nurturant father, his relationship with whom could heal the wound.

Chapter 4, "*Blutbrüderschaft* and Self Psychology in *Women in Love,*" is a study of how these themes form an important structural element in the attempt, through *Blutbrüderschaft,* to resolve these masculine tensions. *Women in Love,* one of Lawrence's greatest novels—rich in symbolism and complexity of character—explores further development of both male-male and male-female relationships. Although Birkin and Ursula experience renewal in their sexuality through an experience of "bestiality," at the end of the novel Birkin continues to long, in addition, for "another kind of love," a relationship with an ideal male whom he can establish irrevocable blood brotherhood. These themes are considered from the perspective of Kohut's clinical application of his concepts of the psychology of the self.

Chapter 5, "Lawrence, Idealization, and Masculine Identity," relates Lawrence's search for an idealizable man to the deficit in his own intrapsychic structure, or in his words, the "wound to the soul." Idealization is discussed first as one of the two major poles of developmental self structure in Kohut's self psychology, then in terms of the cost of idealization in subsequent relationships according to Stephen A. Mitchell's relational theory. Turning to the "leadership novels," Lawrence considers what might happen if the ideal man could attain political leadership and engender a society that would respond to his ideals and values. Could the protagonist find in such a figure the idealizable and nurturant male he seeks, and could this figure's leadership engender the healing society? In two of these novels the male protagonist is in search of a nurturant man, while the leader wants submission from the seeker and other potential followers. This common feature raises the critical question of the "cost of idealization" in the seemingly arbitrary quality of the leader's power.

In the next three chapters, I turn to a consideration of several problematic issues of human sexuality in Lawrence's work. Chapter 6, "Lawrence's Sexual Fallacies," discusses Lawrence's primarily culture-based issues of male dominance, male sexual performance, and phallic veneration and penis size. Issues that are predominantly personal to Lawrence, such as his early phobic response to female pubic hair and the related myth of the vagina dentata are also considered. Finally, issues that are both culturally derived and personal to Lawrence, including the question of female vaginal orgasm versus clitoral orgasm, and Lawrence's insistence on the importance of mutual or simultaneous coital orgasms are discussed.

Chapter 7, "Lawrence, Freud, and Masturbation," focuses on Lawrence's acceptance of the culturally based fallacy, endorsed by Freud and others in the early psychoanalytic movement and promulgated in their published works, that masturbation is medically and psychologically harmful, the prevailing attitude of their time that is not confirmed or upheld by medical knowledge of the present day. I also employ Moses Laufer's psychoanalytically significant concept of the central masturbation fantasy.

Following this fallacious view of masturbation as a medically and psychologically dangerous practice, in chapter 8, "'The Rocking-Horse Winner' as Self-State Tale," first I survey the extensive psychoanalytic criticism of the story, which has typically interpreted little Paul's rocking frenziedly to a climax as a symbolic equivalent of masturbation. I then propose a new reading of the story in terms of Kohut's self psychology, emphasizing the dissolution of the self and its concurrent overwhelming anxiety as the causes of little Paul's death.

During the writing of the later works discussed here, it had become progressively difficult for Lawrence to deny his failing health and the reality and effects of his tuberculosis. In chapter 9, "The Fall of John Thomas," after briefly presenting a medical perspective on Lawrence's loss of sexual function as his health progressively deteriorated in the last four years of his life, I turn to a discussion of the contrasting idealized and negative presentations of the gamekeeper Oliver Mellors and his paraplegic employer, Sir Clifford Chatterley, in *Lady Chatterley's Lover,* and to a consideration of the theme of loss in the "loss of desire" sequence in *Pansies* in the context of Lawrence's erectile dysfunction as his illness advanced at the time he was writing these works.

In the concluding chapter, "Lawrence, the True Self, and Dying," I follow Lawrence as he moves beyond his concern with loss of sexual function to his poetic and psychological strategies in *Last Poems* for creatively confronting his knowledge of his impending death and incorporating it with integrity. Some of these poems, written in spiritual preparation for his dying, are among the finest poetic meditations in modern literature. In discussing the process in which Lawrence was engaged, I draw on D. W. Winnicott's concept of the true and false self and Erik Erikson's definition of ego integrity as the task of the last stage of life.

~

My own interests in psychoanalysis and human sexuality are not new. For most of my professional life, I have been a professor and scholar of modern English literature, with a special interest in D. H. Lawrence. My earliest criticism often employed a psychological reading of the literary subject. Several experiences have also significantly shaped the convergence of a medicine and literature perspective and the psychoanalytic view of Lawrence and his work presented here.

Some years ago, I was a member of a stimulating dialogue group convened to explore the relationships between literature and medicine. Chaired by Joanne Trautmann, the nine members of our group—including physicians, poets, other creative writers, and teachers of literature—met for two years under the auspices of the Institute for Human Values in Medicine with support from the National Endowment for the Humanities. Subsequently, I taught a course for medical students on literature and medicine, organized around the tasks of eight stages of life as presented in Erik Erikson's psychoanalytic theory of ego development throughout life, in his *Identity and the Life Cycle,* paired with corresponding works of literature illustrative of each stage of life. If literature can give to medicine a humanities perspective, medicine can contribute to literary criticism a view of health and informed medical criteria in an attempt to enlarge our understanding of the human condition.

Subsequently I was admitted as an academic candidate in the University of North Carolina–Duke University Psychoanalytic Education Program, a training institute of the American Psychoanalytic Association. The curriculum consists of four years of seminars in psychoanalysis, with two seminars running concurrently. Candidates in the clinical track, including psychiatrists, psychologists, and social workers, undergo personal training analyses and work under supervision with patients in psychoanalysis. After completing extensive requirements in clinical psychoanalytic practice, writing a substantial, and acceptable, paper derived from original research, and performing satisfactorily on an oral examination, a clinician could be graduated and certified as a psychoanalyst by the American Psychoanalytic Association. As an academic candidate, not in the clinical track, I wrote several papers and, after completing the four-year program, received a certificate qualifying me as an Academic Associate in Psychoanalysis. In its original form, my paper "The Two Analyses of D. H. Lawrence" was presented at a program of the North Carolina Psychoanalytic Society. I was pleased that, in preparation, a number of those attending had read, or reread, *Sons and Lovers.*

Although I have never thought of my literary subjects as "patients" or "analysands," I am engaged in a critical method that employs psychoanalytic principles in an effort to understand a modern writer and his work. This method may be designated generally as a form of applied psychoanalysis. As Charles M. T. Hanly points out, "The writer is conscious neither of some of his or her ideas (fantasies) nor of their influence upon the writing." "Psycho-analytic interpretation, in applied as in clinical work, requires that what is unconscious be rendered conscious," Hanly says. "Thus, in applied psycho-analysis one seeks to construct interpretations of meanings that ordinarily remain unconscious or preconscious but are substantiated by thematic and formal elements in the work itself that are conscious." Unlike the analyst in clinical psychoanalysis, the critic in psychoanalytic literary criticism has nei-ther the free associations nor the dreams of the author in response to the ana-lytic process as means of uncovering unconscious material, though letters and other personal materials may afford partial access to the author's inner world. Although the analysand's transference in clinical psychoanalysis is not paral-leled by the writer's comparable transference in applied psychoanalysis, the psychoanalytic critic, like the analyst, has his or her own preconscious responses to the individual who is the subject of analysis. These responses—countertransferences, as it were—to both the author and his work, if rigor-ously analyzed, may provide valuable clues to the less conscious aspects of the writer's communications in the text. In both applied and clinical psycho-analysis, one's effort is to steer a course, "as recommended by Freud, between the Scylla of attributing too much to the unconscious and the Charybdis of attributing too little to it."[1]

∼

Why should a scholar originally schooled in the "New Criticism" of Cleanth Brooks and other distinguished critics of his time in the methods of *explica-tion de texte* even have an interest in understanding D. H. Lawrence's personal psychological issues or the status and validity of his views on human sexual-ity? I am not sure that I can identify all of the reasons for my own compelling interest in Lawrence in these terms. I do recall that on my first reading of *Sons and Lovers,* I thought, mistakenly, that the novel was entirely oedipal. I felt that Lawrence had plunged me into reliving with insight my own early oedi-pal issues in the context of trying to deal with the constant tumescent urge of young manhood and my concern to resolve internalized social and religious prohibitions in order to express this urge in adult sexuality. Lawrence, of course, had his own sexual concerns, not necessarily identical with mine, though from what I have known of other men, I think that male sexual con-cerns are fairly universal. Lawrence's literary work emerges from the matrix of his personal psychological experience, including his psychosexual experience.

That alone is reason enough to make an effort to understand him in these terms. From that source comes the sensitive man, attempting to establish masculine identity by means of blood brotherhood and idealization; the sexual liberator who, though not always able to transcend the sexual misconceptions of his culture, continued the effort to make sex available for literature, and literature available for the treatment of sex; the eloquent voice for the central significance and richness of human sexuality; and the self striving to define and to live out the true self with integrity.

CHAPTER I

Lawrence Criticism and the Four Psychologies of Psychoanalysis

Psychoanalytic criticism of D. H. Lawrence, from *Sons and Lovers* on, reflects the history of psychoanalysis as it has developed in four successive psychological models, focusing on drive, ego, object relations, and self (Pine 1988, 1990).[1] None, taken alone, is a tightly knit scheme representing the full complexity of human development and the dynamics of relationship. Each emphasizes different concepts, asks different questions, and employs differing therapeutic interventions. All four share the basic assumptions of psychoanalysis: the principles of psychic determinism, of unconscious mental functioning, and of primary process thinking. All purport that character is shaped by early body-based experience in relation to important early objects.

Sons and Lovers was hailed by members and friends of the London Psychoanalytic Society as a novel "about the Oedipus complex."[2] Most members of that society would have viewed the novel from the perspective of an early Freudian developmental psychology of instinctive drives and the topographical theory of the mind. In this model, the postulated mental structure is a topography of unconscious, preconscious, and conscious levels of the mind. Important concepts include the presence of unacceptable drives, primarily sexual, resulting in conflict signified by anxiety, shame, and pathological character traits. Sigmund Freud postulated an unfolding of psychosexual stages of development (oral, anal, phallic latency, and genital) that are inherent in the organism. The major clinical (or critical) questions to be asked concern unconscious wishes: What wish is being expressed? How is the individual defending against the forbidden wish? Are particular drives met with over- or under-gratification, resulting in early fixations or subsequent stage regressions? In this model, the tasks of human development are taming, socialization, and finding effective and acceptable modes of drive gratification. In the Freudian model, change is produced by making the unconscious conscious and by replacing conflict with sublimation in regard to drive wishes. Despite the impossibility of a totally objective stance of "analytic neutrality," it is important for the analyst, or the critic, to try to preserve a nonjudgmental attitude, in so far as possible, in an effort to avoid imposing his own biases on the patient or the literary subject. When Alfred Booth Kuttner, an American psychoanalyst, reviewed *Sons and Lovers* in 1915 and published an article on it in the *Psychoanalytic Review*, 1916,[3] Freudian drive theory was his frame of reference.

Freud's essay "On Narcissism: An Introduction" (1914) introduced significantly new ideas. As Joseph Sandler, Ethel Spector Person, and Peter Fonagy point out, "Here he first suggests that there are two types of libido—object libido and ego libido—and that an increase in one causes a decrease in the other since libido is regarded as a fixed quantity." The narcissism of childhood is succeeded in the adult by self-regard and the ego ideal.[4] This modification of instinct theory prepared the way for further theoretical development. Although he remained a drive theorist, Freud, in *The Ego and the Id* (1923), supplemented his topographical theory (the conscious, preconscious, and unconscious systems) with the tripartite model of intrapsychic structure (id, ego, and superego), in which his later writings were grounded.

Freudian theory informed psychoanalytic criticism of Lawrence for some years to come. Several critics draw comparisons, and contrasts, between Lawrence's ideas and psychoanalysis. Frederick J. Hoffman, in his chapter "Lawrence's Quarrel with Freud," in *Freudianism and the Literary Mind* (1945),[5] demonstrates the divergences between classic Freudianism and Lawrence's theories in *Psychoanalysis and the Unconscious* and *Fantasia of the Unconscious*. It is worth mentioning, however, that Adrian Stephen, Virginia Woolf's brother, who was to become a prominent psychoanalyst, reviewed *Fantasia* favorably in *The Nation and the Athenaeum*.[6] Philip Rieff, in his chapter "The Therapeutic as Mythmaker: Lawrence's True Christian Philosophy," in *The Triumph of the Therapeutic: Uses of Faith After Freud* (1966), sees the attack on Freud in Lawrence's psychoanalytic essays on the unconscious as integral to his effort to confront the problem of how man in a post-Christian world can find his own god.[7] In *D. H. Lawrence: The Artist as Psychologist* (1984), Daniel J. Schneider discusses Lawrence's psychological ideas, from their sources in Schopenhauer and Nietzsche to their parallels in Freud, Jung, Adler, Trigant Burrow, and Erich Fromm.[8]

Several critics have examined Lawrence from the perspective of other theorists within the Freudian psychoanalytic movement. For example, David Boadella's *The Spiral Flame: A Study in the Meaning of D. H. Lawrence* (1959), reprinted in *Paunch* (1977), employs the sexual theories and character psychology of Wilhelm Reich, originally a member of Freud's circle in Vienna, who expanded concepts of character defenses. Using such Reichian concepts as body armor, orgastic potency, and the function of the orgasm, Boadella draws significant parallels between Reich's ideas and Lawrence's body-centered psychology. Arthur Efron also employs Reich in his article "The Mind-Body Problem in Lawrence, Pepper, and Reich" and in his book *The Sexual Body: An Interdisciplinary Perspective,* both published in the *Journal of Mind and Behavior* (1980 and 1985), as well as in his collection of essays, *Life-Energy Reading: Wilhelm Reich and Literature,* in *Paunch* (1997).[9]

An avowed Freudian commitment in criticism is affirmed by Daniel A. Weiss in *Oedipus in Nottingham: D. H. Lawrence* (1962). His chapters "The Mother in the Mind" and "The Father in the Blood" are fine, authoritative studies of *Sons and Lovers* from a classic Freudian perspective.[10]

Psychoanalytic theory, however, was evolving. The implications for psychic functioning of Freud's structural theory were set forth in Anna Freud's *The Ego and the Mechanisms of Defence* (1936). Heinz Hartmann, Ernst Kris, and Rudolph Loewenstein further elaborated ego psychology. What emerged was a theory of psychoanalysis as a general psychology of the mind, in which Hartmann's ego-based "adaptive point of view" became a model for ego functioning.[11]

In ego psychology, the postulated mental structure is the organization of the personality in the form of id, ego, and superego, with the ego in the position of negotiating between the pressure of id impulses and the prohibitions of the superego. Important concepts include specific defense mechanisms as outlined by Anna Freud (1936), adaptation to average expectable environment as discussed by Heinz Hartmann (1939), and ego identity as postulated by Erik Erikson (1959). Additional concerns are reality testing and ego deficits (adaptational incapacity). The major questions to be asked concern the individual's capacity for adaptation: What tools of adaptation have failed to develop? Is there capacity for delay? Has object constancy been established? Has appropriate socialization occurred? In this model, the essential tasks of human development are the development of ego defenses with respect to the inner world, adaptation with respect to the external world, and reality testing with respect to both. It is important to note that an ego deficit is not a conflict, as in drive theory, but a state that requires the learning of new ego skills, the acquisition of which is essential to positive change. In criticism it is important for the critic to maintain an objective, nonjudgmental stance, again to avoid projecting one's own adaptational skills and ego deficits upon the writer and text in order to understand the subject, whatever his human strengths or frailties, with empathy for the human condition. In *Identity and the Life Cycle* (1959), Erik Erikson supplemented the Freudian stages of development rooted in instinctive drives with the concept of identity as it develops in terms of the psychological tasks to be confronted in each of eight stages of the life cycle. A very good example of criticism informed by Eriksonian psychology of ego identity is Marguerite Beede Howe's *The Art of the Self in D. H. Lawrence* (1977). Howe uses Erikson to support her thesis that Lawrence's "main concern is identity, and the fragmented self. It is not 'blood' religion, nor modern sexuality, nor the vicissitudes of the industrial age."[12] She also draws eclectically on the work of C. G. Jung and R. D. Laing, and discusses Lawrence's two psychoanalytic books in terms of an existential ego psychology.

One group of analysts in the British school of psychoanalysis (Melanie Klein, D. W. Winnicott, W. R. D. Fairbairn, Harry Guntrip, and others), starting from Freud's concept of introjection, developed an object relations theory that conceptualizes the intrapsychic structure as comprised of elements taken in from outside by a process of internalization, and that sees psychic functioning and relationships with others in terms of the relation of the ego to the internal objects of one's representational world.[13] Important concepts include a view of the individual in terms of a series of internal dramas, derived from early childhood and carried within memory, including unconscious memory. New experiences are colored by these old dramas. Early memories are based in intense affective and wishful experiences of childhood, prior to object constancy, and are preoedipal by definition. Hence, Melanie Klein uses language that evokes the good breast/bad breast duality, or the nourishing mother/devouring mother opposition. An experience or event is laid down in memory and so cannot be called objective in its own right. There is a need to repeat old family dramas in current relationships. The essential questions concern what old object relationship is being repeated. Is it being repeated in an effort to gain mastery, or to hold on to old parental relationships no matter how painful? In this model change is produced by understanding early internalizations, thus reducing distortion of new events, and by healing old splits based on good-bad dichotomies, in this way achieving emotional integration. The essential tasks of human development are carrying within oneself the record of one's personal history through internalized relationships and freeing oneself sufficiently from these internal relationships in order to meet new experiences on their own terms. Because of the intensity of preoedipal affect and its accompanying distortion of the perception of the other, the attitude of the analyst or critic should be as nonjudgmental as possible in order to preserve an empathic relation to the material being considered.

Margaret Storch's *Sons and Adversaries: Women in William Blake and D. H. Lawrence* (1991) is an excellent study informed by Kleinian theory, with its concepts of splitting the maternal object into good and bad aspects, leading to an unconscious intrapsychic view of the breast as a part object to be preserved as a nurturing object or attacked as a persecutory object. Storch amply demonstrates the relevance of such concepts to a reading of Lawrence. In a chapter on "Images of Women in Lawrence," Storch focuses on three scenes in *Sons and Lovers*—the sacrifice of the doll Arabella, the bread-burning scene, and the death of Mrs. Morel, hastened by Paul's giving her an overdose of morphia. Storch argues that "the three acts, two fantasied and one actual, are linked by several similarities, indicating that they arise from the same psychic source" (105). Furthermore, "the female accomplice who assists him in the three episodes of killing the mother is a symbol of the sexual liberation he hopes to achieve through destruction; that ultimate act of rebellion is finally, however, ineffectual" (107). In another chapter, Storch applies Kleinian theory to "Patterns of Maternal Loss in Early Lawrence: *The White Peacock*" to reveal "the paradigms of infantile emotion" underlying the novel. Finally, in "The Triumph of Masculinity in *The Plumed Serpent*," Storch demonstrates that although "the novel apparently begins with a revulsion from blood and violence, the higher reaches of masculinity . . . are often associated with exquisite violence detached from moral censure," as in the ruthless killing of the prisoners followed by Cipriano's dipping his hands into a bowl of blood and raising his red fist before the altar of Huitzilopochtli in a ceremony from which women are excluded (158–60).[14]

Two key concepts in D. W. Winnicott's object relations theory are skillfully and informatively employed by John F. Turner in two articles, "The Perversion of Play in D. H. Lawrence's 'The Rocking-Horse Winner'" and "The Capacity to Be Alone and Its Failure in D. H. Lawrence's 'The Man Who Loved Islands'" (both published in *The D. H. Lawrence Review*, 1982 and 1983).[15]

Less happily, David Holbrook, in *The Quest for Love* (1965), and in various recyclings of this material, in *Where D. H. Lawrence Was Wrong about Women* (1992) and elsewhere, cites D. W. Winnicott, without Winnicott's humanity and empathy, in what amounts to the critic's own judgmental attack on Lawrence. Citing object relations theories of Harry Guntrip, who was the analysand first of Fairbairn, then of Winnicott, Holbrook says, "Lawrence failed in *Lady Chatterley's Lover* to approach adult relationship at all," depicting instead "a neurotic genitality, conditioned by oral aggressiveness: thus, both the book and its direction are virtually an act of oral sadism." Failing "to leave behind infantile concepts," Lawrence "tries to solve the problem of love in terms of erotic pleasure merely." In the "coition between Connie and Mellors," says Holbrook, Lawrence fantasizes "his own unconsciously desired coition . . . in the place of his father with his mother"—but also with himself. *Mellors* is an anagram for *Morel*, and thus equals *Lawrence*, whose name is also embedded in the second syllable, *ance*, in *Constance*. "This verbal anagram also suggests that when Mellors is making love to Constance there is an aspect of Lawrence making love to himself," which points "to the narcissism of the book." "Lawrence in this was embracing himself, and ends by making an anal possession of himself, in final oral-anal aggressive verbal sensuality."[16]

The widening scope of mainstream psychoanalysis today, moving beyond the primary focus on interpretation of oedipal conflicts, has opened for analysis the difficult issues rooted in the preoedipal experience of very early childhood. Margaret Mahler's concept, based on direct infant research, of the process of separation-individuation from the early symbiotic fusion or merger with the mother is employed, to my knowledge, for the first time in Lawrence criticism by Judith Ruderman in *D. H. Lawrence and the Devouring Mother* (1984). As Ruderman observes, the prevalence of the Paul-mother dyad points to early psychological issues "manifested in strongly dyadic relationships, those involving chiefly two people, mother and child—rather than the oedipal triangle that includes the father" (8–9).[17] A major psychoanalytic significance of Ruderman's study is that it demonstrates the preoedipal basis of Paul Morel's psychology and, by extension, of Lawrence's, in his ambivalent attraction to and conscious rejection of the merger relationship that Birkin refers to as "meeting and mingling" (*Women in Love*, 148), and more problematically, in the defense against devourment and absorption in Lawrence's leadership novels.

The critical concern with preoedipal issues opens Lawrence criticism to further consideration of deficits in the self as distinguished from personality conflicts. Daniel Dervin's *A "Strange Sapience": The Creative Imagination of D. H. Lawrence* (1984) masterfully employs Michael Balint's concept of "the basic fault," the sense of a fundamental lack or deficiency in one's self, which Balint understands as deriving from insufficient responses to a basic psychic need in one's very early preoedipal development, which is then carried forward into later life and experienced as a deficit, not as a drive-based conflict or complex. In this regard, Balint anticipates Kohut's self psychology.

Dervin's focus on object relations issues, using Balint and Winnicott, enables him to make a significant study of Lawrence's artistic maturation and the creative process that enabled him ultimately to move beyond the stage of primary narcissism toward adulthood. "As applied to Lawrence," Dervin writes, "creativity is more analogous to therapeutic working-through than to catharsis, more akin to self-emergence than to circular-repetition, and so in the long run favoring maturity over the tenacious lures of childhood or the recurring grips of disease" (10). Elsewhere Dervin demonstrates Balint's usefulness for critics in his essay "Michael Balint's Contribution to the Psychoanalysis of Literature," in the *Psychoanalytic Review* (1979–1980).[18]

John J. Clayton, in *Gestures of Healing: Anxiety and the Modern Novel* (1991), finds the essential impetus of the work of modern U.S. and British novelists to be psychic injuries to the self, sustained in early object relations. Authoritatively informed by the psychoanalytic theories of the British object relations school, including Klein, Winnicott, and Fairbairn, and in part by the U.S. self psychology school of Heinz Kohut, Clayton sees the human psychological situation of the modern novel as characterized by deficits in the development of the self. Paradoxically, it is also a condition of creative growth, even in the face of deprivation of psychic needs; of mourning for lost objects, even those in whom one was most severely disappointed; and of human longing to find in the external world the idealized object that for most people can exist only as an internal imago. The book concludes with individual chapters on "Psychological Strategy in Henry James," "Moments of Healing: Virginia Woolf," and "D. H. Lawrence as Healer."

In his search to recognize and establish the "true self," "Only gradually over the years does Lawrence grow to appreciate his father," says Clayton. "Yet even in *Sons and Lovers*, . . . and far more than Lawrence himself realized, the father (for all his crudeness) is a more attractive figure than the frozen, impinging, guilt-producing mother, who is the 'voice of my education,' the voice of the cultural surface beneath which the artist needs to mine" (192). "Lawrence's childhood devotion [to his mother] was complicated by unacknowledged rage," which was "grounded in pre-oedipal fury at the split-off 'bad' mother, the devouring, engulfing, rejecting, all-powerful mother of infancy. What seems clear is not mother love but fierce ambivalence rooted in infancy—a separation anxiety that flowered ambivalently into yearning for regression to a symbiotic or fused attachment while raging against engulfment" (193). Without envisioning anything so definitive as a "cure," Clayton sees Lawrence's literary work as a "gesture of healing" for both the writer and his reader.

In *The Analysis of the Self* (1971), *The Restoration of the Self* (1977), *How Does Analysis Cure?* (1984), and other clinically based theoretical works, Heinz Kohut posits a separate line of development for the self apart from that of the instinctive drives. Kohut locates the origin of disturbances in the self, such as shame, lowered self-esteem, perversions, and "disintegration anxiety," in injuries to the nuclear self and deficits in self structure left by flawed responses or nonresponses to early psychic needs, especially needs for mirroring by and idealization of parental objects. Kohut emphasizes the individual's fundamental need to organize the psyche into a cohesive configuration and to establish sustaining relationships with significant others, who serve as "self-objects," objects that help one to maintain self-cohesion and strengthen harmonious functioning among the constituents of the self. Self psychology has continued in the work of Ernest Wolf, Joseph Lichtenberg, and others.

In these various theories of narcissistic development, the postulated mental structure is that of the self. Mahler and Pine posit a definite sense of "self experience," without elaborating on its origin. Kohut posits a separate line of development for the "self" not derived from drives. Important concepts for a psychology of the self include differentiation of the self from others, as in Mahler's concept of separation-individuation; issues of boundary, merger, wholeness/fragmentation, continuity/discontinuity in the sense of self, early narcissistic wounds producing deficits in the self; and subjective experience regarding self definition in relation to others. The major questions concern the stability of differentiated self-boundaries. To what extent are fantasies of merger important to the individual? To what extent is panic about loss of boundaries a factor for the individual? In a psychology of the self the essential tasks of human development are forming a differentiated and whole sense of self. This means establishing the self as a center of initiative and oneself as the owner of one's inner life with an ongoing sense of self-worth. In this model of psychoanalysis, the individual is working with pre-dominantly preoedipal self-fragments that are primitive, disconnected, and nonverbal. Change is produced by a psychoanalytic interaction in the form of describing, explaining, and reconstructing self concepts in a holding environment provided by the analyst.

Kenneth Bragan's article "D. H. Lawrence and Self Psychology" (*Australian and New Zealand Journal of Psychiatry*, 1986) finds a correspondence between Lawrence's ideas and the tenets of self psychology.[19] Both Jeffrey Berman, in "Echoes of Rejection in *Sons and Lovers*," *Narcissism and the Novel* (1990) and Marshall W. Alcorn, Jr., in *Narcissism and the Literary Libido: Rhetoric, Text and Subjectivity* (1993), discuss narcissistic injury and other self issues in Lawrence.[20] Five of my chapters in the present study employ Kohut's self psychology in attempting a psychoanalytic understanding of the kind of self issues in Lawrence that he refers to as "wounds to the soul, to the deep emotional self."[21]

Barbara Schapiro, in *Literature and the Relational Self* (1993), includes a chapter on Lawrence and Woolf, comparing identity and self issues in their works from the perspective of relational theories. In *D. H. Lawrence and the Paradoxes of Psychic Life* (1999), Schapiro employs Stephen A. Mitchell's *Relational Concepts in Psychoanalysis: An Integration* (1988) and other relational theories in a fine study of Lawrence and his work from this perspective.

I probably do not need to comment extensively on Jacques Lacan's theory, which has been more widely employed in recent academic criticism than in clinical psychoanalysis. A neo-Freudian on his own terms, Lacan attempts to return psychoanalysis to a pre-1923 Freudian topographical theory centered in instinctive drives, and thus to lead it away from what he sees as the repres-sive privileging of the ego in such concepts as adaptation, synthesis, and inte-gration. Unlike Freud, he rejects the notion that psychoanalysis is healing or in any way ameliorative. Lacan's most original contribution to psychoanalytic thought, the idea that the unconscious has the structure of a language, may partly explain why his main audience in the United States is literary and academic rather than clinical.

In addition to several periodical articles employing Lacan's theories in studies of Lawrence's texts, two books—Eugene Goodheart's *Desire and Its Discontents* (1991) and Ben Stoltzfus's *Lacan and Literature: Purloined Pretexts* (1996), both outstanding studies—include chapters applying Lacan's concepts to Lawrence. "Lacanian desire," says Goodheart, "is ultimately the matter of literature, specifically a modernist literature that specializes in the disrupted narrative, the resistances to origins and closure, a hermetic and opaque rhetoric, and a bewildering polyvalent language."[22] In his chapter on Lawrence, Goodheart suggests that far from being the sexual liberator he has often been considered, Lawrence is painfully aware of the "tyranny of desire." Lawrence, he points out, saw the oedipal drama as an expression not of the creative unconscious but of a mental idea—"a deliberate, calculated erotic stimulation of the male child by the mother"—in consequence of her failure to achieve erotic satisfaction with her husband and leading in turn to the son's inability to mature emotionally and sexually (Goodheart, 61). Otherwise Goodheart is concerned with the tragic implications of desire, not with the origin of issues of desire in the writer. Thus, his psychoanalytic observations on Lawrence are often right on target about the end result of a psychic process, while showing no interest in understanding where any particular psychological issue came from—a marked distinction between this model of psychoanalysis and almost any other theoretical perspective I can name.

Ben Stoltzfus briefly addresses the reason for this difference: "If the unconscious is structured like a language, then literature contains repressed material that engenders a never-ending dialog with the Other—a fictitious self made up of the confluence of the Imaginary and Symbolic."[23] "Lacan privileges the text over the artist's life because the text already contains everything we need to know" (Stoltzfus, 20). Stoltzfus's chapters on *The Escaped Cock* and "The Rocking-Horse Winner" illustrate his thesis. In *The Escaped Cock,* "The sexual union of the man and the priestess of Isis is, in Lacanian terms, a metaphor for moving the contents of the unconscious into the light of day." "What had been silenced and repressed by ideology was the phallus. The man's erection is the resurrection and retrieval of wholeness" (29). Stoltzfus's astute analysis of "The Rocking-Horse Winner" will be discussed in chapter 8, which is centered in that story.

Earl G. Ingersoll, in *D. H. Lawrence, Desire, and Narrative* (2001), instead of applying Lacan's theory directly to Lawrence's novels, places Lawrence in a postmodern context by employing the Lacanian-influenced

theories of postmodernist readers of Lacan, including Peter Brooks, Shoshana
Felman, Jane Gallop, and Barbara Johnson, to establish a frame for reading
desire in Lawrence's narratives. Rather than adducing desire as the subject of
Lawrence's novels, Ingersoll closely studies how desire informs the texts,
whether in the narrative desire for an ending or in the desire of the reader's
gaze. As in other Lacanian studies, Ingersoll focuses on the texts rather than
the biographical origins of desire. This strategy allows Ingersoll to reconsider
traditional and previous psychoanalytic interpretations of Lawrence's work in
a series of markedly original chapters on "De-Oedipalizing *Sons and Lovers*,"
"The Sense of an Ending in *The Rainbow*," "Staging the Gaze in *Women in
Love*," "*Mr. Noon* as Postmodernist Text," and, most strikingly, "Revisiting
Mellors's Penis in *Lady Chatterley's Lover*," in which a Lacanian distinction
between "phallus" and "penis" informs the narrator's and the reader's gaze in
viewing Mellors's genital organ both at rest and aroused in erection.[24]

~

Finally, there is no monolithic, "correct" psychoanalytic interpretation of
Lawrence. The various psychoanalytic approaches that I have described,
because they ask different questions, lead the critic to focus on different
aspects of Lawrence and his work. Within their particular frames of reference,
these differing perspectives may all be valid in terms of the analytic or critical
focus produced by each. Notwithstanding the importance of theoretical clar-
ity and precision, the quality of criticism ultimately depends on the critic's
insight, not on which theory is *in* or *out* in the vicissitudes of critical fashion
at any given time.

   The question now is, where do we go from here? My sense of the present
direction is that we will see more psychoanalytic studies of Lawrence in terms
of preoedipal issues, which will usually be approached from a relational perspective—from relational psychology and theories of intersubjectivity as well
as from object relations theory and self psychology. Citing the contrast
between the Freudian oedipal readings set forth by Weiss and others and the
preoedipal perspectives of Ruderman, Dervin, and Storch, Barbara Ann
Schapiro observes: "While psychoanalytic criticism of Lawrence was originally dominated by classical Oedipal interpretations . . . the emphasis has
shifted in recent years to a pre-Oedipal and object relational focus."[25] The
change in critical perspective that she describes is correlated with the similar
shift in emphasis in mainstream psychoanalysis from drive theory to a concern after Freud's structural theory with ego functions and defenses, and
thence to the relation of the ego to the internal objects of one's representational world and to the analysis of the self and its constituents. In theoretical

terms this can be seen in Kohut's shift in emphasis from conflict to deficit. In terms of Stephen A. Mitchell's relational psychology, the shift in focus is from the Freudian "oedipal conflict" to "relational conflict" between competing self-representations or self-organizations. These changes have been brought about largely in response to the change in the kind of patients being encountered in psychoanalysis and psychoanalytic psychotherapy in the latter half of the twentieth century. In Kohut's self psychology, this change is reflected in the shift in emphasis from guilty man to tragic man.

Psychoanalytic critics may still take their point of departure from Freud, but we will probably see more criticism from the perspective of theorists like Winnicott and Kohut—and from contemporary relational theorists like Stephen A. Mitchell and the feminist psychoanalyst Jessica Benjamin. Schapiro's recent fine criticism of Lawrence reflects the changed perspective she describes.[26] My own understanding of Lawrence's psychological situation, though shaped by my interest in self psychological issues in Lawrence, does not differ substantively from the concerns addressed by Ruderman, Dervin, Storch, and Schapiro.

CHAPTER 2

The Two Analyses of
D. H. Lawrence

In a now famous case study, Heinz Kohut in 1979 gave an account of "The Two Analyses of Mr. Z," as a means of showing the clinical relevance of the new psychoanalytic theories of self psychology that he had been developing for twelve years. Each analysis lasted about four years, and the two were separated by an interval of five and a half years. During the first analysis, Kohut says, he "was viewing analytic material entirely from the point of view of classical analysis." The second analysis, which was in progress while Kohut was deeply involved in writing *The Analysis of the Self* (1971), coincided with his development and testing of a new frame of reference—his emerging theory of a separate line of development for the self. This theory allowed the analyst "to perceive meanings" he had not "consciously perceived" before and thus to give the patient "access to certain sectors of his personality that had not been reached in the first part of the treatment."[1] I intend to return to the contrasting psychoanalytic theories on which these two analyses were based, but I turn now to an analogous situation in the psychoanalytic reception and criticism of the work of D. H. Lawrence.

First Analysis: The Oedipus Complex

When *Sons and Lovers* was published in 1913,[2] it was almost immediately perceived by members of the London psychoanalytic community as a masterpiece illustrating such Freudian theories as the Oedipus complex, psychosexual development, and unconscious motivation. Ivy Low, whose aunt, Barbara Low, and uncle by marriage, David Eder, M.D.,[3] were both London psychoanalysts, wrote enthusiastic postcards to friends: "Be sure to read *Sons and Lovers*!" "This is a book about the Oedipus complex!"[4] Further consideration of both the novel and Lawrence's early life also suggests the influence of preoedipal issues, such as those articulated by Margaret Mahler and by Heinz Kohut.

Among those who initially saw the theme in oedipal terms was D. H. Lawrence himself, whose letter to his editor, Edward Garnett (19 November

1912) (*Letters* 1:476–77) presents a basically oedipal synopsis of the novel. Earlier (26 April 1911), Lawrence describes the *Oedipus Rex* of Sophocles as "the finest drama of *all* times" (*Letters* 1:261). In the unpublished "Foreword to *Sons and Lovers*," he writes: "The old son-lover was Oedipus. The name of the new one is legion. And if a son-lover take a wife, then is she not his wife, she is only his bed" (*Letters*, ed. Aldous Huxley, 104). It is fair to say, however, that Lawrence saw himself as adapting the materials of his own childhood, adolescence, and young manhood to the fictional form of the realistic English bildungsroman rather than as writing a case history to illustrate the theories of Sigmund Freud, whose work he had not read.

Lawrence met Frieda von Richthofen Weekley (17? March 1912) and eloped with her six weeks later (3 May 1912). Frieda was acquainted with Freud's theories through Otto Gross, a brilliant but erratic young psychiatrist, who was briefly on the fringes of Freud's circle in Vienna. Frieda had had a love affair and a passionate correspondence with Gross while she was married to Professor Ernest Weekley.[5] During Lawrence's final revision of *Sons and Lovers*, Frieda influenced the psychoanalytic emphasis on oedipal material and sexual symbolism that was already inherent in the manuscript. She may also have influenced the oedipal slant that Edward Garnett gave the manuscript by editing out some realistic material unrelated to that theme. Frieda wrote to Garnett (September 1912): "I think L. quite missed the point in 'Paul Morel.' He really loved his mother more than anybody, even with his other women, real love, sort of Oedipus. . . . He is writing P.M. again, reads bits to me and we fight like blazes over it, he is so often beside the point." Later she reinforces her view of the delineating theme by telling Garnett: "The mother is really the thread, the domineering note."[6] On their return to England in 1914, Lawrence became friends with psychoanalysts Barbara Low and David Eder and was acquainted with Ernest Jones, then president of the London Psycho-Analytical Society.[7]

The first psychoanalytic criticism of the novel came in a review by the American critic Alfred Booth Kuttner (1915), which he expanded into an article for the *Psychoanalytic Review* (1916), which Barbara Low sent to Lawrence.[8] *Sons and Lovers*, Kuttner says, has the "double quality" of ranking "very high as a piece of literature," while embodying a scientific theory and illustrating it with astonishing completeness. Kuttner, the analysand of early Freud translator Abraham Arden Brill, M.D., clearly sets forth the classic psychoanalytic issues underlying the novel:

- The contrast between the parents, Walter Morel, warm, sensuous, and indulgent, whom Gertrude Morel, puritanical like her father, comes to loathe;

- Her determination to atone to her third baby, Paul, for his having been unwanted (*SL*, 73–74);
- The children's common hatred and contempt for their sometimes drunken and violent father (*SL*, 101);
- The psychologically incestuous relationship that develops between mother and son, as presented in scenes that often resemble courtship, such as their visit to Lincoln (*SL*, 297–303);
- Paul's praying for his father's death (*SL*, 99), while bringing to his mother the tributes of flowers, his school prizes (*SL*, 102), and his artwork;
- The rivalry between Mrs. Morel and Paul's adolescent girlfriend, Miriam Leivers, whose love he rejects in preference for his mother (*SL*, 267);
- Paul's elaborate fantasy of not marrying but of sharing his life with his mother in a cozy little house, perhaps in middle age taking a staid wife who would be no rival for his mother (*SL*, 130, 420)—which Kuttner calls a remarkably childish picture of the good life for a young man to have;
- His passionate involvement with Clara Dawes, married though separated from her working-class husband, and thus suitably debased to be available sexually while not competing with his mother for his spiritual side (*SL*, 418);
- Paul's inability to love another woman while his mother lives (*SL*, 418), yet his finding no freedom in her death but only increased allegiance to her internalized imago;
- His breaking off his relationships with both Miriam and Clara out of fidelity to his mother;
- His finally drifting derelict without the mooring his mother had provided (*SL*, chap. 15).

Kuttner's discussion briefly develops several related psychoanalytic issues: Because of the father's "unnatural position in the family," "where there should have been an attractive standard of masculinity to imitate," Paul "can only fear and despise" (95). Paul's inability to detach himself from dependency on the mother by means of the father's countervailing influence is further distorted in that his "early fixation" on his mother is actively encouraged by her "abnormally concentrated affection for her son" as a surrogate for her "unappeased love" in the marital situation (95). Paul's infatuation with his mother has a "paralyzing influence" on his lovemaking (95). Unable to "free himself from the incubus of his parents," Paul "remains enslaved by his parent complex" in "a kind of bottomless childishness." "Paul goes to pieces because he can never make the mature sexual decision away from his mother" nor "accomplish the physical and emotional transfer" (96).

There are several classically psychoanalytic elements that Kuttner does not notice, most of them clearly interpreted in a later applied Freudian analysis by Daniel A. Weiss[9] or in psychoanalytically tinged discussions by others. Kuttner does not comment on the role of Clara's husband, Baxter Dawes, who, as Weiss points out, resembles Paul's father closely enough to serve as a father surrogate (26), to whom Paul responds with the same marked ambivalence (30–31), and with whom he can enact reparation by proxy. First, in a fight over Clara, Paul allows himself to be beaten by Dawes as if in acceptance of deserved punishment (*SL*, 433–35; Weiss, 31–33); then he placates the man, staging a "rescue fantasy" and befriending him when he is in hospital (*SL*, 448–51); and finally he returns Clara to Dawes and reunites husband and wife as he could never do with his parents (*SL*, 474, 478–80; Weiss, 33–35).

Following Ernest Jones's psychoanalytic study of *Hamlet* (1949), Weiss develops several rich parallels between Hamlet and Paul:

• Their intense oedipal love for their mothers, both of whom are named Gertrude (Weiss, 17–18);
• Their projection of incest guilt as hatred of the father, degraded as the brutal stepfather, whom they request the mother to refrain from sleeping with (*SL*, 269; Weiss, 18, 20, 24);
• Their attributing excessive purity to Ophelia and Miriam, whom they refer to as nuns (*SL*, 309; Weiss, 50);
• Finally, their use of parental surrogates to resolve issues relating to the "family romance," with Paul employing Baxter and Clara Dawes as Hamlet employs the player king and queen for this purpose (Weiss, 67).

Certainly, for both Hamlet and Paul, these psychological issues come down to the question of whether "to be or not to be."

Kuttner does not acknowledge the ambiguity of the final paragraph, in which Paul, clenching his jaw and his fist and turning sharply, walks "towards the faintly humming, glowing town, quickly" (*SL*, 492), as most readers see it, toward life. To which Mark Schorer appends the reservation: "as nothing in his previous history persuades us that he could unfalteringly do" (Schorer, 12). Kuttner foresees for Paul only a compulsion to repeat in an endless round of temporary relationships with women, each of whom will be compared to his mother, found wanting, and then rejected as he moves on to the next woman.

Kuttner's article is quite favorable, but Lawrence reacted with dismay to find his creative work reduced, as he saw it, to a set of complexes. As he wrote to Barbara Low: "You know I think 'complexes' are vicious half-statements of the Freudians. . . . My poor book: it was, as art, a fairly complete truth: so they carve a half lie out of it and say 'Voila.' Swine!" (*Letters* 2:655). Lawrence's strong resistance to having his psychological issues uncovered and analyzed without the mask of art was activated by his reading of Kuttner's article.

Sons and Lovers as Self Analysis

The oedipal meanings of *Sons and Lovers* were obvious not only to Frieda Weekley but also to Jessie Chambers, the original of Miriam, who, aware that Lawrence had placed her in a hopeless position of rivalry with his mother, wrote to their mutual friend Helen Corke (23 March 1913): "The Miriam part of the novel is a slander, a fearful treachery. David has selected every point which sets off Miriam at a disadvantage, and he has interpreted her every word and action, and thought in the light of Mrs. Morel's hatred of her."[10] "In *Sons and Lovers,*" she says, "Lawrence handed his mother the laurels of victory."[11]

Although such statements as these are colored by Jessie Chambers's emotional involvement in the situation, her perspective also provides insights that warrant being taken seriously. When she and Lawrence read Shakespeare's *Coriolanus,* Jessie felt the play had a special significance for him: "'You see, it's the mother who counts,' he said, 'the wife hardly at all. The mother is everything to him'" (Chambers, *D. H. Lawrence,* 62). After his mother's death, Lawrence told Jessie: "I've loved her—like a lover—that's why I could never love you" (Chambers, *Collected Letters,* 54). This insight is echoed in his subsequent statement to Frieda, "If my mother had lived I could never have loved you, she wouldn't have let me go."[12] Jessie believes that "the necessity he felt to justify his mother" in the novel resulted in his utter failure to face the issue (Chambers, *Collected Letters,* 66).

Without recourse to Freudian theory, Jessie Chambers accurately observes: "It seems to me that one result of D. H. L.'s relationship with his mother was the complete divorce in his mind and attitude between love and sex" (Chambers, *Collected Letters,* 78). Lawrence's critical biographer Emile Delavenay, who does know his Freud, comments: "With every woman he approached, Lawrence experienced the same split: he found himself incapable of loving those he respected and of respecting those he dared desire" (156). The implications of drive theory for the classically oedipal material are still apparent today.

These oedipal elements were, I believe, the issues Lawrence was referring to earlier when he wrote to his friend Arthur McLeod (26 October 1913) with reference to *Sons and Lovers:* "[O]ne sheds ones sicknesses in books—repeats and presents again ones emotions, to be master of them" (*Letters* 2:90). Kuttner expresses a similar idea: "Mr. Lawrence has escaped the destructive fate that dogs the hapless Paul by the grace of expression. . . . He cures himself by expression in his art" (100).

These are the first two statements of the widespread but questionable view of *Sons and Lovers* as a kind of self-analysis, in which Lawrence, by *remembering* his experience in relation to his mother and representing it in fictionalized detail, employed the transformations of art in *working through* his Oedipus complex and so freed himself from it and healed his major psychological splits. Both Harry T. Moore (52) and Father Martin Jarrett-Kerr (25) subscribed to this view.[13] In Freud's terms in "Remembering, Repeating, and Working Through" (Freud, *SE,* 12:145–56), Lawrence's statement is not about *remembering* but about *repeating* one's emotions in an effort to master them. Such personal growth can be achieved, however, only by means of a more distanced perspective than is possible in the midst of emotional repetition. Mark Schorer comments that Lawrence's theory is acceptable "only with the qualification that technique, which objectifies," affords this perspective: "For merely to repeat one's emotions . . . is also merely to repeat the round of emotional bondage."[14] Frieda's account of Lawrence's rewriting *Sons and Lovers* in Italy confirms that he was not only remembering the original experiences, but reliving the emotional situation with abreaction: "[W]hen he wrote his mother's death he was ill and his grief made me ill too" (F. Lawrence, *"Not I, But the Wind,"* 56). But nothing Frieda says would support the conclusion that Lawrence's task of mourning was thereby completed, and he continued to struggle with the original emotional constellation in countless repetitions throughout his life.

Later psychoanalytic interpretations have found defensive maneuvers that suggest Lawrence may have wanted to avoid shedding too many sicknesses. Mark Schorer, linking the issues of artistic technique and therapeutic effectiveness, points out that "Morel and Lawrence are never separated. . . . Lawrence maintains for himself in this book the confused attitude of his character" (Schorer, 13). In a Freudian interpretation that runs counter to much previously received opinion, Daniel A. Weiss finds a psychoanalytic subtext of defenses and resistance: "In *Sons and Lovers* the artistic recognition of the material becomes itself a false recognition, a feint to catch the artist's eye while the real legerdemain of symbolic transformation does its work below the surface." Weiss approvingly summarizes Schorer's view that "Lawrence failed to resolve his ambivalent feelings toward his parents—his identity with and his alienation from his father, his wish to be free of and his dependence on his mother" (Weiss, 14; Schorer, 13). Schorer proposes: "If our books are to be exercises in self-analysis, then technique must—and alone can—take the place of the absent analyst" (12). Émile Delavenay, who does not address the question of aesthetic distance, comments: "The attempt at self-analysis is a failure, not as a novel, but as a cure: it does not enable Lawrence to make a new start" (516).

Kuttner also must have recognized the limitations and incompleteness of *Sons and Lovers* as self analysis when, as a consultant to the publisher on another Lawrence manuscript, "The Wedding Ring," he was pained by signs of "deterioration . . . in a gifted writer, knowing as I do that it is of neurotic origin." In his opinion, "A rigorous Freudian analysis would make Mr. Lawrence both a happier man and a greater artist."[15] ("Report and Letter on 'The Wedding Ring,'" in *The Rainbow*, 483–85).

Lawrence, of course, was never psychoanalyzed, and the analogy I have drawn is just that: a parallel between the two analyses of Mr. Z and the two applied analyses of Lawrence, the first being the classical Freudian analysis set forth by Kuttner, Weiss, and others, and the second being the Kohutian self psychological analysis that I will put forward here. Both of these applied psychoanalyses are, of course, in the form of psychoanalytic literary criticism at some distance from the deeply invested transference and uncovering process of a clinical psychoanalysis. If the synthesis of Lawrence's literary art may be seen as a major personal factor enabling him to build up a compensatory structure, it is not to see it reductively, but to recognize its importance to the artist in the maintenance of self-cohesion.

Second Analysis: Preoedipal Issues and the Self

What would it add to our understanding to reanalyze the Lawrence of *Sons and Lovers* along lines developed in more recent psychoanalytic theory? Although oedipal issues are consciously addressed, preoedipal issues are also implicit in the novel, but are not worked through or understood on a conscious level. My observations on Lawrence's preoedipal issues must be considered as materials for a second analysis that is still in progress, for at this point I am unable to draw any final conclusions, and I do not want to foreclose what may yet emerge. Fred Pine, who has attempted an integrative approach to "the four psychologies of psychoanalysis" (i.e., the psychologies of drive, ego, object relations, and self), suggests that from the perspective of a "psychology of the self" (not specifically Kohutian self psychology), among the useful questions "are those having to do with boundaries, integration, and esteem" (Pine, 582).[16] Keeping these and related questions in mind "as potential modes of conceptualizing" the subject, I will focus, in the remainder of this chapter, on two of the most important of Lawrence's preoedipal self issues: (1) the difficulties of separation-individuation deriving from Lawrence's symbiotic relationship with his mother, and (2) the internal deficit resulting from his inability as a child to make a positive identification with his devalued father.

Despite the obvious activation of oedipal feelings in the split between sexual and spiritual love in Paul Morel, Lawrence's emphasis throughout much of his work on the dangers of merger versus respect for otherness as Judith Ruderman has pointed out, does not derive from triadic oedipal conflicts, but from the dyadic relationship of mother and child.[17] Jessie Chambers recognizes the psychic injury left by Lawrence's relationship with his mother: "What seems to me perhaps the most sinister feature is that intellectual awareness of the part his mother had played in his life was not sufficient to set him free. Some real inner injury had been done to him, and he could not heal himself" (Collected Letters, 70). In self psychological terms, the cognitive understanding of the oedipal issues, even with abreaction and some attempt at working through, could not heal the narcissistic injury.

In a letter to Rachel Annand Taylor (3 December 1910),[18] Lawrence examines his family history, or mythology, to explain how that situation came about and what its effects were (Letters 1:190–91). Written one week before Lydia Lawrence's death, this letter expresses some remarkable perceptions that would enable Lawrence ultimately, with relative success, to negotiate the passage through separation-individuation. This task was made even more difficult in Lawrence's childhood by the familial rejection of the father and his unavailability as an idealizable object who could provide a way out of the dilemma. In the letter to Mrs. Taylor, Lawrence recognizes the attractive, desirable qualities of his father: "My father was dark, ruddy, with a fine laugh. He is a coal miner. He was one of the sanguine temperament, warm and hearty." The father's less attractive qualities, seen entirely from the mother's perspective, are magnified: "He lacked principle, as my mother would have said. He deceived her and lied to her. She despised him—he drank" (Letters 1:190). In the symbiotic merger with the mother, instituted from his birth, the boundaries of the self were seemingly dissolved and mother and son shared, as it were, a common boundary. The father, hated and rejected from birth, occupied a position outside that merger; consequently, both the good paternal qualities of dark, ruddy life and fine laughter and the bad paternal qualities of instability and lack of principle were consciously defined as outside the self, even while, on a deeper level, Lawrence also unconsciously identified his masculine self with the vitality as well as the irrationality and violence of the only masculine model he had.

The fusion with his mother that Lawrence describes in the letter to Rachel Annand Taylor was a world unto itself, seemingly containing everything necessary for life, a golden globe in which empathic immersion afforded almost total access to the mother so that sensitivity replaced the need for speech. There is, however, a further split. Lawrence's description of the experience sounds so idyllic at first that the gratification seems close to ecstasy. Yet the feeling of merger is also potentially destructive: "It has been rather terrible, and has made me, in some respects, abnormal" (*Letters* 1:190).

"This peculiar fusion of soul," Lawrence says, "never comes twice in a lifetime." When it does come, it is in the form of total immersion in the flood of shared consciousness that affords mutual, intuitive "understanding." Lawrence's relation to his mother was his only model for love, and his sense of reality was grounded in this relationship. The impending loss, then, poses the threat of self dissolution, and he must find an anchor in reality elsewhere. As the experience of merger has left him with a feeling of abnormality, Louisa Burrows, an old girlfriend, suddenly emerges as the representative of healthy normality, and he impulsively asks her to marry him. The two feelings are simultaneous: "There is no hostility between the warm happiness and the crush of misery: but one is concentrated in my chest, and one is diffuse—a suffusion, vague." "Muriel," Lawrence's poetic name for Jessie Chambers, cannot provide a mooring in reality against such identity diffusion, since his mother has hated the girl and he believes that she, like his mother, wants to devour his soul (see *SL*, 211). Louisa, with her "healthy, natural love," "will never plunge her hands through my blood and feel for my soul," he says. "Nobody can have the soul of me. My mother has had it, and nobody can have it again. Nobody can come into my very self again, and breathe me like an atmosphere" (*Letters* 1:190–91).

The threatened loss of self cohesion—in Kohut's term, the *disintegration anxiety*[19]—which Lawrence describes in the last chapter of *Sons and Lovers*, was real. Eighteen years later he recalled: "I was twenty-five, and from the death of my mother the world began to dissolve around me, beautiful, iridescent, but passing away substanceless, till I almost dissolved away myself, and was very ill: when I was twenty-six" ("Foreword to *Collected Poems*," 851). Lawrence's lung diseases, his bilateral pneumonia in that year and later the pulmonary tuberculosis that ultimately caused his death, with their common symptom of breathing difficulties, served psychologically, by his own account, to convey the effects of a smothering love. In *Fantasia of the Unconscious*, Lawrence attributes the etiology of such diseases to exploitation of the child's love: "[A]ny excess in the sympathetic mode . . . tends to burn the lungs with oxygen, weaken them with stress, and cause consumption. . . . No child should be induced to love too much. It means derangement and death at last" (97). This statement, as unscientific as it may be, speaks to the need to dispel the devouring mother.

According to Margaret S. Mahler and her associates, "the child with a predominantly symbiotic organization seems to treat the mother as if she were part of the self, that is, as not separate from the self but rather fused with it" (Mahler, Pine, and Bergman, 7). In Mahler's conception, the "process of separation-individuation has two intertwined . . . developmental tracks": "the track of individuation, the evolution of intrapsychic autonomy, perception, memory, cognition, reality testing"; and "the track of separation that runs along differentiation, distancing, boundary formation, and disengagement from mother. All these structuralization processes will eventually culminate in internalized self-representations, as distinct from internal object representations."[20] In these terms, at twenty-five, Lawrence's separation-individuation was ambivalent and less than complete. Employing Mahler's concept of separation-individuation and its subphases (176–77), Judith Ruderman suggests that Lawrence's difficulty in separating from the mother is "evidenced by the tension between the desire for merger and the need for independence that informs all his work" (175–76).

What evidence do we find in *Sons and Lovers* of the symbiotic relationship I am discussing? In an early childhood scene, Lawrence describes Mrs. Morel's feelings toward the infant Paul:

> In her arms lay the delicate baby. Its deep blue eyes, always looking up at her unblinking, seemed to draw her innermost thoughts out of her. She no longer loved her husband; she had not wanted this child to come, and there it lay in her arms and pulled at her heart. She felt as if the navel string that had connected its frail little body with hers had not been broken. A wave of hot love went over her to the infant. She held it close to her face and breast. With all her force, with all her soul she would make up to it for having brought it into the world unloved. She would love it all the more now it was here; carry it in her love. Its clear, knowing eyes gave her pain and fear. Did it know all about her? When it lay under her heart, had it been listening then? Was there a reproach in the look? She felt the marrow melt in her bones, with fear, and pain. [*SL,* 74]

Psychoanalytically, what is striking about this passage is not only the young adult male author's intuitive grasp of his mother's most intimate feelings, but also his fantasies about his infantile relationship with her. As Lawrence presents the situation imaginatively, since the mother no longer loves her husband, the infant son, early in the oral incorporative stage, has already effectively won the oedipal rivalry with his father. Thus, although originally unwanted, he has been chosen as her favorite. They are bound together as if by an uncut umbilical cord. Although in time this tie will become a tether from which even his mother's death will not entirely free him, it is, at this point, a source of strength. Through Paul, Lawrence presents himself, not only in infancy but throughout childhood and even beyond, as a delicate, physically frail youngster whose strength lies in his ability to gain intuitive knowledge of the other, an ability this passage suggests he may have acquired prenatally and further developed in the strong empathic relationship he shared with his mother.

That Paul Morel as a child shares everything with his mother is a given. Beyond that, he feels nothing has really happened until it has been shared with her (*SL*, 102). More significantly, I want to reconsider two passages that are sometimes cited as evidence of Paul's oedipal fixation. The first is from his childhood:

> Paul loved to sleep with his mother. Sleep is still most perfect, in spite of hygienists, when it is shared with a beloved. The warmth, the security and peace of soul, the utter comfort from the touch of the other, knits the sleep, so that it takes the body and soul completely in its healing. Paul lay against her and slept, and got better; whilst she, always a bad sleeper, fell later on into a profound sleep that seemed to give her faith. [*SL*, 107]

To my mind, what the passage illustrates is not only the triumph of Paul's oedipal wishes but, more profoundly, the gratification of his merger needs in the global union with his mother. In the fantasy he returns in sleep to a pre-separation state in which mother and child share, in effect, a single consciousness.

As Paul develops into adolescence, his mother exploits both his oedipal wishes and his dependency needs to preserve the symbiosis for the gratification of her own needs. When Mrs. Morel bitterly objects to Paul's growing interest in Miriam, "Instinctively he realized that he was life to her. And, after all, she was the chief thing to him, the only supreme thing." Paul immediately declares, "I talk to her, but I want to come home to you." When his mother pleads, "And I've never—you know, Paul—I've never had a husband—not really—," he accedes to the obvious manipulation of his oedipal feelings and accepts the role of surrogate (*SL*, 267).

This is something more than the usual Oedipus complex that is resolved in the normal stages of development. I believe that the strength and persistence of Lawrence's oedipal pathology is to be understood in terms of the preoedipal issues it served, in Jessie Chambers's words, the "inner injury," or as he put it, the "wounds to the soul, to the deep emotional self" (*Complete Poems*, 620). Lawrence says of his autobiographical character: "There was one place in the world that stood solid and did not melt into unreality: the place where his mother was. Everybody else could grow shadowy, almost non-existent to him, but she could not. It was as if the pivot and pole of his life, from which he could not escape, was his mother" (*SL*, 278). As the letter to Rachel Annand Taylor makes clear, Lawrence's relationship with his mother was the ground of his reality.

~

The psychoanalyst Jessica Benjamin traces the roots of idealizing love to the rapprochement subphase of separation-individuation, the period from about sixteen to twenty-four months during which the child must resolve the conflict between the wish to remain in symbiotic union with the mother and the wish for autonomy as a separate individual (Moore and Fine 1990, 181). As "the father begins to assume the crucial role of standing for freedom, separation, and desire," Benjamin says, "Here begins the child's relationship to the father that has been adduced to explain the power of the phallus." It is through identification with the father "that boys escape the depressive mood of rapprochement and deny the feeling of helplessness that comes with the realization of separateness." "The father of rapprochement is internalized as the ego ideal of separation and, like the oedipal superego, can be seen as a psychic agency that embodies a specific resolution of the rapprochement conflict." "The upshot of this analysis is that for boys . . . the issues of recognition and independence become organized within the frame of gender."[21]

What happens, however, if the father is not available for idealization and identification? In Lawrence's family of origin, and in *Sons and Lovers,* the position of the depreciated father, living in internal exile in his own home, precluded his providing a stable model for safe passage through separation-individuation to individual identity and autonomy. For Lawrence, the rapprochement conflict of dependency versus independence could not be resolved at a phase-appropriate age, the splitting characteristic of the preoedipal period continued, and his childhood gender identity was at best unstable.

Sons and Lovers provides evidence that despite his protestations, Paul Morel needed the idealizing relationship he had never had with his father. He takes delight in Walter Morel's stories about Taffy, the pit pony who likes a bit of tobacco, though the stories seem to go nowhere (*SL*, 103–4). Jessie Chambers mentions Lawrence's pleasure in the dancing skills of the father he generally despised (*D. H. Lawrence*, 30).

The potential relationship with his father, however, derailed from birth, could not be restored. The letter to Rachel Annand Taylor shows clearly how that situation came about. "I was born hating my father: as early as ever I can remember, I shivered with horror when he touched me. He was very bad before I was born," Lawrence writes. Then in juxtaposition that implies a causal connection, he adds: "This has been a kind of bond between me and my mother" (*Letters* 1:190). It is not his personal recoil but his mother's active interference that prevented Lawrence from developing any positive relationship with his father.

Heinz Kohut says that in this kind of situation, behind the mother's "depreciating attitude" toward the father, and her "manifest preference for the (thus overstimulated) child (the son)," there is "regularly a covert attitude of admiration and awe toward her own oedipal love object," her father. "The son participates in the mother's defensive belittling of his father, and elaborates this emotional situation by spinning out grandiose fantasies; he senses, however, the mother's fear of the strong male figure with the adult penis and realizes (unconsciously) that her exaltation of him, the son, is maintained only so long as he does not develop into an independent male" (Kohut 1971, 146–47). Kohut's interpretation describes the emotional situation between Lawrence and his mother with uncanny accuracy.

Despite his need for paternal connection, Lawrence rejected his father's overtures. Lawrence's boyhood friend George Neville recalls Arthur Lawrence's coming to the sickroom with awkward, unspoken concern for his son when Lawrence was ill (Neville, 63). In the parallel scene in *Sons and Lovers,* instead of responding to his father's solicitous inquiry, Paul says, "No; is my mother comin'?" "How long will she be?" (*SL,* 106). But in the return of the repressed in later novels—notably in Lilly's therapeutic massage of the flu-stricken Aaron in *Aaron's Rod* (96) and Birkin's fantasy of being taken care of in his delicate health by stronger, working-class men in the "Prologue" to *Women in Love* (502)—Lawrence enacts the fantasy of being the recipient of masculine tenderness during illness.

I postulate an additional psychic element as a constituent of Lawrence's difficult separation-individuation: the function his phallic-stage discovery of his penis must have had in his gradually developing sense of separateness from his mother and as a part object that he came to regard with the idealization he could not invest in the whole object, his father. In his fiction, Lawrence came to idealize the phallus as object and sign of separateness and independence. In his novel *Aaron's Rod,* Aaron's phallic flute, metaphorically recalling Moses's brother Aaron's miraculous rod, is associated with Aaron Sisson's individual, creative self (*Aaron's Rod,* 108, 129). In *Lady Chatterley's Lover,* the penis is represented as the phallus with quasi-sacral properties and personified with a separate identity, culminating in Mellors's memorable address to his phallus as an autonomous being with a will of its own (*Lady Chatterley's Lover,* 210). In Lawrence's novella *The Escaped Cock,* the risen Christ figure's erect phallus becomes the source of his resurrection and the sacramental sign of his transcendence (*The Escaped Cock*, 57). If one may take a great leap back to the childhood psychological situation depicted in *Sons and Lovers,* Lawrence's later pervasive use of the phallus as an image of autonomous selfhood suggests that the penis early came to represent an area of the self that was independent of the relationship with the mother. If this hypothesis is correct, then idealizing the penis was a way of avoiding the danger that he might fall into and be engulfed by the mother or her female surrogates. The first part of his life that Paul Morel does not share with his mother is his sexuality in what Peter Blos has called "the second individuation process of adolescence." "There was now a good deal of his life of which necessarily he could not speak to his mother. He had a life apart from her—his sexual life. The rest she still kept" (*SL,* 411–12). Despite his split between spiritual and sexual love, Paul's allowing himself in late adolescence this single area of relative independence from his mother is a positive sign that foreshadows his ultimate success, however attenuated or incomplete, in establishing his own separate identity.[22]

Whatever John Arthur Lawrence's limitations, the family constellation already in place when D. H. Lawrence was born required the son's rejection of the father as the price of the simultaneously sustaining and devouring relationship with the mother. The father's abdication meant that he could meet few if any of his son's early psychic needs. In Jessica Benjamin's theory, what "boys get from their fathers in the normal course of rapprochement" is "a vehicle of solving that conflict between separation and dependency that preserves grandiosity and omnipotence, salvaging self-esteem and independent will and desire" (Benjamin, 132). Lacking such a vehicle, Lawrence must fight that battle as best he can without it.

In his young manhood, Lawrence's individuation, like Paul Morel's, was conditioned not only by the strength of his overidentification with his mother, but also by the perceived deficits in his relation to his father. In face of the father's unavailability, such a son must look elsewhere for masculine identification, as Lawrence sought to do in his idealization of male bonding; in the homoerotic impulses that tended to return in the anxiety of crisis situations such as he experienced in the Cornwall period; in the attempted sublimation of his longing in rituals of *Blutbrüderschaft* or leadership; and in his mythic idealization of the phallus. However overdetermined these masculine elements may be, and whatever literary themes they may embody, I believe that all of them derive in large part from Lawrence's unmet need in relation to his father.

Lawrence's continuing issues in this regard, his repeated attempts to find a nurturant man, an idealizable man, or viable male bonding, are related "to the reactivation of the needs of the unconscious nuclear self," with regard to the pole of its masculine ideals. In Heinz Kohut's terms, Lawrence, unable to idealize his father but massively disappointed in his unavailability, had no opportunity to de-idealize him gradually as he inevitably discovered the father's realistic flaws. Hence, Lawrence had no means of making transmuting internalization of the paternal selfobject in the integration of the ideals with other parts of his personality.[23] In the figure of Walter Morel, Lawrence depicts his father as exiled from family life and raging alone in his own home (*SL*, 101–2). But his absence left a deficit that Lawrence tried to fill in the compulsion to repeat the ambivalent pattern of overidealization, inevitable disappointment, disruption, and undervaluation in relation to other men.

The wide emotional swings of this pattern derived, I believe, from Lawrence's wishful fantasies regarding the earliest objects of his internal representational world. For all his insistence on otherness and the repeated strictures against merging throughout his work, Lawrence's only early model for closeness was his relationship with his mother. Whereas the repetition compulsion in relation to men derived from his sense of deprivation and longing for the relationship he felt he had never had, its emotional intensity came from his overgratification in the relationship he had had and lost. Although Lawrence was able to work through the disintegration anxiety of his "sick year" following his mother's death, his mourning for the lost feeling of merger with her was lifelong, and he could not entirely suppress the wish to reinstate this model in other close relationships. This wish may have returned whenever the possibility of closeness presented itself, but it returned with particular strength in his repeated fantasies of being tenderly nurtured by another, usually stronger, man. So did his disappointment at the inevitable failure of the attempt and his underlying despair about the impossibility of such a relationship.

In Kohut's second analysis of Mr. Z, idealization of the analyst was "replaced by a mirror transference of the merger-type": "the patient became self-centered, demanding, insisting on perfect empathy, and inclined to react with rage at the slightest out-of-tuneness with his psychological states, with the slightest misunderstanding of his communications." Although in the first analysis Kohut had seen such behavior as defensive, he now looked on it as an "analytically valuable replica" of a time in early childhood, when Mr. Z "had been alone with his mother, who was ready to provide him with the bliss of narcissistic fulfillment at all times," "when a condition of overgratification had prevailed which, in turn, led to the fixation that hampered further development" ("Two Analyses of Mr. Z," 11–12).

In his introduction to Kohut's correspondence, Geoffrey Cocks has put forth the hypothesis that "The Two Analyses of Mr. Z" contains "[t]he most revealing account of Kohut's early years": "It is likely that this essay describes Kohut's training analysis with Ruth Eissler in the 1940s . . . and a subsequent self-analysis in the 1960s." Cocks, who says that Kohut's wife and son as well as colleagues and friends had intuited that he was Mr. Z, supports his argument with a series of striking parallels between Kohut and the pseudonymous patient: "An examination of the case study in fact reveals only lightly camouflaged events in Kohut's life."[24] If Cocks is correct in his view of the autobiographical origin and "personal status of what [Kohut] regarded as the seminal case for self psychology," then Kohut stands in relation to "The Two Analyses of Mr. Z" in a position comparable to Lawrence's in relation to *Sons and Lovers.* Possibly both men were "shedding sicknesses."

Kohut's comments, both in the essay and elsewhere, open a fascinating area for further exploration in regard to Lawrence. In a typical Lawrentian split, if women potentially threatened to repeat the danger of engulfment by the devouring mother, men could be seen in wish-fulfillment fantasy not only as the available and idealizable father but also as the potentially nurturing father, who could provide the kind of gratification Lawrence had experienced in the merger with his mother but not in relation to his father. In several late autobiographical pieces, Lawrence revised the view of his parents as presented in his letter to Rachel Annand Taylor of 3 December 1910. This change implies an attempt to revise the internal representation of his earliest objects. In one unpublished manuscript, he writes:

> My mother fought with deadly hostility against my father, all her life. He was not hostile, till provoked, then he too was a devil. But my mother began it. She seemed to begrudge his very existence. She begrudged and hated her own love for him, she fought against his natural charm, vindictively. And by the time she died, at the age of fifty-five, she neither loved him nor hated him any more. She had got over her feeling for him, and was "free." So she died of cancer. ["Getting On" (1926)][25]

In the revised version of Lawrence's family myth, his mother's fatal cancer has a psychosomatic etiology in her vindictive hatred of his father, and the father has become the model of natural charm and instinctuality. In later years Lawrence said to Frieda: "I would write a different 'Sons and Lovers' now; my mother was wrong, and I thought she was absolutely right." (F. Lawrence, *"Not I, But the Wind,"* 56). Where the father was concerned, Lawrence did write a correction to *Sons and Lovers.* It is in *Lady Chatterley's Lover,* in the idealized portrait of the gamekeeper, Oliver Mellors, a working-class man who speaks in the Midlands dialect, delivers a strong polemic for life and against a corrupt society based on mechanism and money, and expresses genuine tenderness in a heroic masculine sexuality.

CHAPTER 3

Lawrence and the
Sensitive Man

D. H. Lawrence, from early childhood, was extremely sensitive to slights or blame communicated by or absorbed unconsciously from his environment. John Worthen describes how Lawrence, at "three or four," would burst into tears and cry "for no apparent reason." Worthen relates this crying to what D. W. Winnicott has called "sad crying," in which the small child, instead of reacting to circumstances, feels responsible for the circumstances: "The trouble is that he starts off feeling *totally* responsible for what happens to him and for the external factors in his life. Only gradually does he sort out what he *is* responsible for from all that he *feels* responsible for."[1]

Lawrence's early sensitivity affected his feelings about himself and his relation to other males throughout his childhood and young adulthood. The issue of homosexuality, I believe, became for Lawrence a magnet for feelings of shame and masculine inadequacy that long predated either his conscious homoerotic attractions or his homosexual fears. According to his childhood schoolmate J. E. Hobbs, he was considered "a delicate boy," one who "never played with boys, never joined in their games," even if asked. When he refused, the boys wagged their fingers and jeered: "Th'art a mard-arsed kid" (Nehls, 1:33). Lawrence's brother George says, "it was a grief to him that he wasn't able to enter the boys' games."[2] The sense of shame extended to other areas of his young life.

As Mabel Thurlby Collishaw recalls, "The most unhappy day of Bertie Lawrence's week was Friday when, with a calico bag clutched in his hand, he had to go to the offices on Nether Green to draw his father's wages" (Nehls, 1:29). For a differently constituted child, being entrusted with such a responsibility might have been a source of pride. Lawrence's sense of humiliation and shame in this and similar circumstances was probably an overdetermined response to a situation that for him encompassed the repeated feelings of exposure and masculine inadequacy that were only partially compensated by his intellectual and artistic achievements.

William E. Hopkin remembers the young Lawrence as "very sensitive, or as his schoolfellows said, 'Mardy,' which is a term used to signify a sort of babyish disposition. Never in his life could he bear anything like severe criticism. He either got extremely angry or worried and upset. In his later school and college days he had a few male friends, but in his elementary school days he did not get on with other boys. They despised him because he couldn't take part in their games" (Nehls, 1:23). Hopkin describes the scene he observed one day when he was passing the school: "He was walking between two girls, and a number of Breach Boys walked behind him monotonously chanting, 'Dicky Dicky Denches plays with the Wenches.' That charge branded any boy as effeminate—the local term is 'Mardarse.' Bert's chin was in the air as though he cared no jot but his eyes were full of anger and mortification" (Nehls, 1:23).

Whatever the other boys may have understood of the effect of their cruelty, the adult William Hopkin empathically recognized that assaults of this kind on the self do cause injury. The insult sticks and the wound lasts long after the initial injury is presumed to be healed or at least grown over. In a state of dormancy that is more apparent than real, the original injury awaits reactivation, even many years later, by the almost inevitable recurrence of another wound that reinstates the feelings that surrounded the first. As Heinz Kohut puts it: "Stated in general terms we can say that . . . a current narcissistic injury may be followed by the emergence of specific unconscious narcissistic and autoerotic configurations—i.e., of early stages of the self, and of its fragmented precursors—the analysis of which leads to the recall of narcissistic and autoerotic responses in childhood."[3]

The question is why his relationship to his two parental objects did not enable the young Lawrence to deal more effectively with the thoughtless cruelties he endured from his peers. I argue that the failure derives from two sources: First, the early and continued merger with his mother was extremely gratifying. By enclosing him in an exclusive union with her, it was also dangerous. It made the separation-individuation process especially difficult, so much so that even in his late adolescence and continuing into his young adult years, Lawrence felt that he could not love another woman so long as his mother was alive. Second, since the father was placed outside this global merger, his qualities—both good and bad—were defined as outside the self. Arthur Lawrence's isolation from the family and his rejection by both Lawrence and his mother meant that the man could not provide for his son, in Margaret Mahler's terms, the early paternal function of standing as a model for separation and independence. Lawrence's father was, however, the most immediate masculine model in the young Lawrence's life, and Lawrence absorbed more of his father's qualities and psychic makeup than he may have consciously recognized. By his own account, in his letter to Rachel Annand Taylor (3 December 1910), Lawrence "was born hating" his father. What we know of Lawrence's early life suggests that he was taught from birth to hate and despise his father. Both the father's less attractive qualities and the attitude toward him that Lawrence shared with his mother made it impossible for the son to idealize his father or for the father to stand as a model for his young son's masculine ideals.

The sensitivity that Lawrence had experienced in the relationship with his mother became the model for the sensitive sensibility that was essential to him as an artist and as a man. But the sensitivity cultivated in that relationship had also robbed him as a boy of aggressive masculinity. As an adult Lawrence came to recognize that his sensitivity had come at the cost of being partially cut off from his instinctual needs.

In an early version of "The Crown," part 4 (written 1915, but unpublished at the time), Lawrence comments extensively on "the sensitive man" in relation to reduction of the self, sexuality, and the wounded sense of self. The immediate context is his contrast in the process of reduction between two kinds of men: on the one hand, the men "whose souls are coarsely compounded, so that the reduction is coarse, a sort of activity of coarse hate," and on the other, "the men of finer sensibility and finer development, sensuous or conscious, they must proceed more gradually and subtly and finely in the process of reduction" (*Reflections on the Death of a Porcupine*, 284. See also Appendix 2: The "Crown 1915 Variants," 469–79, in *Textual Apparatus*, esp. 472–74.).

In the manuscript of *The Crown*, part 4, Lawrence describes the sensitive man's sexual situation as follows: While "coarse, insensitive men" can obtain "the prime gratification of reduction" with a woman, the sensitive man is too conscious and too subtle to "come like a perverse animal, straight to the reduction of the self in the sex." The soldier who rapes a captive woman, knowing the extreme reduction of death, "becomes almost a carrion creature, feeding on dead organisms, on real corruption." The sensitive man, on the other hand, "caught within the flux of reduction, seeking a woman, knows the destruction of some basic self in him, while the complexity and unity of his consciousness remains intact above the reduction." "Horrified at his own mangled, maimed condition, of which he is painfully aware in his complete consciousness," he finds such a connection with a woman gross and repulsive. From the perspective of Freudian drive theory, Lawrence's description of the maiming may appear to be a reference to castration anxiety. But the next sentence—"Instead of obtaining the gratification of reduction, he has got only a wound in his unified soul, a sort of maiming"—clarifies Lawrence's meaning. The sensitive man's "maimed condition" is the result of the "wound in his unified soul," the narcissistic injury which, reactivated in the current situation, threatens the sensitive man's self cohesion. Lawrence's description of the two types of men encompasses an ambivalent value judgment of each: The sensitive man is presented not only as a man of higher sensibility but also as one injured by a wound to the soul. The coarser man is presented as one who proceeds without hesitation to reduction of the self in sex but also as one who may become a brute in the process.

As Lawrence presents the sensitive man's situation, loving a man who is "less developed than himself, he can proceed to reduce himself to this level": "He loves men, really. This is the inevitable part of the activity of reduction, of the flux of dissolution, analysis, disintegration, this homosexuality." Wishing to reduce himself back to the simplicity and undeveloped state of a boy or to that of a lower type of man, he basically wants "to get back to a state which he has long surpassed." According to Lawrence, "This is the significance of the myths, of Leda, of Europa. This is David turning to Jonathan, Achilles to Patroclus. This is always the higher, more developed type seeking to revert to the lower."

Although he does not apply his conception of the sensitive man directly to himself, Lawrence describes the effects of the narcissistic injury in terms that correspond to his own early experience and to his responses to subsequent situations that evoke its repetition. In terms of masculine identification, the massive disappointment in the relationship with his father left a structural deficit in the self that Lawrence repeatedly sought to fill in relation to other men. Since his early and continuing experience of the gratifying fusion with his mother was characterized by an extreme empathy that he describes as sensitivity, a merger form of relationship became his early model for a loving relationship. When he sought to establish a satisfying relationship with another man to fill the paternal deficit, his first temptation may have been to do so by attempting to reinstate a new version of the only gratifying love relationship of his early experience, the symbiotic merger with his mother.

Lawrence's attitude toward merger, however, was also marked by ambivalence. Although the possibility of reinstating the gratifying merger relationship with another man may have been an initially alluring temptation, Lawrence was also wary of the danger of engulfment. He repeatedly opposed the kind of relationship that Birkin refers to as "meeting and mingling." Indeed, I would argue that one function of Birkin's concepts of both "star polarity" with a woman and *Blutbrüderschaft* with a man is to make intimacy possible by defining the relationship in terms designed to protect the self against the danger of being engulfed by or fusing with the other. As I have suggested, the unmet need that Lawrence was trying to satisfy came from the relationship he had never had with his father, but its emotional intensity came from the relationship he had had with his mother and had lost at her death.

These two motives were too powerful to resist altogether. The gratification of the merger with the mother—"We have been like one, so sensitive to each other that we never needed words" (*Letters* 1:190)—is expressed in the extraordinary sensitivity of the sensitive man. As Lawrence describes it, however, the sensitive man's countervailing motive is the reduction of his cultivated, sensitive self back to a less refined, basic or primitive stage of development. Lawrence's own motivation is directed not toward reinstating a similar fusion with a woman, who would thus be cast as still another competitor for the place his mother had occupied, but rather toward filling the paternal deficit in relation to another man. In his partial, and temporary, identification with the other man, who is often seen as a stronger, rougher, more robust, and less refined being than himself, the sensitive man seeks the gratification of sensual reduction of the sensitive self in relation to another man who more than a little resembles Lawrence's father. The intense feeling that characterizes this longing is easily mistaken for true homosexuality.

Lawrence continues in this vein in a markedly intellectualized theory of homosexuality. Part 4 of "The Crown" was not published, as the first three parts were, in *The Signature* (1915), because publication of the little magazine, a literary venture of John Middleton Murry, Katherine Mansfield, and D. H. Lawrence, was discontinued after three issues. When Lawrence subsequently included "The Crown" (all six parts) in his collection *Reflections on the Death of a Porcupine and Other Essays* (1925), he extensively revised part 4 for publication, retaining the theme of reduction of the self but omitting the discussion of homosexuality. With its emphasis on sensitivity, the sense of a wound to the self, and the struggle with a longing that, although it derived from the paternal deficit and the early difficulties in masculine identification that followed, Lawrence had felt as homoerotic, this material may have seemed too personal to be retained in a book published ten years later when the issue was not so pressing as it was in the crisis situation of 1915. The issue, however, was not entirely resolved. It reappears in Birkin's attraction to Crich in *Women in Love* and in partially sublimated form in Don Ramón Carrasco's need for Cipriano Viedma in *The Plumed Serpent* (1926).

The composition of the "sensitive man" material in 1915 is contemporaneous with the suppression of *The Rainbow* (1915) and immediately precedes the stressful situation of the Cornwall period of 1916–17. Taken together these conditions represented for Lawrence the kind of personal crisis that would almost inevitably give rise to a renewed need and longing for the support of a masculine bond that was missing in his early development. Lawrence's emotional involvement with the young Cornish farmer William

Henry Hocking during the Cornwall period illustrates the "reduction" he describes: the sensitive man's effort to reduce himself back to the level of a less culturally developed man.

As W. R. D. Fairbairn observes, the homoerotic search for the father's penis "resolves itself, so to speak, into a search for [the] father's breast."[4] It should be noted that psychoanalytic writing employs a kind of anatomical geometry, full of "breast," "penis," "nipple," "baby," and so forth. As Freud's designation of developmental stages as oral, anal, phallic, latency, and genital emphasizes the body-based function that becomes the focus of each stage, so too the symbolic equations evoked by Klein, Fairbairn, and others have their physiological counterparts in the primitive wishes encoded in the unconscious fantasies that give rise to the mental imagery.

Emphasizing the motivational goals of the homosexual conflict, Lionel Ovesey says: "This conflict . . . can be broken down into three component parts: sexual, dependency, and power. Only the first is truly sexual in motivation. The other two are not sexual at all, although they make use of the sexual apparatus to achieve their ends. They are in reality pseudohomosexual components of the homosexual conflict."[5]

Ovesey explains the psychodynamics involved: "The dependent person aspires on the most primitive level to recapture the maternal breast. Such persons will have repeated dreams of food, all symbolic of the infantile desire to have one's every need gratified by an all-powerful parent. The breast-fantasy is the most direct reparative approach to the problem of dependency. There is, however, an alternative route; it is based on the equation, penis = breast" (Ovesey, 22–23).

Ovesey explains the complex origin of the equation "penis = breast" in the early development of multiple inhibitions in several areas of behavior, each of which reinforces the others: "The unconscious ideation . . . forms the basis for a magical reparative fantasy in which the penis is ultimately equated with the breast. The dependent person, instead of relying on the breast, may achieve the same effect by invoking a compensatory fantasy of oral or anal incorporation of a stronger man's penis, thus undoing his castration and making the donor's strength available to him" (Ovesey, 23–24).

According to Ovesey, "In the overt homosexual, the sexual component is primary, and the primary motivational goal is therefore orgastic satisfaction. The dependency and power components are secondary" (Ovesey, 29). Similarly, he defines "the latent homosexual as one in whom the homosexual impulse was either conscious or unconscious, but not overtly acted out." Ovesey adds that the term "latent" is correctly applied only "to the purely sexual component of the complex." "The great majority of so-called homosexual anxieties are motivated by strivings for dependency and power. These anxieties," says Ovesey, "stem from pseudohomosexual fantasies that are misinterpreted . . . as being evidence of frank homosexuality. In reality, the sexual component, if present at all, is very much in abeyance" (Ovesey, 31).

Where Lawrence is concerned, the early and continuing merger with his mother suggests an underlying unconscious fantasy of the idealized breast. Why did he at a disturbing time of crisis and transition such as the Cornwall period apparently make the unconscious equation "penis = breast" and look for nurturance in relationship with another man? Logically, I think that the "penis = breast" equation would emerge at times when Lawrence felt threatened by the possible dissolution of the self. Although his actual father did nothing to protect him from the danger of devourment in the relationship with his mother, the introjected image of the penis, idealized as the quasi-mythic phallus, was, I believe, the imago through which in the intrapsychic self Lawrence sought masculine support in the compensatory fantasy. Turning to the alternative part object of the father's penis in the unconscious oral fantasy of substituting it for the breast could also serve the defense of reparation, both by restoring the lost breast by means of the equation and by repairing his own sense of emasculation in his present situation. That is, in the intrapsychic sphere, he could turn to the idealized part object, the phallus, as a partial imago of the father for the male nurturance he had never received or perhaps had never been able to accept from his actual father. In the homoerotic fantasy, he could also placate the father, make reparation for his guilt in the oedipal triumph with the mother, and thus repair his own fantasied castration.

In terms of current psychoanalytic theory of narcissism, as Barbara Schapiro argues, "the idealization defense, however, is invariably threatened by the shame and envy that initiated it. The empty, deficient self dreads being overwhelmed by the very power and vitality it has projected outward, onto the other." Thus, in Schapiro's view of Lawrence's situation, "While loving another man is connected in the fiction with an infusing male potency, it is also tangled up with profound, unconscious shame, with self-contempt, and with a terror of dissolution and absorption."[6]

∼

The real issue in Lawrence is not homosexuality per se but the injury to the self. Whereas earlier psychoanalytic criticism of Lawrence tended to emphasize oedipal conflicts (Kuttner, Weiss), recent psychoanalytic criticism tends to emphasize preoedipal deficits (Dervin) or relational conflicts (Schapiro). In Kohut's conception, "relationships may exist between the phallic-oedipal structures in which the child's wounded narcissism plays only a secondary role, and the narcissistic structures (phallic and pre-phallic) which are the leading pathogenic determinants in a narcissistic transference." Moreover, while "a manifestly narcissistic disorder" may hide "a nuclear oedipal conflict," Kohut points out that the reverse is also true: "a narcissistic personality disorder" may be "covered by manifestly oedipal structures" (Kohut 1971, 155).

Late in his literary canon, Lawrence returns to the theme of narcissistic injury or, as he expresses it, "wounds to the soul." In *Lady Chatterley's Lover*, Connie recognizes that the most devastating injury her paraplegic husband, Clifford, has sustained is the wound to his soul:

> And dimly she realised one of the great laws of the human soul: that when the emotional soul receives a wounding shock, which does not kill the body, the soul seems to recover as the body recovers. But this is only appearance. It is, really, only the mechanism of re-assumed habit. Slowly, slowly the wound to the soul begins to make itself felt, like a bruise, which only slowly deepens its terrible ache, till it fills all the psyche. And when we think we have recovered and forgotten, it is then that the terrible after-effects have to be encountered at their worst. [*Lady Chatterley's Lover*, 49]

In the three successive versions of *Lady Chatterley's Lover*, as Michael Squires has shown, Clifford increasingly comes to resemble Lawrence himself. Viewed in this context, the narrator's frequent attacks on Sir Clifford Chatterley may be understood, as savage self criticism on the part of the author. Connie's insight on the injury to Clifford's self in the passage cited above is a welcome example of authorial empathy with a character that, for much of the novel, is treated unempathically. When Lawrence speaks of "wounds to the soul," he knows the territory at first hand.

In "Healing," a poem in *More Pansies*, Lawrence insightfully recognizes the psychic connection between the "wounds to the soul" and the compulsion to repeat, and he applies the concept to his own illness:

> I am not a mechanism, an assembly of various sections.
> And it is not because the mechanism is working wrongly that
>   I am ill.
> I am ill because of wounds to the soul, to the deep
>   emotional self
> and the wounds to the soul take a long, long time, only
>   time can help
> and patience, and a certain difficult repentance

> long, difficult repentance, realisation of life's mistake,
>   and the freeing oneself
> from the endless repetition of the mistake
> which mankind at large has chosen to sanctify.
>
> [*Complete Poems*, 620]

In his early response to the exclusively oedipal interpretation of *Sons and Lovers*, Lawrence had rejected what he called the "half lie" of the mother complex (*Letters* 2:655). By the time of *Lady Chatterley's Lover* and *More Pansies*, he understood—well before the concept was recognized and widely employed in psychoanalysis—that his major psychological issues were not primarily the kind of conflicts discussed in Freudian drive theory but "wounds to the soul," the injuries to the self that psychoanalytic self psychology today addresses. These are the kind of wounds that Lawrence cites in his description of "the sensitive man," as discussed in this chapter.

CHAPTER 4

Blutbrüderschaft and Self Psychology in D. H. Lawrence's *Women in Love*

One of the means by which D. H. Lawrence sought to reconcile spiritual and sensual components of the self and to establish a "nourishing creative flow" between the self and the other was the concept of *Blutbrüderschaft*. Long before he introduced the term in *Women in Love*, Lawrence had tentatively explored the theme in *The White Peacock* and *Sons and Lovers*. But the reconciliation of spiritual and sensual modes of consciousness through male bonding was to become a dominant theme in *Women in Love* and in the leadership novels that followed it. Sacramental though the action may be in Cyril and George's bathing scene in *The White Peacock*, the ritual is that of pastoral romance, not the open invitation to vows of blood brotherhood that Rupert Birkin offers to Gerald Crich in *Women in Love*.[1]

Women in Love contrasts the developing relationship of Ursula Brangwen and Rupert Birkin with that of Ursula's sister Gudrun and Gerald Crich and parallels these relationships with that of the two men to each other. Ursula is a teacher and Gudrun an artist, while Birkin is a school inspector and Crich the well-to-do son of a mine owner and, ultimately, a captain of industry who adopts ruthless management policies. Birkin, who emerges as the focal character for most of the novel, is in the process of extricating himself from an unsatisfying love relationship with the socially prominent Hermione Roddice, a relationship he has come to feel as artificial, destructive, and spiritually devouring. He wants to establish his new relationship with Ursula on a structured basis of equal balance and individual autonomy. But he is equally concerned with establishing a complementary, irrevocably bonded, male-male relationship with Crich to counterbalance his male-female relationship with Ursula. Tracing the development of both types of relationship in the interactions among the four young adults, the novel explores psychological themes of merger, marriage, homoeroticism, idealization, sadomasochism, creativity, dissolution, and death. Largely for the artistic maturity of its presentation of the complex interrelationships of characters, imagery, themes, and structure in an apocalyptic anatomy of modern society, *Women in Love* is generally recognized as one of Lawrence's two or three greatest novels.

What Rupert Birkin proposes to Gerald Crich is the kind of *Blutbrüderschaft* the "old German knights" had sworn by making "a little wound in their arms" and rubbing "each other's blood into the cut," swearing "to be true to each other, of one blood, all their lives.—That is what we ought to do," Birkin says. "No wounds, that is obsolete.—But we ought to swear to love each other, you and I, implicitly and perfectly, finally, without any possibility of going back on it" (206–7).

Presented with a proposal that would convert the strong bond between men into something like male marriage, Gerald Crich is understandably bewildered. Confused, ambivalent, pleased but wary of what may seem, on one level, Birkin's sexual advances in a calculated seduction, Gerald demurs: "We'll leave it till I understand it better" (207). Literary critics, not surprisingly, have been equally confused, expressing widely divergent views on the meaning of a proposal that sounds like a homosexual pledge but is not acted out sexually beyond an erotically tinged nude wrestling scene. Critics also disagree on the place and significance of the canceled "Prologue."[2] Since I will use the "Prologue" in my discussion of the novel, I want to clarify my view at the outset. Although the canceled status of the "Prologue" removes it as a structural part of the novel, its textual presence valuably illuminates aspects of the novel. The "Prologue" makes explicit Birkin's self division in relation to women and his homoerotic feelings in relation to men, both of which in the novel remain for the most part implicit. If Lawrence felt that he had been overly explicit in the "Prologue" and needed to develop the *Blutbrüderschaft* theme more gradually, that would have been reason enough, both artistically and personally, for his decision to cancel the "Prologue."[3]

As I try to show, Birkin's wish for blood brotherhood is not disguised homoeroticism; indeed, Birkin's homoerotic fantasies are not disguised at all in the canceled "Prologue" and scarcely so in the novel. Rather, Birkin's concept of *Blutbrüderschaft* as an irrevocable male bond tantamount to marriage in sacramental commitment is a form for experiencing emotional closeness. The relationship includes sensual, physical awareness in which sexual feeling is elevated to noble ideals of male devotion and loyalty rather than expressed directly in sexual behavior. The concept enables Birkin to press into the service of ego defense those feelings that, on an immediate level, are experienced as sexual but that in reality mask a defense against the same psychic danger as his fear of being swallowed up by women, namely, "the threatened dissolution of the self."[4]

To what extent Birkin's meanings reflect Lawrence's is, of course, a critical question. It would be simplistic to identify the authorial voice exclusively with

Birkin's point of view, since Lawrence's literary meaning emerges fully only in the narrator's presentation of the interaction of all the characters along with elements of plot, setting, and style. While Birkin is more fully objectified than such autobiographical characters as Paul Morel in *Sons and Lovers,*[5] most readers have intuitively felt a psychic affinity between the novelist and this protagonist. Sigmund Freud (1908) comments in "Creative Writers and Day-Dreaming" that in such psychological novels "[o]nly one person—once again the hero—is described from within. The author sits inside his mind, as it were, and looks at the other characters from outside" (*SE* 9:150).[6] As Paul Delany observes, "One source of freedom, certainly, was the creation of Birkin as hero: through him Lawrence could both express his own impulses directly and open them to countervailing pressures from other characters."[7] Rather than look for autobiographical equivalence in the narrative action of *Women in Love,* I suggest that Birkin is the carrier of Lawrence's major psychic issues, revived by his stressful situation at the time but actually deriving from his relationships with his earliest selfobjects. Specifically, these issues included, from his close symbiotic merger with his mother, both grandiose merger needs and fears of engulfment, expressed in his ambivalence toward women, and, from his traumatic disappointment in his father, both the need for stable ideals and the longing for paternal nurturance, expressed in various idealizing male friendships and sometimes in homoerotic yearnings.[8]

Persisting in the minds of some readers is the interpretation that the homosexual strivings encoded in the idealization of male bonding in his fiction indicate a primary homosexual motive on Lawrence's part.[9] The unstated assumption of such criticism is that an object-instinctive drive has been uncovered as the underlying motive and that nothing further lies behind it. Lawrence's homoerotic impulses notwithstanding, his basic sexual identity, I believe, was heterosexual. While one may find additional evidence in his fiction of homoerotic feeling between men, this feeling—expressed variously as admiration or close male bonding—is not acted out by his protagonists in overt homosexual behavior. On the contrary, homosexuality in Lawrence's work is usually presented critically in a defensive maneuver that leaves little doubt about the impulses that Lawrence feared in himself enough to defend against them. Male homosexuals are often treated with satiric amusement, as in the association of homosexuality with charming surface wit rather than depth of intellect and feeling in the dialogue of James Argyle and Algy Constable in *Aaron's Rod* (chap. 16, "Florence"); but they are sometimes judged more harshly, as in the characterization of Loerke in *Women in Love* or the captain in "The Prussian Officer," as exploiters of other people for mechanistic sensation. Female homosexuals are usually presented negatively as anti-life, as in the portraits of Winifred Inger in *The Rainbow* (chap. 12, "Shame") and

Jill Banford in *The Fox,* or in Mellors's railing against "Lesbians" in *Lady Chatterley's Lover* (chap. 14).

Sexuality for Lawrence was sacred, and sexual expression a sacrament. Thus, "sex in the head" or sexual activity merely for sensation was a blasphemy against life. As Lawrence writes to the poet Henry Savage (15 November 1915): "Sex is the fountain head, where life bubbles up into the person from the unknown—you conduct life further and further from sex—it becomes movement—expression—logic. The nihilists . . . never tried to love—" (*Letters* 2:102). Since he associates homosexuality with nihilism, Lawrence, in another letter to Savage (2 December 1913) is puzzled by the homosexual motive of most great men, an assumption that remains unproven. In an apparent attempt to resolve the ambivalence of his sexual identification, Lawrence sets forth a theory of human sexuality, drawing a facile, if familiar, distinction between the supposed narcissistic object relationships of homosexuality and instinctual heterosexual object love:

> I should like to know why nearly every man that approaches greatness tends to homosexuality, whether he admits it or not: so that he loves the *body* of a man better than the body of a woman—as I believe the Greeks did, sculptors and all, by far. I believe a man projects his own image on another man, like on a mirror. But from a woman he wants himself re-born, reconstructed. So he can always get satisfaction from a man, but it is the hardest thing in life to get ones [*sic*] soul and body satisfied from a woman, so that one is free from oneself. And one is kept by all tradition and instinct from loving men, or a man—for it means just extinction of all the purposive influences. [*Letters* 2:115]

Lawrence's intellectual theories of this sort were generated in part in an effort to control internal objects and splitting such as the soul-body dichotomy in this letter. After he was introduced to an intellectual coterie of Bloomsbury homosexuals, including John Maynard Keynes, Francis Birrill, and Duncan Grant, Lawrence was so distressed by their mode of living that he said they made him dream of black beetles. The depth of Lawrence's disturbance is revealed in his letter to David Garnett (19 April 1915), in which furious negative feelings about what he saw as their upper-class intellectual nihilism, frivolous lifestyle, lack of reverence for life, and homosexuality are amalgamated in an angry homophobic reaction formation that, in Lawrence's own word, approaches madness (Letters 2:320–21).

Despite his fears and defenses, homosexuality was not the dominant sexual preference in Lawrence's life. For the record, the biographical evidence of overt homosexuality is scant and contradictory, consisting of two possible homosexual contacts, neither of which has been established authoritatively. Writing over forty years after the fact, Compton Mackenzie (1966) remembers Lawrence's once telling him, "I believe that the nearest I've ever come to perfect love was with a young coal-miner when I was about sixteen."[10] Delany thinks Lawrence was alluding to a young farmer, Alan Chambers (Delany, 314). But Derek Britton cites an unsubstantiated account by a "brutish" miner called Tom of an incident in his adolescence when after his bath his mother "came home early to find the young Lawrence kneeling on the floor, biting her son's buttocks." (52).[11] Sexual exploration among boys in adolescence is normative, and experimentation involving polymorphously perverse component instincts is not indicative of the dominant sexual organization that will ultimately emerge. But speculation has also centered on Lawrence's close relationship in his early thirties with the young Cornish farmer William Henry Hocking. Members of the Hocking family were reticent about a subject they had obviously discussed in private. According to Arthur Eddy, an in-law, William Henry had once confided to him that Lawrence was homosexual: "He said Lawrence used to come down to the farm and talk to him about it a lot." But Hocking's younger brother, Stanley, asked if Lawrence was homosexual, replied, "Certainly not! Not to my knowledge. He may have been a bit effeminate. But I refuse to believe that Lawrence was homosexual. He already had a woman to dapple with."[12]

Lawrence's extensive heterosexual experience and lifelong heterosexual commitment indicate a clear sexual preference and primary sexual identity. The evidence for homosexual experience, based almost entirely on hearsay given at third hand, suggests that if Lawrence acted out the homoerotic impulses that he became aware of in adolescence, he did so very briefly in a crisis situation in his young adult life, during the period when he was living in Cornwall following the court-ordered suppression of *The Rainbow* (1915). At work on revisions of the manuscript that became *Women in Love,* Lawrence was struggling with multiple personal difficulties, four examples of which may be cited: First, his ill health following his bilateral pneumonia and long convalescence, accompanied by depression in the year after his mother's death (9 December 1910), continued in his subsequent pulmonary problems, which Ernest Jones, M.D., apparently told him stemmed from his having had tuberculosis (*Letters* 2:623). Second, there was the continuous battle of his marriage to Frieda von Richthofen Weekley, a sexually amoral German aristocrat who had left her English husband, a respected Nottingham professor, and three small children to elope with Lawrence. Frieda's previous extramarital affairs in Germany with an early member of Freud's circle, Otto Gross,[13] and with the painter Ernst Frick were followed by various infidelities during her marriage to Lawrence (Meyers enumerates six such love affairs).[14] Third, the threat of

wartime conscription elicited Lawrence's enraged response to a mass prein-
duction physical examination by medical authorities, which he felt to be willfully intrusive and humiliating (*Letters* 3:287–88; also described graphically
in *Kangaroo,* chap. 12, "The Nightmare"); and repeated official harassment in
Cornwall on the unfounded suspicion that the Lawrences were spying for the
enemy led to their expulsion from Cornwall on 15 October 1917 (Stevens,
99–113). Fourth, though he could still publish poetry and periodical fiction
and essays, Lawrence found it difficult to earn a living in the face of censorship of his work, the notoriety of *The Rainbow* suppression (5 November
1915) delaying trade publication of *Women in Love* for seven years.

The homoerotic feelings that Lawrence experienced in this period of crisis
emerged, I believe, in response to what he felt as multiple assaults on the self.
These feelings, expressed in the passionate attachment to William Henry
Hocking and described explicitly in the canceled "Prologue" to *Women in
Love* (composed 1916), were also channeled into the bond of blood brotherhood that he sought desperately to establish with John Middleton Murry, the
emotional model for Gerald Crich. Murry's self-serving account cannot be
taken at face value: "He wanted me to swear to be his 'blood-brother,' and
there was to be some sort of sacrament between us." Ordinary friendship was
"not enough: there ought to be some mingling of our blood, so that neither
of us *could* go back on it." When Murry, "half-frightened, half-repelled,"
shrank from any such ritual enactment, Lawrence responded with vindictive
narcissistic rage: "'I hate your love, I *hate it*. You're an obscene bug, sucking
my life away'" (Murry 1933, 79). Murry's assumption, vaguely formulated on
drive theory, was that *Blutbrüderschaft* did not represent a relationship "additional to marriage" as Birkin claims, but a substitution for it—Lawrence's
"escape to a man from the misery of his own failure with a woman." Murry's
description of Lawrence's repeated attempts at male bonding virtually implies
a series of brief homosexual affairs: "But always it was brief and fugitive.
Lawrence was always, and inevitably, disappointed." The intensity and
urgency of Lawrence's longing for Murry suggest that archaic selfobject needs
were being remobilized in an effort to establish a selfobject matrix to preserve
self-cohesion in the face of threatened annihilation of the self. The relationship this maneuver required was, however, finally unworkable. "Lawrence's
hunger for a man could never have been satisfied," says Murry, with little
insight on the nature of that hunger.[15]

This interpretation is confirmed by two of Frieda Lawrence's letters. To
Lawrence's friend and biographer Richard Aldington (5 April 1949), she
writes: "Yes, those war years were terrible for Lawrence, he was not quite sane
at times, as you say. . . . You also know (between you and me) in his bewil-
derment he had a passionate attachment for a cornish [*sic*] farmer, but of

course it was a failure."[16] In a subsequent letter (6 August 1953) to Murry about his and Lawrence's failed friendship, she writes: "There was a real bond between you and L. If he had lived longer and had been older, you would have been real friends, he wanted so desperately for you to understand him. I think the homosexuality in him was a short phase out of misery—I fought him and won—and that he wanted a deeper thing from you."[17]

The stress of the crisis situation reactivated, in Kohutian terms, issues that Lawrence felt as sexual but that actually derived from earlier disturbances in the formation of his nuclear self in relation to both parental imagos.[18] What was being activated on an experiential level was a need for affirmation in relation to the idealized paternal imago. It is clear that Lawrence's own father met few if any of his needs for nurturance, although Lawrence's boyhood friend G. H. Neville gives a moving account of John Arthur Lawrence's coming to the door of the sickroom, filled with awkward, unspoken tenderness and concern for his son when Lawrence was ill (Neville, 63). Lawrence's need for male nurturance in his adult life, emerging in times of crisis or transition, was revived in the service of stabilizing a fragile self and would spontaneously disappear, like Birkin's homoerotic attractions (505), whenever a sense of balance could be restored. Lawrence's homoerotic feelings were not a primary psychological configuration but "disintegration products," as the unmet developmental need to merge with the greatness of an idealized omnipotent paternal selfobject was replaced by "the sexualized replica of the original healthy configuration" in a preoccupation with the penis as an isolated symbol of the adult's power (Kohut 1977, 172–73). These homoerotic feelings were expressed primarily by means of fantasy and in a series of idealizing relationships with men. In such relationships Lawrence repeatedly sought to heal the split between sensual and spiritual being and, in the absence of a viable paternal imago, to fill the deficit left by his massive disappointment in his father. As Delany observes: "Lawrence's homoerotic fantasies often seem to involve his being held and soothed by a stronger, usually older man, a desire that might have more to do with his need for security and affection than with any active homosexuality" (Delany, 314). Lawrence's pattern of idealization, attempted merger, and disappointment in regard to significant male figures like John Middleton Murry compulsively repeated the original traumatic disappointment without healing the deficit. Specifically, Lawrence's object hunger, idealizing merger needs, and longing for quasi-sacramental union with another man were fixations on archaic forms deriving from deficits in his frustrating relationship with a father unavailable for idealization.

Lawrence's homoerotic impulses were also, I believe, a screen for more deep-seated and fearful anxieties involving survival and dependency needs in relation to the mirroring maternal imago. While the attraction to men was evoked by deficits in relation to the idealized paternal imago, the intensity of the feelings involved suggests that they originated from a more primitive source less accessible to consciousness than disappointment in the father, that is, from the intensity of the grandiose merger he had had and lost rather than from the idealizing merger he had never had. In *Sons and Lovers* Lawrence consciously aggrandizes the mother and depreciates the father. The role model his own father provided for masculine identification was systematically devalued by the mother. Lawrence's early feelings of weakness, inferiority, sickliness, effeminacy, and shame were dysphoric effects of the gratifying merger with his mother and were reinforced by his father's abdication. The first cost of the merger was Lawrence's participation in rejection of the father and in elaboration of grandiose fantasies of sharing his life with his mother. The lasting cost was his unresolved dependency needs, which were clearly centered in preserving the supportive, if crippling, relationship with his mother since his depreciated father was in no position to provide the alternative idealizing relationship. As Heinz Kohut interprets this kind of emotional situation, the son senses "the mother's fear of the strong male figure with the adult penis and realizes (unconsciously) that her exaltation of him, the son, is maintained only so long as he does not develop into an independent male."[19] Specifically, Lawrence's adult dependency needs and his correlative fear of engulfment in merger, his need for mirroring by an ever changing roster of disciples, the overt grandiosity of his "leadership" novels, and his sudden eruptions of narcissistic rage were fixations on archaic forms deriving from deficits in his symbiotic relationship with the mother, who provided excessive mirroring at times and used him for her own selfobject needs, but who was unable to respond appropriately to his actual needs for separation-individuation and autonomy. It is in this early developmental context in relation to both parental imagos that the homoerotic feelings that emerged from time to time are to be understood.

Women in Love does encode such feelings, but the seduction theory, explicitly rejected by Donaldson and effectively argued by Squires,[20] both on the evidence of persuasive textual analysis, does not fully account for the unconscious motivation behind Birkin's homoerotic impulses or for his overt sexual behavior. Birkin has sexual intercourse with Ursula and other women and experiments with Ursula in sensual touching and manual stimulation (and, possibly, anal penetration) but has none of these with Crich or any other man.[21] What Birkin is offering to Crich is not the acting out of intimacy in overt homosexuality, but the sublimation of homoerotic desire into blood brotherhood through sacramental ritual.

It is misleading to argue that Birkin is a "latent homosexual"[22] that is, by definition, "one in whom the homosexual impulse [is] either conscious or unconscious, but not overtly acted out."[23] Strictly speaking, I believe, Birkin's pressing need, under cover of homosexual striving, derives from motives that are not aimed primarily at sexual gratification but at preservation of the self. In this interpretation, I am extending the distinction that Lionel Ovesey makes between true homosexual identity and "pseudohomosexuality," although this term has not gained wide usage in clinical or theoretical discussions and is not essential to my meaning. Whereas an actual homosexual motive has as its aim the orgastic satisfaction of an instinctive drive, "pseudohomosexual conflict," according to Ovesey, involves dependency and power strivings that are not sexual in origin, though they may employ sexual feelings and genital apparatus in their expression (Ovesey, 31). I would argue that one of the major anxieties that such preoccupations are employed by Birkin to defend against is the fear that the self may be annihilated. My concern, however, is not to deny the homoerotic feelings that Birkin obviously experiences, but to maintain a distinction between a feeling and the acting out of that feeling in overt behavior, between a feeling and its root motive, and between a particular erotic impulse and the basic sexual identity of the individual. The erotic component in Birkin's attraction to Gerald Crich, which in view of Lawrence's canceled "Prologue" cannot even be described as unconscious, is not in question.[24] The real issues are *what it means, where it comes from,* and *what he does with it.*

∼

What Birkin's homoerotic feeling means in terms of psychoanalytic self psychology is not a drive toward object-instinctive gratification, but a search for a magical solution to a condition that Heinz Kohut describes as a "primary narcissistic disturbance," that is, a disturbance in the structure of the nuclear self, which has been sexualized in the present but which is correlated with "an early ego defect" (Kohut 1971, 69). Birkin himself sees his problem as deriving from self-division: "He knew he obtained no real fulfilment in sensuality, he became disgusted and despised the whole process as if it were dirty. And he knew that he had no real fulfilment in his spiritual and aesthetic intercourse with Hermione. That process he also despised, with considerable cynicism." Yet he cannot "unite the two halves of himself" by an act of will (500).

In the "Prologue," Birkin, struggling with the same self-division that had tormented Paul Morel in *Sons and Lovers,* can find no fulfillment in either half: "He would not sacrifice the sensual to the spiritual half of himself, and he could not sacrifice the spiritual to the sensual half" (500). Birkin has been unable to reconcile the two sides of his nature in relation to women, apparently because he finds women too powerful to approach as whole objects and projects his own dichotomy by seeing them as either spiritual or bestial: "To be spiritual, he must have a Hermione, completely without desire: to be sensual, he must have a slightly bestial woman, the very scent of whose skin soon disgusted him, whose manners nauseated him beyond bearing" (500).

From the perspective of Freudian drive theory, Birkin's splitting would seem clearly to illustrate the theory of psychic impotence in response to the incest taboo, as set forth in Freud's essay "On the Universal Tendency to Debasement in the Sphere of Love": "The whole sphere of love in such people remains divided in the two directions personified in art as sacred and profane (or animal) love. Where they love they cannot desire and where they desire they cannot love. They seek objects which they do not need to love, in order to keep their sensuality away from the objects they love" (*SE* 11:183). A further condition for sexual pleasure for men "in whom there has not been a proper confluence of the affectionate and the sensual currents" is that "they have retained perverse sexual aims whose non-fulfilment is felt as a serious loss of pleasure, and whose fulfilment on the other hand seems possible only with a debased and despised sexual object" (*SE* 11:183).

Lawrence, however, does not present Birkin's splitting in the oedipal terms in which, in his letter to Edward Garnett (14 November 1912), he describes Paul Morel's inability to love (*Letters* 1:476–77) but in terms of depressive feelings of emptiness in the self: As Lawrence writes in the "Prologue" to *Women in Love,* "[H]e became more hollow and deathly, more like a spectre with hollow bones. He knew that he was not very far from dissolution" (501). In Kohutian terms, what the developmentally impaired individual is defending against is not castration anxiety and inhibition of desire in relation to love objects associated unconsciously with the mother but the even more devastating threat of loss of the self. According to Kohut (1984), "disintegration anxiety" is "the deepest anxiety man can experience"; it is the fear of "loss of humanness: psychological death" and "the ascendancy of a nonhuman environment." It is "the threatened loss of the self-cohesion-maintaining responses of the empathic selfobject" (16–19), a loss to which the vulnerable self may react with "fragmentation, serious enfeeblement, or uncontrollable rage" (Kohut 1977, 138).

To protect himself from this threatened dissolution of the self, Birkin (in the "Prologue") turns to the magical solution of passionate "friendships with men of no great intelligence, but of pleasant appearance: ruddy, well-nourished fellows, good-natured and easy, who protected him in his delicate health more gently than a woman would protect him" (502). In this situation he also finds himself attracted to men in the street—a policeman, a soldier, a young man in flannels. At twenty-eight and twenty-nine, Birkin feels hopeless of ever escaping the "bondage" of this attraction, yet he will not acquiesce in it.

Unable to tolerate a view of himself as a homosexual, he cannot accept in himself "this keen desire to have and to possess the bodies of such men" (504). In Kohutian terms, the nucleus of Birkin's anxiety is "related to the fact that his self is undergoing an ominous change—and the intensity of the drive is not the cause of the central pathology (precariousness of self-cohesion), but its result. The core of disintegration anxiety is the anticipation of the breakup of the self, not the fear of the drive" (Kohut 1977, 104).

One of Heinz Kohut's case histories, of a heterosexual man with a similar disturbance in nuclear self-structure, strikingly parallels Birkin's situation in several respects:

> Mr. A.'s homosexual tendencies had not exerted a widespread secondary effect on the ego or led to diffuse drive regression. . . . He had never engaged in homosexual activities and—apart from some sexually tinged, playful wrestling in adolescence and the buying of "physical culture" magazines which contained photographs of athletic men—his homosexual preoccupations were consummated only in fantasy, with or without masturbation. The objects of his homosexual fantasies were always men of great bodily strength and of perfect physique. His own fantasied activity consisted in maintaining a quasi-sadistic, absolute control over these men. In his fantasies he manipulated the situations in such a way that, even though he was weak, he was able to enslave the strong man and to make him helpless. [Kohut 1971, 69–70]

In *Women in Love,* when the two men join in naked wrestling in "Gladiatorial" (chap. 20), Birkin, though slighter, weaker, and of frailer health than Gerald, has skills that enable him to dominate the heavier, stronger man. Their bodies are described in phallic terms as "very dissimilar": "Birkin was tall and narrow, his bones were very thin and fine. Gerald was much heavier and more plastic. His bones were strong and round, his limbs were rounded, all his contours were beautifully and fully moulded" (269). Birkin, who cannot accept his desire for sexual contact with another man, substitutes the close body contact of a nude wrestling match, in which his dominance of the other man is conceptualized metaphorically as penetration: "It was as if Birkin's whole physical intelligence interpenetrated into Gerald's body, as if his fine, sublimated energy entered into the flesh of the fuller man, like some potency, . . . through the muscles into the very depths of Gerald's physical being" (270). Lawrence's description does make the union sound something like Iago's "beast with two backs" in *Othello* (1.1.118): "the swift, tight limbs, the solid white backs, the physical junction of two bodies clinched into a oneness" (270). The psychological sensation of an altered state of consciousness is

marked by "the strange tilting and sliding of the world" into darkness (271).
The language is certainly sexual, but as the word *sublimated* suggests, the
"energy" that is being "interpenetrated into Gerald's body" also empowers
Birkin's "physical being" with the "potency" not of literal penile penetration
but of metaphorically phallic incorporation, as homoerotic feeling is transformed into blood brotherhood to defend against the threatened dissolution
of the self, in particular, against the threat of absorption by women. Birkin's
attachment to Gerald is the expression not of an object-instinctive drive, but
of the longing for merger in an idealized selfobject relationship.

Psychologically, the presence of Gerald's penis may provide reassuring evidence that Birkin can wrestle with him without falling into him or being
devoured. Birkin has already sought healing contact with nature by rolling
naked among primroses and hyacinths and stinging his skin with thistles and
fir needles (106–7) to free himself from corruptive contact with Hermione
after she clouts him murderously on the head with a lapis lazuli paperweight.
He now seeks the refuge of male bonding as protection against the disinte-
grative and devouring relationship with a woman. What Birkin seeks to incorporate, however, is not Gerald's actual penis but, through that powerful
imago, the strength that Gerald's athleticism, masculinity, and authority represent in Birkin's idealizing gaze (490). The unconscious motive behind this
wish is not sexual per se but a mechanism of psychic defense against the threat
of dissolution of the self.

In this light, Birkin's homoerotic attractions in the "Prologue" may be
seen as unsuccessful attempts at magical reparation of the injury to his self,
for he inevitably perpetuates the split by relating to men too only in halfness:
"They divided themselves, roughly, into two classes: these white-skinned,
keen-limbed men with eyes like blue-flashing ice and hair like crystals of
winter sunshine, the northmen, inhuman as sharp-crying gulls, distinct like
splinters of ice, like crystals, isolated, individual; and then the men with dark
eyes that one can enter and plunge into, bathe in, as in a liquid darkness,
dark-skinned, supple, night-smelling men, who are the living substance of the
viscous, universal, heavy darkness" (503–4). The rituals of *Blutbrüderschaft*
are a further conscious attempt to heal the split and achieve self-cohesion by
establishing a balance between spiritual and physical being. After the nude
wrestling match, Birkin says to Gerald: "We are mentally, spiritually intimate,
therefore we should be more or less physically intimate too—it is more
whole" (272). Although Birkin sees in the other man parts and qualities that
he himself needs, the narrator presents Gerald as one of the isolate, icy northmen, and Birkin has about as much chance of establishing a relationship of
mutual affirmation and wholeness with this half-being as he does with
Hermione.

~

Where Birkin's homoerotic feeling comes from is not an easy question to answer, since *Women in Love* offers little information about Birkin's early background. His view of Hermione, however, as a possessive female vulture who threatens to devour him psychologically, provides at least a clue. Judith Ruderman, who identifies the twin poles of "[t]he longing for merger and the fear of merger" in Lawrence, observes that "this psychic conflict is rooted in the author's earliest experiences with his caretaker mother. The blood brotherhood . . . a relation of men—allows Lawrence the security of merger without the threat of annihilation that he associates with women."[25]

It will be helpful at this point to survey briefly and sequentially the interpretations of this psychological situation from the perspectives of classical drive theory and of object relations theory in order to point up the unique contribution of self psychology to understanding the issues involved.

A classic Freudian psychoanalytic interpretation would attribute Birkin's sexual aversion in spiritual relationships with women unconsciously associated with the mother to intrapsychic conflicts rooted in unresolved oedipal problems (*SE* 11:182). In Freud's developmental theory, the boy's oedipal guilt feelings and castration anxiety are partially resolved by his identification with the father, as idealization of the father leads to the emergence of the ego ideal and the repression of the Oedipus complex (*SE* 19:31, 34–37). On the theory that "a human being has originally two sexual objects—himself and the woman who nurses him," Freud, in "On Narcissism: An Introduction," postulates "a primary narcissism in everyone," which in homosexuals may reemerge as a narcissistic attachment to self. "[P]eople whose libidinal development has suffered some disturbance, such as perverts and homosexuals, . . . in their later choice of love-objects . . . have taken as a model not their mother but their own selves. They are plainly seeking *themselves* as a love-object, and are exhibiting a type of object-choice which must be termed 'narcissistic'" (*SE* 14:88). The individual most vulnerable to this narcissistic regression has had, "during the first period of childhood," "a very intense erotic attachment" to the mother, which "was evoked or encouraged by too much tenderness on the part of the mother herself, and further reinforced by the small part played by the father" in the boy's early development (*SE* 11:99). In Freudian terms, the son in Lawrence's work, unable to make the identification with the father necessary for full maturation, is caught between two unsatisfactory object choices, each of which presents a dilemma. If he makes a heterosexual object choice, he must choose between a spiritual woman who is a forbidden oedipal object and a degraded woman who is for this very reason an unsatisfactory substitute. If he makes a homosexual object choice, it is inevitably narcissistic, as Lawrence himself indicates in his letter to Savage of 2 December 1913 (*Letters* 2:115).

Object relations theory would see Birkin as driven by the failure of his emotional relationships with external objects to seek the compensatory satisfactions of oral and anal erotic forms of infantile sexuality in an attempt to salvage natural relationships with internal objects that have broken down.[26] Birkin's homoerotic attractions and his longing for *Blutbrüderschaft* would be interpreted in the context of an object relational situation in which the unavailability of the father for idealization means that the son cannot be conclusively assured that he is genuinely loved by the father or that his love for the father is genuinely accepted. Hence, he resorts to the homoerotic search for the father's penis as a substitute for the father himself. As W. R. D. Fairbairn (1941) explains the mechanism, this substitution involves a regression that also revives the original oral relationship with the original part object, the mother's breast.[27] In the search for male nurturance, the son's "search for his father's penis" becomes in effect "a search for his father's breast." In object relational terms, the son in Lawrence's work is playing out in the external world a drama of objects in the internal world, seeking in their external representatives the protection of the internalized paternal imago against the threat of devourment and absorption by the internalized maternal imago.

Finally, in Kohut's nonpejorative theory of narcissism, self psychology proposes a line of development for the self distinct from that of drive-oriented object love. A self psychological interpretation goes beyond earlier psychoanalytic models in attributing the deficits in the child's nuclear self structure to flaws in the responses of his earliest selfobjects. Thus, in Birkin, both the split between spiritual and sensual love, with the concomitant fear of devourment by women, and the search for protective nurturance in an idealizing merger with another man are displacements of the son's needs, derived both from reactivated archaic selfobject needs and from phase-appropriate needs in the present, for a responsive selfobject matrix.[28] The "traumatic disruption" of this selfobject relationship "accounts for the intensity and urgency of the attempts to set up and maintain merger relationships . . . with other selfobjects in a desperate (and often unworkable) effort to resurrect the harmonious selfobject relatedness that obtained prior to its disruption or to install this relatedness as a fresh experience."[29] In Lawrence's case, the self-psychological interpretation of his symbiotic merger with the mother from early childhood until her death and his severe disappointment in the need for idealizing merger with the father explains, more persuasively than either classical drive theory or object relations theory, both his dependency needs and the deficits in his archaic nuclear self structure that he sought repeatedly and urgently to heal.

Kohut's (1977) description of Mr. A. correlates in part with what we know of Lawrence's own early psychic experience. Not having received what he needed from either parent, Mr. A. had "experienced his body-self as fragmented and powerless (as a consequence of the absence of adequate joyful responses from the maternal self-object)," and the "barely established structure of his guiding ideals had been severely weakened (in consequence of the traumatic destruction of the paternal omnipotent self-object)" (126).

The consequent later idealization is attributable as much to dangers in the relation to the mother as to deficiencies in the relation to the father. Kohut (1971) observes that "behind the imagery concerning the relationship of a boy's grandiose self with a depreciated father . . . lies regularly the deeper imago of the dangerous, powerful rival-parent" (146). As a specific example, "[T]he intensity of Mr. A.'s idealization of his father (and thus the traumatic intensity of his disappointment in him) was due to the earlier disappointment in the mirroring self-object" (Kohut 1977, 11n. 2). In Lawrence's case, maternal mirroring served not only his need for support but also his mother's need to tie him dependently to her in symbiotic merger—to feed on his life, as it were, and live through him—and she actively participated in the destruction of the paternal selfobject, leaving the son with a lifelong search, intensely pressing at times, for an idealizable male, instinctual and earthy like his father but, unlike him, a figure of physical power and psychic strength.

The nature of the problem, as Ruderman has shown, indicates that it derives from the preoedipal (i.e., pre-phallic) period, in which divisions in the bipolar self, such as Birkin's split between spiritual and sensual being, originate. According to Kohut (1971), "the basic neutralizing structures of the psyche are acquired during the preoedipal period." In Mr. A.'s case, "a moderate weakness in his basic psychic structure" resulted in "an impairment of its neutralizing capacity" and led to the sexualization of his "narcissistically invested objects" in three areas relating to the two parent imagos and the self: Mr. A. had sexualized and remained fixated on his "idealized father imago," which he needed because he had not internalized a firmly established ego ideal; he had sexualized and remained fixated on the "mirror image" of his "grandiose self," Kohut's term for the ambitious, aspiring, exhibitionistic sector of the self as mirrored by the joyful admiration and encouragement of the maternal selfobject, which he needed because he had not internalized a secure "(pre)conscious image of the self"; and he had sexualized both "his *need* for idealized values and reliable self-esteem" and the "psychological *processes*" of internalization "by which ideals and self-esteem are acquired." Kohut (1971) observes, "The patient's homosexual fantasies can thus be understood as sexualized statements about his narcissistic disturbance, analogous to the theoretical formulations of the analyst. The fantasies stood, of course, in opposition to meaningful insight and progress since they were in the service of pleasure gain and provided an escape route from narcissistic tensions" (70–71).

~

What Birkin does with his homoerotic preoccupations and with his fear of the devouring female that correlates with them is to encode both in theoretical systems that safely structure his concerns about both male-female and male-male relationships. Birkin's elaborate theories of both "star polarity" with a woman and *Blutbrüderschaft* with a man are designed to make intimacy possible by establishing codes of balance and psychic distance that will protect him against the threat of merger and dissolution of the self in the process. Birkin's concept of marriage as "star polarity," in which, as in the solar system, a magnetic force holds the partners in balance like planets and prevents one from plunging into and being absorbed by the other, becomes a male metaphor for the ideal heterosexual relationship. By preserving the separate integrity of each partner, such a relationship provides a psychic defense against the danger that he will fall into or be devoured by the woman.

In the canceled "Prologue," Birkin's homoerotic impulses emerge in the context of his frustrating attempt to force sexual satisfaction out of the spiritual relationship with Hermione (497). As an effect of the split between spiritual and sensual love with women, Birkin turns toward men with "the hot, flushing, roused attraction which a man is supposed to feel for the other sex" (501). Not surprisingly for a man who fears being devoured, his own fantasies center on oral incorporation. Seeing "a strange Cornish type of man" in a restaurant, "Birkin would feel the desire spring up in him, the desire to know this man, to have him, as it were to eat him, to take the very substance of him" (505). As Ovesey (1969) explains the principle, the "dependent pseudohomosexual male," seeking the "protection of an omnipotent father-substitute via the equation, *penis* = *breast*," "aspires to repair his castration through a magical reparative fantasy of oral or anal incorporation of the stronger man's penis, thus making the donor's strength available to him. This maneuver is doomed not only because it is magical and hence cannot succeed in any case, but also because the fantasied act of incorporation is misinterpreted as truly homosexual in its motivation" and thus serves only to intensify the "pseudohomosexual anxiety" (58).

Birkin's reparative fantasies, in Kohutian terms, express the need for self structure. In this kind of "preconscious fellatio fantasy," according to Kohut (1971), "swallowing the magical semen stands for the unachieved internalization and structure formation" of the self (72n. 4). In Kohut's account of the analysis, Mr. A. was able to discern a motivational connection between his feelings of emptiness and "certain intensely sexualized fantasies to which he turned when he felt depressed, in which he imagined himself subduing a powerful male figure with his 'brains,' chaining him through the employment of some clever ruse in order to imbibe, via a preconscious fellatio fantasy, the giant's strength" (Kohut 1977, 126). The "nonsexual significance of the perverse sexual fantasy that accompanied his masturbatory activities" was "the attempt to use the last remnant of his grandiose self (omnipotent thought: the ruse) in order to regain possession of the idealized omnipotent self-object (to exert absolute control over it—to chain it) and then to internalize it via fellatio" (126). In the novel Birkin, who is arguably Lawrence's most intellectual character, does not attempt to actualize his fantasies in overt homosexual activity but to transform them into the highly intellectualized theory of *Blutbrüderschaft*. In other words, he turns again to what has proven to be the most powerful and reliable part of his grandiose self, the mind.

Neither Birkin's attraction to men in the "Prologue" nor the homoerotic feeling evident in *Blutbrüderschaft* derives from an object-instinctive drive toward orgastic satisfaction in a basically homosexual identity. The homosexual yearnings evident in Birkin's fantasies represent an attempt on his part to repair a defect in his nuclear self by magically incorporating the other man's strength. In this light, Birkin's fantasies may be seen, as Kohut sees Mr. A.'s homosexual preoccupations, "as sexualized statements concerning the nature of his psychological defect and of the psychological functions which had to be acquired." In "the absence of a stable system of firmly idealized values" as a source "of the internal regulation of self-esteem," Mr. A. "had in his sexual fantasies replaced the inner ideal with its sexualized external precursor, an athletic powerful man"; and in place of the self-esteem derived from living up to one's standards, he had substituted "the sexualized feeling of triumph" derived from robbing "the external ideal of its power and perfection," thus in fantasy acquiring these qualities for himself and achieving "a temporary feeling of narcissistic balance" (Kohut 1971, 72). There is an obvious parallel in Birkin's temporary feeling of wholeness in physical and spiritual intimacy after robbing Gerald of his power and perfection, triumphing over him by the cunning use of jiujitsu in the wrestling match. In *Blutbrüderschaft*, Birkin takes the process one step further in the attempt to transmute the need for an idealizable omnipotent paternal selfobject underlying his fantasies into a viable ego ideal that he can live by: a standard of commitment and loyalty in male bonding that does not include the exploitation of grossly sensational, overtly sexual acting out.

Birkin's homoerotic feeling is a psychic mechanism thrown up recurrently by the ego during a disturbing transitional period of his life as a defense against dissolution in the service of preservation of the self. But as the narrator comments, "The wrestling had some deep meaning to them—an

unfinished meaning" (272). In his homoerotic fantasies in the "Prologue,"
Birkin, as Kohut says of Mr. A., has sexualized both "his *need* for idealized values and reliable self-esteem" and the *process* of internalization by which these
qualities are acquired (Kohut 1971, 70–71). In the theory of *Blutbrüderschaft*,
a relationship comparable to marriage in commitment, there is still a promi
nent element of magical thinking aimed at pleasure gain rather than realistic
insight. For this reason, Birkin's attempt to transmute the need for an idealizable omnipotent paternal selfobject into the ego ideal by way of male rituals
that dramatize such a relationship cannot be entirely successful.

Where his object relationships with women are concerned, Birkin tries to
make his way out of the impasse through a series of exercises that adapt his
anal eroticism to the task of psychological desensitization. First, he channels
his forbidden sexual inclinations into aesthetic appreciation of a statuette of a
standing female:

> . . . a tall, slim, elegant figure from West Africa, in dark wood, glossy and
> suave. It was a woman, with hair dressed high, like a melon-shaped dome.
> He remembered her vividly; she was one of his soul's intimates. Her body
> was long and elegant, her face was crushed tiny like a beetle's, she had rows
> of round heavy collars, like a column of quoits, on her neck. He remem-
> bered her: her astonishing cultured elegance, her diminished, beetle face,
> the astounding long elegant body, on short, ugly legs, with such protuber-
> ant buttocks, so weighty and unexpected below her slim long loins. [253]

The grace and beauty of the figure's formal aesthetic lines are correlated with
her abstracted beetle face, recalling Lawrence's dream of black beetles in
response to the Cambridge homosexuals, and the arousing grossness of her
protuberant buttocks, encoding Birkin's homoerotic desire.

Later, in "Excurse" (chap. 23), though Birkin initially feels "tight and
unfree," he submits to Ursula's initiative as, "overwhelmed with a sense of a
heavenful of riches," she stimulates him manually by tracing "with her hands
the line of his loins and thighs, at the back." This sensual experimentation
establishes "a new current of passional electric energy, between the two of
them, released from the darkest poles of the body," and leads to "a perfect
passing away for both of them, and at the same time the most intolerable
accession into being, the marvellous fulness of immediate gratification, overwhelming, outflooding from the Source of the deepest life-force, the darkest,
deepest, strangest life-source of the human body, at the back and base of the
loins" (313–14). While Lawrence evokes the prostatic and sacral chakras of
kundalini yoga in his reference to the "mystically-physically satisfying"
"strange fountains of his body," he alludes, on a more mundane level, to erotic

satisfaction at the anal erogenous zone: "And now, behold, from the smitten rock of the man's body, from the strange marvellous flanks and thighs, deeper, further in mystery than the phallic source, came the floods of ineffable darkness and ineffable riches" (314). By means of this unconventional sexual experience with a woman he can both love and desire, Birkin begins the healing process that can restore his self-division.

Finally, Birkin channels these impulses into a conscious process of debasement from the spiritual to the profane in love. Like the West African statuette, he seems to Ursula both fascinating and repellant at once: "His licentiousness was repulsively attractive. But he was self-responsible. . ." (412–13). The result is uninhibited sex with Ursula, and her developing response conveys the liberating effect of the experience for both partners:

They might do as they liked—this she realised as she went to sleep. How could anything that gave one satisfaction be excluded? What was degrading?—Who cared? Degrading things were real, with a different reality. And he was so unabashed and unrestrained. Wasn't it rather horrible, a man who could be so soulful and spiritual, now to be so—she balked at her own thoughts and memories: then she added—so bestial? So bestial, they two!—so degraded! She winced.—But after all, why not? She exulted as well. Why not be bestial, and go the whole round of experience? She exulted in it. She was bestial. How good it was to be really shameful! There would be no shameful thing she had not experienced.—Yet she was unabashed, she was herself. Why not?—She was free, when she knew everything, and no dark shameful things were denied her. [413]

Their precise sexual practices, veiled in shadowy, suggestive, but generic language, are not specified, but the emphasis upon anality in the protruding buttocks of the West African statuette, in the anal eroticism of the sexual experimentation in "Excurse," and in the sense of liberation through "degrading," "shameful," and "bestial" sexuality suggests that their activities included anal intercourse. What is involved is not the simple substitution of the female body for the preferred male body of Birkin's fantasies in the "Prologue." Rather, a familiar pattern of arousal has been adapted in a process of de-idealization that makes possible a relationship with a woman on a basis other than either spiritual elevation or sexual disgust.

Birkin has achieved in some measure the restructuring that Lawrence sees as an aim of heterosexual relationships. The need for affirmation of the self by means of an irrevocable bonding with a stronger male remains. In their

poignant dialogue after Gerald's death at the end of *Women in Love,* Birkin's
longing and Ursula's insistent reality are both reasserted. Birkin's compromise
has been to accept the "sheer intimacy" of heterosexual marriage as sufficient
for overt sexuality, provided he could also have the emotionally satisfying
bond of "eternal union with a man too: another kind of love." In Ursula's
view, "It's an obstinacy, a theory, a perversity." "You can't have two kinds of
love," she declares. "It seems as if I can't," Birkin admits. "Yet I wanted it"
(481). Ursula's final comment, "You can't have it, because it's false, impossible," suggests her insight on why he is prevented from having what he wants:
because he will not, or cannot, accept the realistic limits of such a relationship. His intransigent reply, "I don't believe that" (481), is more ambiguous.
He has not given up his longing for merger with an idealizable male, but his
tone is wistful and sad and the intensity of his need seems somewhat diminished in strength. The dialogue has shown that *Blutbrüderschaft,* as a prac-
tical means of gratifying Birkin's longing, is doomed to tragic failure and
disappointment. But as a psychological maneuver, the concept has enabled
him to incorporate this longing and to preserve the self-cohesion needed to
function creatively.

For Lawrence, as for Birkin, the subject was not closed. He returns to the
issue of blood brotherhood in two essays in *Studies in Classic American Literature,* in which Herman Melville becomes the proxy through whom he criticizes his own hopeless quest for blood brotherhood: "Yet to the end he pined
for this: a perfect relationship; perfect mating; perfect mutual understanding.
A perfect friend" (142). The lost merger was not to be restored: "Right to the
end he could never accept the fact that *perfect* relationships cannot be" (142).
As hard as it was for Lawrence to hear it above the insistent demands of his
own needs and wishes, that was the voice of the reality principle.

CHAPTER 5

D. H. Lawrence, Idealization, and Masculine Identity

It seems clear that as Lawrence completes *Women in Love* and *Studies in Classic American Literature,* he does not and cannot stop the search for the male figure who can serve to bridge and unify the divided male consciousness. This theme must have been a significant factor in Lawrence's conscious and unconscious thought processes.

As Jacob A. Arlow explains the concept of unconscious fantasy, one's fantasy life is idiosyncratic and specific to the individual, deriving from childhood experience of "object relations, traumatic events, unfulfilled wishes." "These decisive forces of the individual's life are organized into a number of leading unconscious fantasies that persist throughout life," forming "a stream of organized mental representations and wishes which act as a constant source of inner stimulation to the mind." "The evidence is clear," Arlow concludes, "that the influence of unconscious fantasy is a constant feature of mental life, operating all the time we are awake and some of the time we are asleep."[1] Arlow's emphasis on the idea that leading unconscious fantasies persist throughout life is borne out in the flow of Lawrence's creative work. His preoccupation with the search for an integrated masculine identity through relationship with another man continues in his next major works.

For boys, the penis is the defining organ in the establishment of male sexual identity. It remains for men the central imago in the organization of masculine gender identity. In psychoanalytic terms, the search for masculine identity is embodied in the search for an effective penis. Phyllis Tyson and Robert L. Tyson have defined the difference between gender role and gender identity and have discussed the importance of the father in this process. Much recent gender criticism based in cultural theory is essentially concerned not with identity but with gender role, a term derived from the sociological concept of role, here referring to social features of behavior relating to gender. Tyson and Tyson define more precisely what they call "gender role identity" as "a gender-based patterning of conscious and unconscious interactions with other people." Gender role identity, as differentiated from the earlier concept of gender role, "should not be confused with socially determined learned roles; rather it refers to an intrapsychic, interactional representation."[2]

In the preoedipal period, idealization of the father and identification with him emerge as significant experiences for the boy. As early as the second year of life, "paternal availability plays an important role in helping the boy establish a phallic body image."[3] According to the Tysons, "The father is so important in encouraging masculine attitudes that his availability as a role model is crucial." "As he approaches the phallic phase, the boy looks increasingly to his father as an adored ideal. He wishes to be with his idealized father and to be gratified by him, and builds a wished-for view of himself on the model of this paragon of perfection he has created in his mind." They add: "The father's easy availability to his son in a variety of activities clearly is important if the boy is to identify with a male gender role" (Tyson and Tyson, 283).

In psychoanalytic terms, Lawrence's apparent wish, in early childhood, to blend with girls suggests an unconscious fantasy of being loved by his father as if he were a girl. On a less accessible level, this suggests an unacknowledged wish to be loved by his father just as his mother was. If he were loved by his father in this way, he would be receiving a penis, and he would be assured of the masculinity he had wanted to obtain from his father.[4] Stated in conscious terms this idea may come across to some as metaphorical and to others as absurdly literal. Young children, however, do not so easily distinguish between figurative and literal meanings. In the timeless unconscious, as well, no such distinctions are made.

In Heinz Kohut's self psychological terms, "personality may be organized around a grandiose, exhibitionistic trend, expressed as healthy ambition or assertiveness and derived from the mirroring selfobject, usually the mother. Alternatively, the idealizing selfobject relationship may be the dominant force. Usually derived from the relationship with the father (especially for the boy), this would be expressed in terms of healthy and strongly held ideals and values." Kohut emphasizes "the importance of the parents' role in the reflection of infantile grandiosity and the provision of opportunities for idealization."[5]

Lawrence's merger relationship with his mother certainly encouraged his grandiose exhibition of his talents and ambitions; but as supportive and gratifying as this relationship seemed to be, it also posed the threat of engulfment. In this psychological situation, the usual course would be to turn to the other parental selfobject, the father, to gain confirmation of the self through an idealizing relationship with him. It is extremely doubtful that Arthur Lawrence could have served as a selfobject for his son. The inability of the father to respond appropriately to his son's needs was the result, in part, of the alliance of mother and son in rejection of him. The interactional relationship with the father and its internalization as an intrapsychic representation that psychoanalysts like Phyllis Tyson and Robert L. Tyson regard as the norm for establishing a masculine gender role identity was largely unavailable for Lawrence.

As Barbara Schapiro has pointed out, "The son's rejection of his father, of course, only intensifies his need for paternal identificatory love. That need is made all the more desperate by the original failure of recognition in the mother-child relationship. Lawrence looks to an idealized father-figure not only to defend against the omnipotent mother of unconscious fantasy, as Storch and Ruderman insist, but also to bestow recognition of the bodily, passionate self that, having been unrealized, has become idealized."[6]

The two major poles of the developing self in the preoedipal matrix, according to Kohut, derive from selfobject relationships based on mirroring and idealization—the former primarily, though not exclusively, maternal mirroring in the development of the grandiose self, the latter primarily, though not exclusively, in response to the father as an omnipotent paternal ideal. Kohut's chapter "The Idealizing Transference" in *The Analysis of the Self* and his clinical illustration of these principles in the case history of Mr. A. are particularly useful in understanding the effect of Lawrence's massive disappointment in his depreciated father. If his merger relationship with his supportive and mirroring but possessive mother left him with a lifelong attraction to, and fear of, merging, his disappointment in his father left him with a lifelong unsatisfied need to find a male figure he could idealize in his effort to establish and maintain a stable self structure and masculine identity. The unavailability of Lawrence's father for idealization meant that the process of making a masculine identification with him could not be completed through the "optimal frustration" of experiencing a series of lesser disappointments as the son gradually encounters and incorporates the realistic limitations of the idealized object, leading to the necessary internalization of ideals originally attributed to the father as one of the two major poles of preoedipal self structure.

Kohut's description of his analysand Mr. U. illustrates the issues that may arise for the son in such a situation. In early childhood, turning away from the "unreliable empathy" of his mother, he had tried to gain "confirmation of his self" through an idealizing relationship with his father. The "self-absorbed" father, however, unable "to respond appropriately," "rebuffed his son's attempt to be close to him, depriving him of the needed merger with the idealized self-object and, hence, of the opportunity for gradually recognizing the self-object's shortcomings." The son "remained fixated on two sets of opposite responses to ideals—responses he repeated again and again." "He either felt depressed and hopeless vis-à-vis an unreachable ideal, or he felt that the ideal was worthless and that he, in grandiose arrogance, was vastly superior to

it." "These swings in Mr. U.'s self-esteem were an outgrowth of his not having achieved the gradual and thus secure internalization of the idealized
parental imago." A further effect of the child's "failure to form reliable ideals,
which would have regulated his self-esteem," was the intensification of his fixation on a fetish associated with the mother.[7]

The effect of the paternal abdication and emotional abandonment was
for Lawrence the compulsion to repeat the unmet need for idealization and
for male nurturance in relation to various other men. The ambivalent reen-
actment, as in his relationship with John Middleton Murry, was characterized by wide swings between the opposite poles of overvaluing idealization
of the other and grandiosity on his own part with concomitant devaluation
of the other.

As Lawrence writes to Lady Ottoline Morrell (22 February 1915), early in
his friendship with Murry: "He is one of the men of the future—you will see.
He is with me for the Revolution. He is just finishing his novel—his first—
very good. At present he is my partner—the only man who quite simply is
with me.—One day he'll be ahead of me. Because he'll build up the temple if
I carve out the way—the place" (*Letters* 2:291). Ten years later (28 January
1925), near the end of their relationship, he writes to Murry: "You remember
that charming dinner at the Café Royal that night? You remember saying: I
love you Lorenzo, but I won't promise not to betray you?—Well, you *can't*
betray me, and that's all there is to that. Ergo, just leave off loving me. Let's
wipe off all that Judas-Jesus slime" (*Letters* 5:205). Finally, in direct contra-
diction of the evaluation of Murry expressed in the letter to Lady Ottoline
Morrell (22 February 1915), he writes to Murry (19 January 1926): "I would
rather you didn't publish my things in the Adelphi. As man to man, if ever we
were man to man, you and I, I would give them to you willingly. But as writer
to writer, I feel it is a sort of self-betrayal. Surely you realise the complete
incompatibility of my say with your say. Say your say, Caro!—and let *me* say
mine. But for heavens sake, dont let us pretend to mix them" (*Letters* 5:380).

Lawrence's treatment of the relationship between Rupert Birkin and Gerald Crich in *Women in Love*, drawing in part on his relationship with Murry,
reflects a similar pattern. One is struck by the inconsistency of Birkin's longing
for a formalized *Blutbrüderschaft* with Crich, who is presented as a mechanistic and exploitative captain of industry, exactly the sort of man an organicist
like Birkin (or Lawrence) might be expected to despise. The discordance is
explicable in terms of the author's ambivalence, which was inevitably embedded in the text. Birkin's longing and his disappointment at its unfulfillment,
remain unresolved at the end of the novel.

Women in Love does not set forth the failure of the original paternal selfobject from which a relationship such as Birkin's with Crich would probably

derive. *Sons and Lovers,* however, does illustrate this principle. As different as they are in many respects, there is a psychological continuity between the two novels. Alfred Booth Kuttner makes a striking observation on this continuity in his report to the publisher Mitchell Kennerley (10 November 1914), on the manuscript of "The Wedding Ring," which was ultimately the source of both *The Rainbow* and *Women in Love:* "'The Wedding Ring' contains simply chunks and chunks of psychological motivation almost literally transferred from 'Sons and Lovers.' This is particularly notic[e]able in the men. The Brangwens, Skrebensky, Birkin, all take what is practically Paul's attitude towards love and marriage. . . . Birkin is simply an older Paul, more wretched and more pitiless" (Kuttner, Appendix III, 483–84). One difference between the two novels is that in *Sons and Lovers* the developmental source from which the protagonist's psychological motivation originates is made clear, whereas in *Women in Love* it is not.

Our understanding of the situation is reinforced by what we know of Lawrence's own relationship with his father. Unable to admire his father and consciously aware only of hating him (*Letters* 1:190), Lawrence nevertheless felt keenly the lack of male nurturance. It is not a matter of Lawrence's father's mistreating him, but of his abdication and unavailability for idealization as a viable paternal selfobject, which left the paternal deficit that Lawrence, for much of his life, tried to fill in the repetition of an ambivalent pattern of adulation, inevitable disappointment, and devaluation in relation to other men.

In self psychological terms, Lawrence's extreme disappointment in his father was the opposite of optimal frustration insofar as rejection of the father from early childhood (Lawrence says from birth) gave him no opportunity to de-idealize his father gradually as he inevitably encountered the father's realistic flaws. Hence the son had no means of transmuting internalization of the ideals that would normally have been attributed to the father and thus of integrating these ideals with other parts of his own self structure. Lawrence sought to fill the deficit in self structure in an idealizing relationship with another, seemingly stronger, man, but this attempt led inevitably to further splitting and it ended in disillusionment.

Kohut explains the significance of idealization of the paternal selfobject with reference to another analysand, Mr. X., whose "transference related to the reactivation of the needs of the unconscious nuclear self," specifically in "the pole that carried its masculine ideals." As Kohut explains in self psychological terms: "Specific disturbances of the relation between the developing self and the self-objects during the patient's childhood had not permitted the completion of the developmental sequence of (a) merger with the paternal ideal, (b) de-idealization and transmuting internalization of the idealized omnipotent self-object, and (c) integration of the ideals with the other constituents of the self and with the rest of the personality" (Kohut 1977, 217). In the psychoanalytic process, "the reactivation of a specific incompleted developmental task" leads to "the reintensification of the attempt to fill in a specific structural defect." According to Kohut, "The increased sexual activities and especially the so-called sexualization of the transference encountered in the early phases of some analyses of narcissistic personality disorders are usually manifestations of the intensification of the patients' need to fill in a structural defect. These manifestations should not be understood as an eruption of drives but as the expression of the patients' hope that the selfobject will now supply them with the needed psychological structure" (Kohut 1977, 217–18n). The need to fill in a structural defect may also account for the sexualization of an otherwise nonsexual relationship in a disturbing situation in the course of life. This, I believe, is how the sexualization of Lawrence's feelings in the relationship with William Henry Hocking during the Cornwall period is to be understood.

In another context, Kohut speaks of "the decisive difference between instinctually cathected objects who are the targets of our drives and selfobjects who maintain the cohesion, vitality, strength, and harmony of the self." Furthermore, says Kohut, "the archaic selfobject need" does not "proceed from the loss of a love object but from the loss of a more mature selfobject experience."[8] The distinction between the two, the instinctually cathected love object and the cohesion maintaining selfobject, derives from Kohut's theoretical position that "narcissism has a separate line of development" from drive development (Kohut 1984, 226n. 2).

If one or the other of the two earliest, or in Kohut's word "archaic," selfobjects fails to respond appropriately to the needs of the self, the effect may be an impairment or deficit in the self. But as Kohut elaborates: "the self will be seriously impaired only if, after one of the selfobjects of the child has failed to respond, the attempt to acquire compensatory structures via the adequate responses of another selfobject has also come to grief" (Kohut 1984, 205–6). In Lawrence's development, despite his father's unavailability, in the family situation in place even before Lawrence's birth, and the danger of engulfment that the merger with his mother posed, his mirroring relationship with her left him with a basic core that enabled him to establish compensatory structures and prevented serious impairment of the self. But the structural deficit left by the unsatisfied need for an idealizing relationship with the paternal selfobject was one that Lawrence sought to fill as he continued to look for an idealizable man with whom he could establish such a relationship.

Although Arthur Lawrence, as virtually an outsider in the family, was largely unavailable for idealization, there are some indications in texts of Lawrence's felt need in this regard. The father's body could still become a focal point for admiration—as in Paul's admiring gaze upon his father's naked body when Morel is at his bath. The description is of a once powerful male body, at middle age scarred by overwork in the coal mining industry, but still impressively vital and young looking: "He still had a wonderfully young body, muscular, without any fat. His skin was smooth and clear. It might have been the body of a man of twenty eight, except that there were perhaps too many blue scars, like tattoo marks, where the coal-dust remained under the skin, and that his chest was too hairy." To Paul, "It seemed strange they were the same flesh." A brief conversation about the father's body ensues:

"I suppose," he said to his father, "you had a good figure once."

"Eh!" exclaimed the miner, glancing round, startled and timid, like a child.

"He had," exclaimed Mrs. Morel. "If he didn't hurtle himself up as if he was trying to get in the smallest space he could."

"Me!" exclaimed Morel. "Me a good figure! I wor niver much mor n'r a skeleton."

"You've had a constitution like iron," she said; "and never a man had a better start, if it was body that counted. You should have seen him as a young man—" she cried suddenly to Paul, drawing herself up to imitate her husband's once handsome bearing. [*Sons and Lovers,* 235–36]

As an adolescent, Lawrence sought to reassure himself of his own masculinity in part by his association with friends like Alan Chambers and George Neville. In a striking scene described in his memoir of Lawrence, Neville's body becomes the object of Lawrence's gaze of intense admiration.

According to Neville, Lawrence, who was trying to paint a copy of Maurice Greiffenhagen's *An Idyll,* was unable to reproduce the male figure without distorting the back. Neville's response was to lock the door and undress, as he told Lawrence, to show him "what a man's back is really like—if he *is* anything of a man." As Neville recounts the scene, Lawrence was "dreadfully puzzled. . . . But as my bare limbs began to come into view his eyes began to shine and they positively glittered when at last I stood naked before him and said, 'There now! For God's sake have a good look at a man with a decent shape while you have the chance.'" Flexing his muscles, Neville displayed some of the showmanship he had picked up at the gymnasium. Turning his back to show Lawrence "what a fellow's back ought to look like when he was grabbing a girl in that fashion," he "maintained the pose for a time and there was a deep silence in the room." When he turned to see Lawrence's reaction, "he was leaning forward in his chair, his elbows resting on the table, the cup of his hands supporting his face, upon which was an expression of perfectly rapt adoration." As Neville recognizes, "That is a very strong expression to use, but it is the only one that will express to you what I wish to convey. Lawrence adored strength and beauty with a kind of envious adoration; and in the same way he adored practically all personal characteristics he did not himself possess." Lawrence's verbal response was to gasp, "I had no idea. Good gracious! You're positively a pocket Hercules."[9]

Both of these two scenes, Paul Morel's gaze of admiration at his father's still vital body and Lawrence's gaze of "rapt adoration" at Neville's athletic physique, involve the male observer's response to the naked male body. There is no reference to the man's penis in either scene, but clearly neither Paul Morel at his father's bath nor Lawrence at the revelation of Neville's body could have avoided being intensely aware of this powerful imago of masculine identity. In the absence of a supportive relationship with his father, Lawrence's association with a physically stronger, more conventionally masculine friend like Neville may have been a means of reassuring himself about his own masculinity. Although Lawrence could not have been described like Neville as "a pocket Hercules," it must have been encouraging to see that they both had penises.

The strength and beauty that Lawrence had discovered in the male body may be understood as a form of the idealization that he was unable to experience fully in the masculine character of his father. Neville's account presents Lawrence's response to this revelation of the body as a profound emotional and aesthetic experience. In his subsequent novels, Lawrence often glorifies the male body, male relationships, and male leadership. In later years, he comes more and more to regard with respect the particular manifestation of qualities, characteristic of his father, that he identifies as masculine.

Kohut hypothesizes that "the baby's archaic merger-idealizations of fusing with the calm body of the adult who picks him up gradually lead to the reassuring and self-organizing experiences embodied in our admiration for great political leaders, artists, scientists, and their inspiring ideas . . ." (Kohut 1984, 206). Lawrence's extreme disappointment in his father led almost inevitably to the emergence of the imagined figure of the strong leader that he formulated in the novels of his leadership period. Yet for Lawrence, this strategy may not have been entirely satisfactory in that it belonged to a closed circuit governed by deficit needs rather than by the reality principle.

Psychologically, idealization in the present as a repetition of a need unsatisfied in early development seems destined to repeat the original disappointment. Arriving at a more realistic acceptance of one's self-experience in the present must finally entail working through the disappointment in the original paternal figure rather than attempting to short-circuit or bypass this disappointment. To the extent that the process of working through enables the individual to internalize the ideals, he may be able to discontinue repetition in the present of the previously unsatisfied idealization needs.

Stephen A. Mitchell suggests that both "[g]randiosity and idealization are efforts to reach the object through familiar, preferred modes of connection and intimacy."[10] In the psychoanalytic process, G. Atwood and A. Stolorow, "drawing on the self-psychology tradition, regard these narcissistic illusions as the product of the patient's effort 'to establish in the analytic transference the requisite intersubjective context that had been absent or insufficient during the formative years and that now permitted the arrested developmental process to resume'" (*Structures of Subjectivity*, 83, qtd. in Mitchell, 206). The assumption of this theory of psychoanalysis, which follows the "developmental arrest" model of neurosis, is that the analytic process will be used to facilitate the individual's resuming development from the point at which it had been arrested and completing it. Whatever the merits of this assumption—and the concept is debatable in light of other schools of psychoanalytic thought—there are people who, in the face of numerous failures to acquire the desired results, seem compulsively driven to repeat the same maneuvers that have not worked in the past.

Where Lawrence is concerned, there is a close connection between the impulse to integrate relationships with others around grandiose claims, his wish to be the leader who attracts followers to himself, and the opposing impulse to integrate relationships around idealization of the other, his wish to ally himself to such a figure. The former is seen in his repeatedly expressed need to have his own grandiosity reflected in the mirroring response of a select, but changing, group of disciples. The latter is seen in his veneration of various figures of heroic masculinity in a way that he could not venerate his father.

In the unpublished "Prologue to *Women in Love*," Lawrence discusses at length Birkin's attraction to men and his wish for friendship with "passionate young men, ruddy, well-nourished fellows, good-natured and easy, who protected him in his delicate health more gently than a woman would protect him" ("Prologue to *Women in Love*," 502). In the novel, in his relationship with Gerald Crich, Birkin looks for a brother, a friend, an alter ego and does not emphasize the "maternal" elements of the description in the "Prologue." At this point in his fiction, Lawrence looks directly for a man to whom he can submit himself and gain his "selfhood" through that experience with a nurturing father. His "leadership" novels reveal some of the problems that may derive from such a strategy.

As Mitchell points out, people "who integrate relations around idealizing others tend to believe passionately that this is the best sort of relationship to have." For such people, life is "complicated and perilous." Hence, "the safest strategy for living is to find someone who seems to be secure and successful, who has all the answers, and to apprentice oneself to that person." This strategy, however, is not without expense. "For the price of considerable devotion, the idealized object will take the disciple under his wing, protecting him, leading him, guiding him along the path they have already cut through the obstacles of life." While those who integrate relationships on this basis are convinced of the preciousness of such a bond, Harry Stack Sullivan would ask, "Can they afford it?" According to Mitchell, "It is precisely the cost of idealization" that the idealizing person "does not notice" (Mitchell, 209).

Aaron Sisson's idealizing relationship with Rawdon Lilly in Lawrence's *Aaron's Rod* is an example. Aaron's disillusionment with marriage and the demands of intimate family life comes to a head at Christmastime with the shattering of a Christmas ornament, the blue ball, which metaphorically encompasses the cultural ideal of a unified world of faith, fidelity, family, and personal integration, while alluding subliminally to his depressive frustration in the actual situation. Leaving home and family with only his flute (in a psychoanalytic context, his phallus), Aaron sets out consciously in search of individual selfhood but, as soon becomes apparent, unconsciously in quest of the elusive masculine ideal. Men such as Jim Bricknell fall far short of this masculine ideal, and trendy personalities, like the homosexuals Algy Constable and James Argyle, with their amusing but superficial chatter, and Francis Dekker, "flinging his hand and twisting his waist and then laying his hand on his breast" (213), bear little resemblance to the ideal.

Aaron finds the aesthetic embodiment of the internal idealized masculine imago in Florence in the large marble sculptures of male figures in the Piazza della Signoria, especially in the *David* of Michelangelo: "standing forward stripped and exposed and eternally half-shrinking, half-wishing to expose himself, he is the genius of Florence," but also, in a somewhat cruder form, in the marble colossi, *Hercules and Cacus* of Baccio Bandinelli: "the big, lumpy Bandinelli men are in keeping too. They may be ugly—but they are there in their place, and they have their own lumpy reality" (211–12).

Aaron experiences Florence as a city of men: "Here men had been at their intensest, most naked pitch." "Aaron felt a new self, a new life-urge rising inside himself. Florence seemed to start a new man in him" (212). The feeling is almost rhapsodic. "But men! Men! A town of men, in spite of everything. The one manly quality, undying, acrid fearlessness. The eternal challenge of the unquenched human soul. Perhaps too acrid and challenging today, when there is nothing left to challenge. But men—who existed without apology, and without justification. Men who would neither justify themselves nor apologise for themselves. Just men. The rarest thing left in our sweet Christendom" (213).

Ultimately Aaron believes that he has found the masculine ideal in the person of Rawdon Lilly, who in the much discussed massage scene during Aaron's serious illness with flu accompanied by an underlying depression bordering on despair, provides Aaron with the needed male nurturance that was largely missing in Lawrence's own early psychological development. After the destruction of Aaron's flute, which is identified throughout as both the instrument of individual artistic creation and the symbol of his phallic sexuality and individuality, he turns to Lilly as an admired source of strength, a psychological maneuver that Lilly tacitly encourages. Implicitly contrasting himself to political figures like Prime Minister David Lloyd George, whom he describes as a mere "instrument" of the "mob power" to which the "popular will" yields rather than "submit to a bit of healthy individual authority" (96–97). Returning to this theme at the end of the novel, Lilly explains: "We must either love, or rule. And once the love-mode changes, . . . then the other mode will take place in us. And there will be profound, profound obedience in place of this love-crying, obedience to the incalculable power-urge. And men must submit to the greater soul in a man, for their guidance: and women must submit to the positive power-soul in man, for their being." "You'll never get it!" Aaron responds skeptically. If the line of power and submission sounds arbitrary, Lilly insists: "It's the deep, fathomless submission to the heroic soul in a greater man. You, Aaron, you too have the need to submit. You, too, have the need livingly to yield to a more heroic soul, to give yourself. . . . And you know it isn't love. It is life-submission" (299). This final scene illustrates the idealizing relationship that Aaron Sisson, and at this time perhaps Lawrence himself, regards as most desirable:

> There was a long pause. Then Aaron looked up into Lilly's face. It was dark and remote-seeming. It was like a Byzantine eikon at the moment.
> "And whom shall I submit to?" he said.
> "Your soul will tell you," replied the other.
>
> [*Aaron's Rod*, 299]

Although the problems inherent in such a relationship may seem obvious to many readers, "the cost of idealization" is not apparent to any Lawrentian protagonist until Richard Lovatt Somers's sudden insight that the Australian fascist leader Ben Cooley in *Kangaroo* really wants to put him in his pocket. "Don't thwart me," Cooley pleads. "Don't—or I shall have to break all connection with you, and I love you so. I love you so. Don't be perverse and put yourself against me." As Cooley clasps Somers to his own "warm passionate body," Somers recognizes the total control behind the profession of love. "He doesn't love me," he thinks to himself. "He just turns a great, general emotion on me, like a tap. . . . Damn his love. He wants to force me." "Let's be hard, separate men," he says to Cooley. "Let's understand one another deeper than love." "Is any understanding deeper than love?" Cooley asks. "Why, yes, you know it is. At least between men," Somers replies. "But you're such a Kangaroo, wanting to carry mankind in your belly-pouch, cosy, with its head and long ears peeping out." Male kangaroos, of course, do not have pouches. Far from being the idealizable and nurturant father that Somers has been searching for, Cooley is revealed as yet another possessive, controlling, and engulfing mother. "I'm sorry I have made a mistake in you," Cooley tells him, then adds: "I think the best thing you can do is to leave Australia" (*Kangaroo*, 208–10).

Did the cost of idealization in his own life escape Lawrence? The search for an idealizable male in an effort to fill the paternal deficit is understandable in self psychological terms. The cost of idealization as a way of life without transmuting internalization of the masculine ideals as self structure is a dependent self. Clearly, at this point in his life Lawrence wrestled with these issues. In *Aaron's Rod,* in a time of alienation and need, Aaron Sisson is drawn to idealize a seemingly stronger, more self possessed man, Rawdon Lilly, who has provided him with a limited experience of the male nurturance he needs. But what Lilly wants from Sisson is submission, submission absolute, from his very soul. In *Kangaroo,* Richard Lovatt Somers, tempted to submit to the will of a would-be fascist leader, recognizes the threat to the self behind the profession of love, and states his preference for a relationship of mutual respect between independent men. If this clear choice represents on Lawrence's part an internalization of his masculine ideals, he was not yet finished with idealization.

In his next novel, *The Plumed Serpent,* Don Ramón Carrasco, the leader of a Mexican revolutionary movement based in the revival of the ancient Aztec religion and the imagined mode and rituals of leadership, is perhaps Lawrence's most idealized character. Ultimately assuming godhead, Ramón becomes the living Quetzalcoatl. Kate Leslie, who marries his second in command, Don Cipriano Viedma, continues to struggle with the question announced earlier in the title of chapter 4: "To Stay or Not to Stay." Less inclined toward idealization than some of Lawrence's male protagonists, Kate nevertheless admires Ramón. Despite her reservations, she is drawn into the Quetzalcoatl movement, even while recognizing its male pretensions. L. D. Clark, adducing textual and manuscript evidence, makes a strong argument that she stays. If so, the last page of the published novel still demonstrates the ambivalence with which Kate continues to struggle, despite her undeniable admiration for Ramón.

Among the many studies concerning Lawrence's imagined leaders in the novels of this period, I will cite a statement by Judith Ruderman, who observes: "Lawrence himself was in constant conflict with, and flight from, the Magna Mater, and his embrace of the dark gods at this time signifies not so much an acceptance of his own coalmining father as it signifies a last-ditch effort, through acceptance of a fantasy father, to escape the smothering embrace of woman." The features common to the fiction of this period, she says, "suggest a pattern of pre-oedipal concerns and conflicts." Ruderman is acutely aware of what those who accede to the leader in all three of the leadership novels are searching for—a nurturant father.[11]

CHAPTER 6

Lawrence's Sexual Fallacies

D. H. Lawrence's status as the major modern English literary advocate for the central significance and seriousness of human sexuality is well established. His attempts to foster greater openness about sexuality in the culture earned him the approbation of several generations of supporters who were seeking a way out of the Victorian impasse between officially sanctioned ideals of sexual "purity" and unofficial but tolerated forms of sexual exploitation, including easily available prostitution and under-the-counter pornography. The dilemma that this conflict posed for young men of Lawrence's generation, described in Sigmund Freud's essay "On the Universal Tendency to Debasement in the Sphere of Love" (1912),[1] is clearly set forth in the split between spiritual and sexual love in *Sons and Lovers* and *Women in Love*. Lawrence's purpose was to heal the split, beginning with himself. In this effort, he was a pioneer in his courageous stand for the honest treatment of human sexuality in modern literature. The forward thrust of his ideas, the vitality of his characters, and the vivid sense of life conveyed in his presentation of scenes have made him one of the most influential of modern writers.

Lawrence's attempts to establish greater freedom of expression in the presentation of sexual themes in literature also earned him the reprobation of censors throughout his career. When his first novel, *The White Peacock* (1911), was already printed and ready to be bound, self-censorship on the part of the publisher forced Lawrence to rewrite an offending paragraph in tepid language. Official censorship became more virulent in the prosecution and suppression of *The Rainbow* (1915) six weeks after its publication, and the resulting notoriety necessitated issuing *Women in Love* in both the United States and England in a privately printed edition for subscribers in 1920, amid charges of obscenity and threats of action for libel, while a trade edition was delayed until 1922. *Lady Chatterley's Lover* was more explicit than Lawrence's earlier novels in its direct descriptions of both passionate experience and relational problems in sexual intercourse and in its use of dialogue employing the "four-letter words" and Derbyshire dialect of a Midlands gamekeeper. It could be published in 1928 only in a privately printed edition, which Lawrence chose rather than accepting the heavy-handed expurgation required for a trade edition. Although expurgated editions were subsequently published to protect copyright, an unexpurgated trade edition was delayed until 1959 in the United States and 1960 in England, and in both instances resulted in landmark censorship trials.[2] The manuscript of *Pansies,* a volume of poems that Lawrence sent from Florence to his literary agent in London in 1929, was intercepted and seized in the mails by the postmaster general, acting on warrants issued by the home secretary. In the same year, an exhibition of twenty-five of Lawrence's paintings, including male and female nudes, in the Warren Gallery in London was raided, and thirteen of the paintings were impounded by the police.[3]

In the first decade of the twenty-first century, D. H. Lawrence's status as a sexual polemicist is no longer what it was in earlier generations. For a quarter of a century, his literary reputation has been under attack by forces that, though motivated by an interest in promoting their own sexual and political agendas, have revealed how dated Lawrence's views of male and female sexual roles have become. The rise of feminist criticism in the last three decades and increased awareness of Lawrence's own sexual issues have somewhat undercut his reputation as a sexual liberator. In my view, neither the fact that Lawrence's sexual theories did not always transcend the culture of his time nor the fact that he had sexual issues of his own in some areas can invalidate his insights on the central significance and richness of human sexuality. When his views derive from erroneous information, the fantasy model of sex, or sexual stereotypes that he apparently accepts and presents as achieved truths, they must be identified as sexual fallacies. One of these theories—Lawrence's belief that masturbation is intrinsically harmful to both the individual and society—is treated so extensively that I must defer discussion of this issue to a separate chapter (see chapter 7: "Lawrence, Freud, and Masturbation"). It would be easy to assert cynically that, as beauty is said to be in the eye of the beholder, the distinction between sexual fallacy and sexual truth lies in the genital response of the perceiving subject. Too many other considerations—social, moral, and scientific—condition our thinking on this issue. It is fair to say, however, that Lawrence accepted and promulgated in his writings some sexual theories that by today's standards are seen as fallacious or questionable. These misconceptions about sex provide an informative context for the self psychological view of Lawrence's personality organization as characterized primarily by narcissistic deficits rather than predominantly by oedipal conflicts. The following examples illustrate the kind of Lawrentian sexual theories that might be reconsidered in light of subsequent medical research and cultural change.

Male Dominance

Lawrence believed that a satisfactory state of affairs between the sexes is achievable only through male dominance in sexual relations. As an adolescent, Lawrence's fixed belief in male dominance in sex could not be shaken even by the rational challenge of his friend George H. Neville, who was far more experienced sexually than he. According to Neville,

> It is certain that from somewhere he developed a personal ideal, vision or state which had for its foundation the utter dominance of the male. If my idea be right and he did develop such an ideal at this time, it is perfectly clear proof that he was very much lacking in the practical application of his observations. In nature, and on the farm, there can be no male dominance in matters of sex relationship, for such relationship is only possible under given conditions; and those conditions are usually particular and personal to the female. The male is the seeker, the competitor. The intrinsic difference lies in the fact that, in the male, there is the ever constant urge, the subconscious readiness, while in the female, the urge appears only at certain definitely fixed periods.

Neville, whose comparison of women's personal conditions for sexual relations to the female estrus found in other mammals is itself erroneous, was attempting to rationalize his position that, although their sexual roles are different— the male as seeker, the female as the setter of conditions—male and female are sexually equal.

Lawrence's male protagonists accept the woman's participation in and enjoyment of sex, but on the man's terms. In *Lady Chatterley's Lover,* for example, Mellors wants both partners to be involved, but reserves the activity to himself. When Lawrence's male protagonists feel their masculinity threatened and become more defensive in protecting it, they usually think the woman should just lie still and make herself passively available. In sex, this tendency leads to the man's requiring the woman to cease all activity. In *The Plumed Serpent,* Cipriano's insistence that Kate forgo movement to let him probe the depths is a case in point.

At worst, in two of Lawrence's Mexican stories, his determination to reinstate male dominance leads to direct violence against women. In "None of That!" the spoiled, rich American woman Ethel Cane, who has toyed with the Mexican bullfighter Cuesta by willfully leading him on, is handed over by him to be gang-raped by "half a dozen of his bull-ring gang." Later she commits suicide by poisoning herself, but leaves half her fortune to Cuesta.[5] "It is important to remember," observes feminist critic Sandra Eagleton, "that

Lawrence did not kill anyone, even if he created characters who did. Fictional characters cannot be taken as synonymous with the author": "we can convict only Cuesta and his bull-ring gang of the appalling and vindictive act."[6] I agree. The name of the bullfighter, however, is a homonym for Questa, the village near Taos, New Mexico, which was the postal address of the Lawrence ranch. This allusion places the hostility closer to home than one might otherwise suspect.

In "The Woman Who Rode Away," the unnamed white wife of an American mine owner rides alone into the mountains to a mythic enactment in which the Chilchui Indians (Lawrence's name for the Huichol tribe) deceptively lead the bewildered, and drugged, woman into acquiescing to her own human sacrifice to restore sun and moon, long the captives of the white race, according to the Indians' mythology, by returning the masculine power of the sun to the Indian men and freeing the feminine power of the moon to enter the caves of their women.[7] As the story ends, the aged Indian *cacique,* poised with his knife, awaits the moment of sacrifice, conceptualized in a sexual metaphor as the entry of the red sun through the shaft of ice into the funnel-shaped cave. Unlike Ethel Cane's rape, the confused woman is not to die for her own willful transgressions but for those attributed to her race and gender. As pharmakos, she is paralleled throughout with Christ and made to serve a larger mythic purpose of restoration: "The mastery that man must hold, and that passes from race to race" ("The Woman Who Rode Away," 71).

Male Sexual Performance

In sexual relations, male dominance leads to the assumption that the quality of sexual experience equals the quality of male performance. Lawrence seems to have bought the prevalent male myth that the man is responsible for orchestrating the entire sexual encounter, and all the woman is supposed to do is to cooperate and admire. Hence, the male's performance is inevitably felt as a test. If all goes well, a good performance on the test is a large part of the gratification.

Unlike the female orgasm, which does not require a refractory period afterwards, the male orgasm, usually associated or synchronous with ejaculation, is followed by a necessary refractory period before the man can get another erection. This pattern is contradicted by the phenomenon of multiple orgasms in some men, who experience one or more non-ejaculatory orgasms either before or after ejaculation.[8] William H. Masters and Virginia E. Johnson's research demonstrated that "[m]any males below the age of 30, but relatively few thereafter, have the ability to ejaculate frequently and are subject to only very short refractory periods during the resolution phase." One of their male study subjects was "observed to ejaculate three times within 10 minutes from the onset of stimulative activity," although the volume of semen was progressively reduced with each ejaculation.[9] In a subsequent study, Rutgers University researchers Beverly Whipple, Barry Komisaruk, and Brent R. Myers documented the multiorgasmic ability of a thirty-five-year-old research subject who, under observation in controlled laboratory conditions, achieved six natural, fully ejaculatory orgasms in thirty-six minutes, maintaining a full erection throughout with no refractory periods. Again, the seminal volume was progressively reduced after the first ejaculation.[10]

Evidence of Lawrence's youthful experience in this regard, which reportedly included the capacity for repeated orgasms in rapid succession with incredibly brief refractory periods, makes the contrast between his sexual strength as a young man and his later erectile dysfunction the more poignant. One of his early lovers (Alice Dax) confided to a friend (Enid Hopkin Hilton) that as a young man he could "come back to a woman time after time."[11]

Lawrence seems to confirm this assessment of his sexual capacity as a young man in the second part of *Mr. Noon*, which in part fictionalizes his and Frieda's elopement and early life together,[12] when Johanna says to Gilbert Noon: "Do you know, I was rather frightened that you weren't a good lover. But it isn't every man who can love a woman three times in a quarter of an hour—so *well*—is it—?"[13] Mark Kinkead-Weekes thinks that "the sexual episodes, much as one might have hoped otherwise, were very probably invented for comic and ironic purposes." He comments, "'three times in a quarter of an hour'—Bing-bang-bump—is heroic-*comic*, and part of a tease of women, not autobiographical boasting, or lie" (Kinkead-Weekes, 618, 619–20).

The Lawrentian narrator comments, whether with Fieldingesque comic irony or not: "I can see absolutely no sounder ground for a permanent marriage than Johanna's—three times in a quarter of an hour, and so *well*. . . . Then you're down at the bedrock of marriage" (*Mr. Noon*, 145). The serious, or mock-serious, tone, however, covers an assumption that in retrospect seems particularly hubristic. Lawrence may have thought that his youthful sexual powers could be expected to last. If so, their subsequent diminution must have revealed the unreliability of anything so uncertain as rapidly repeated male orgasms as a bedrock for marriage.

If Lawrence's perspective at the time included any part of ironic distance, he nevertheless, for some years, continued to present the capacity for multiple orgasms in male performance as an index of male dominance. In the poem "He-Goat," written in Taormina in December 1921 or January 1922,[14] the he-goat, like a true satyr, asserts his mastery in the triple pattern of "Orgasm after orgasm after orgasm" (line 59).[15]

Lawrence's revisionist view of the triple orgasm emerges in *The Plumed*

Serpent: Kate had loved her late husband, Joachim, "for this, that again, and again, and again he could give her this orgiastic 'satisfaction,' in spasms that made her cry aloud." Cipriano teaches her to forgo what Lawrence now regarded as the superficial thrills of rapidly repeated clitoral orgasms and introduces her to the deeper, and in his view more fulfilling, satisfaction of vaginal orgasms.[16] Despite Lawrence's revised view of the *female* orgasm, it should be noted that Cipriano remains firmly in charge of the situation and, like Gilbert Noon, meets the performance test brilliantly.

When the sexual encounter is felt to be unsuccessful or unfulfilling, the responsibility is often displaced to the woman. In "The Test on Miriam" chapter of *Sons and Lovers,* Paul Morel attributes his temporary loss of erection ("all his blood fell back") to Miriam's attitude of resignation in approaching sexual relations as a sacrifice to be immolated.[17] In *Lady Chatterley's Lover,* Michaelis, who tends to ejaculate quickly and, for Connie's needs, prematurely, blames her bitterly for not reaching climax at the same time he does. There is sometimes, however, a better alternative in dealing with an unsatisfactory sexual experience. Later in the novel, when Connie and Mellors's fourth sexual encounter turns out badly because of Connie's adopting the role of ironic observer, Mellors, with an achieved empathy that was clearly beyond either Paul Morel's or Michaelis's capacity, accepts the situation nonjudgmentally and observes realistically that she "wasn't there" that time.[18] The problem can be resolved by effective communication. They can establish greater mutuality when they have sexual relations a second time the same night, because he does not see the previous encounter as her failure of some ultimate test or treat it as if it were the end of the world.

Penis Size and Phallic Veneration

Male power, which Lawrence sees as proportionate to the significance placed on the phallus, is related symbolically to the popular male equation between penis size and sexual effectiveness. Usually in Lawrence's work this idea is expressed indirectly or metaphorically, as in the following passage on Cipriano and Kate in *The Plumed Serpent:*

> When the power of his blood rose in him, the dark aura streamed from him like a cloud pregnant with power, like thunder, and rose like a whirlwind that rises suddenly in the twilight and raises a great pliant column, swaying and leaning with power, clear between heaven and earth.
> Ah! and what a mystery of prone submission, on her part, this huge erection would imply! Submission absolute, like the earth under the sky. Beneath an over-arching absolute. [311]

If women reasonably object to the role of submission and passivity assigned to them here, men are assigned the no less stereotyped role of producing the giant erection as the signifier of innate power. The internal conflict involved in trying to conform to this kind of reified picture of male and female sexual roles, with its absolutist language and iconographic imagery of "huge erection" and "prone submission," is inevitably vitiating to the humanity of both participants.

The equivalence of male power and effectiveness with penis size is such a widespread male myth that it would be surprising if Lawrence did not, either consciously or unconsciously, subscribe to it. I suspect there is hardly a man alive, no matter how well endowed, who has not at some point wished that his penis were bigger. Both C. G. Jung's concept of the sacral power of phallos and Sigmund Freud's theory of penis envy are related to this issue.

There is a long tradition, in both Western and Eastern cultures, of worship of the phallus as a transpersonal image of masculine spiritual power.[19] Jung records his early dream at age three of finding in a subterranean cavern something like "a tree trunk twelve to fifteen feet high and about one and a half to two feet thick. It was a huge thing, reaching almost to the ceiling. . . . It was made of skin and naked flesh, and on top there was something like a rounded head with no face and no hair. On the very top of the head was a single eye, gazing motionlessly upward." In the dream his mother called out, "Yes, just look at him. That is the man-eater." Jung adds, "Only much later did I realize that what I had seen was a phallus, and it was decades before I understood that it was a ritual phallus. . . . At all events, the phallus of this dream seems to be a subterranean God 'not to be named.'"[20]

In a passage in *John Thomas and Lady Jane,* containing comparable elements of phallic pride, subterranean (unconscious) being, sightlessness, and unnamed deity, but no reference to size, Connie contemplates "that other strange creature in him, the erect, sightless, overweening phallus":[21] "It was like some primitive, grotesque god: but alive, and unspeakably vivid, alert with its own weird life, apart from both their personalities. Sightless, it seemed to look round, like a mole risen from the depths of the earth. The resurrection of the flesh, it was called in joke. But wasn't it really so? Wasn't there a weird, grotesque godhead in it?" (233)

In a letter to Earl Brewster (27 February 1927), Lawrence writes: "I stick to what I told you, and put a phallus, a lingam you call it, in each one of my pictures somewhere. . . . I do this out of positive belief, that the phallus is a great sacred image: it represents a deep, deep life which has been denied in us, and still is denied."[22]

The association of the penis with innate sacral power, from which Lawrence's use of the phallus as a literary symbol derives, has been dismissed in recent years on political grounds, but it cannot be understood psychologically solely in sociopolitical terms. Freud noted "two corresponding themes" in the psychical life of human beings: "in the female, an *envy for the penis*—a positive striving to possess a male genital—and, in the male, a struggle against his passive or feminine attitude to another male." The common element in both themes is the castration complex: in the girl, the belief that she has been deprived of this "superior organ"; in the boy, the fear that as punishment for oedipal wishes, he may yet lose what he has (*SE* 23:250). As Freud describes it, the size of the penis in comparison to the clitoris is the decisive factor for girls: "They notice the penis of a brother or playmate, strikingly visible and of large proportions, at once recognize it as the superior counterpart of their own small and inconspicuous organ, and from that time forward fall a victim to envy for the penis" (*SE* 19:252).

Obviously Freud's drive-centered theoretical construct has been roundly attacked from the perspective of feminist theory. It has also been criticized within psychoanalysis itself. According to psychoanalyst Arnold M. Cooper, while Freud hesitated to "perturb or interfere with the assumption of unquestioned male authority," most analysts today "believe that a significant portion of penis envy relates not to anatomy but to two aspects of penis symbolization—the penis as representative of male privilege, and the penis as a representation of successful separation from the powerful mother of the pre-Oedipal period. There are also important problems of self-esteem and object-relations that are not reducible to penis envy in any form."[23] I would add, there are also aspects of penis symbolization that are not reducible to conscious social concerns. Although Lawrence's employment of the penis in the developmental process of separation-individuation is demonstrable, the revisionist interpretation of penis envy, as enlightened as it seems from a sociopolitical perspective, does not account for the primitive intensity of either the ritual image of the Jungian archetype or the "drivenness" of the Freudian wish, both of which originate in the unconscious.

In Lawrence's fiction, the contrast between male characters is stated in terms of innate phallic power, which is often presented in symbols of erectile potency employing linguistic metaphors of relative firmness and size. In the dénouement of "The Border-Line," the returned first husband, Alan Anstruther, even as a ghost, reclaims his wife, Katharine, in a phallic embrace, while his rival, her present husband, Philip Farquhar, freezes to death. Katharine and her sister belittle Philip sexually as "the little one" and "the stand-up-mannikin." The contrast between Alan's towering potency and Philip's sexual inadequacy is emphasized as the erect Alan is phallically compared to "a great round fir-trunk that stood so alive and potent, so physical, bristling all its vast drooping greenness above the snow," while the flaccid Philip, "who never would walk firm on his legs," "just flopped."[24]

Although Freud does not exactly say so, penis envy, in the literal sense, is, if anything, as prevalent among men as among women. A boy, comparing his small penis to his father's larger one, experiences envy of the father's big penis.[25] In the phallic stage, "This part of the body, which is easily excitable, prone to changes and so rich in sensations, occupies the boy's interest to a high degree," Freud observes. "He wants to see it in other people as well, so as to compare it with his own; and he behaves as though he had a vague idea that this organ could and should be bigger" (*SE* 19:142–43). Boys at around the age of puberty will engage in "circle jerks" and make direct comparisons of their penile erections. Morris A. Sklansky points out that as the pubescent boy's "penis becomes elongated and widened . . . and the testes larger," this focal interest is reasserted. "Young adolescent males are much preoccupied with the size of the penis, and comparisons are made regularly, whenever exposure and examination are possible."[26] In any close male group, individuals usually know the size of the other males' flaccid penises. Envy and veneration are among the unconscious affects, and anxieties, of the locker room. Men visually check each other out surreptitiously and fear the preconscious wish to touch or the embarrassment of being caught looking. The impulse expressed in this kind of behavior is very primitive. The large phallus confers status on the man who possesses it and becomes a totemic object to others. But a totemic object evokes both awe and the taboo.

Psychoanalyst Lionel Ovesey relates a male patient's account of "a marvelous athlete known in fraternity circles as 'Stud'" for the size of his penis. When "a group of students prevailed upon this man to expose himself for purposes of measurement," first flaccid, then erect, "in the latter state somebody suddenly grabbed the penis and masturbated it to climax on the spot, to the great amusement of everyone present"—with the "lone exception" of Ovesey's patient, who turned away in disgust and revulsion from the anxiety of his own homoerotic impulse.[27] Ovesey's psychoanalytic interpretation sees the ostensibly sexual response as a screen for dependency needs rather than as the expression of an instinctual drive.

In Lawrence's story "Sun," the penis becomes a totemic object to a woman, as Juliet submits her naked body to the phallic power of the sun itself, which Lawrence at one point metaphorically equates to the peasant's penis, rising inside his pants in response to the visual stimulation: "But now the strange challenge of his eyes had held her, blue and overwhelming like the blue sun's heart. And she had seen the fierce striving of the phallus under his thin trousers: for her. And with his red face, and with his broad body, he was like the sun to her, the sun in its broad heat."[28] Under the aegis of the sun, the woman fantasizes, "Why shouldn't I go to him! Why shouldn't I bear his child?" But the reality is otherwise. She knows the peasant will not come for her and that she will return to the futile, meaningless life with her "grey faced" husband, Maurice. The contrast between the two men is presented graphically through the metaphor of penis size:

> She had seen the flushed blood in the peasant's burnt face, and felt the jetting, sudden blue heat pouring over her from his kindled eyes, and the rousing of his big penis against his body—for her, surging for her. Yet she would never come to him—she daren't, so much was against her. And the little etiolated body of her husband, city-branded, would possess her, and his little, frantic penis would beget another child in her. She could not help it. She was bound to the vast, fixed wheel of circumstance, and there was no Perseus in the universe to cut the bonds. ["Sun," 38]

Michael Ross comments: "The most obvious 'unexpurgated' details—the 'big penis' of the peasant, unkindly juxtaposed against the 'little, frantic penis' of the husband—fit naturally and even unobtrusively into the passage, and into the entire narrative. The anatomical contrast itself strikes one as neither funny nor reductive, because it is not the determining factor in Juliet's attitude; it is, rather, an apt and concrete reflection of the richer and more complex conflict of values that Lawrence has evoked throughout the tale."[29]

Awe of the erect penis at full engorgement makes it easy to overestimate its size. Phallic awe may originate in an early childhood experience of seeing the father's erect penis, or it may be related to penis envy.[30] The anonymous narrator of the erotic Victorian memoir *My Secret Life* persuades a woman to display another lover's "donkey sized" penis as the narrator peeps through the door left ajar to see the man standing naked with a "glorious erection." "It was worth seeing, a noble, well proportioned shaft standing out seven or eight inches from the belly, and perhaps nine from his balls, and looking an inch and a half in diameter," the memoirist writes. "Altogether, it was the biggest prick but one I've ever seen, and the handsomest."[31] Subsequently in the narrative, when he gets the woman to take accurate measurements of several lovers' penises, the results, he says, showed "how much smaller the two large pricks were than she had supposed them to be." "She had often spoken of both as seven or eight inches long or more," he adds, perhaps forgetting that he had the same impression when, peeping through the door, he had seen the other man's erect penis. In the actual case, the measurements taken by the woman were as follows: for the man called "donkey prick": 6 3/4 inches long, 5 inches circumference; for the "poor lover": 6 1/4 inches long, 4 3/4 inches circumference; and for "Philip": 5 1/4 inches long, 4 1/8 inches circumference. The narrator modestly omits giving his own measurements, but says "it's neither so short or so long as the extremes.—Once I was ignorantly ashamed of its size—I knew no better then." The memoirist's informal research has revealed what more recent scientific investigations have confirmed: that despite exaggerated estimates, "six inches is more than the average length of stiff pricks measured in the way described."[32]

As urologists W. A. Schonfeld and G. W. Beebe state: "The true physiological length of the penis is its erect length"; but in the early 1940s, they did not find it feasible to collect data by direct observation and measurement of a large number of erections and chose instead to use stretched length as an approximation for erect length.[33] Later in the forties, Alfred C. Kinsey, Wardell B. Pomeroy, and Clyde E. Martin published their findings on penis size based on their extensive data in *Sexual Behavior in the Human Male* (1948).[34] Subsequently, in an effort to determine the "average" penis size, Kinsey measured the erect penises of 3,500 college males.[35]

To test several widely accepted beliefs regarding penis size, William H. Masters measured the penises of eighty research subjects "from the anterior border of the symphysis at the base of the penis along the dorsal surface to the distal tip of the glans." Masters and co-researcher Virginia E. Johnson compared the penile measurements of forty men whose penises in the flaccid state measured 7.5 to 9 centimeters in length and forty men whose flaccid penises measured 10 to 11.5 centimeters. "All 80 penises were measured on three different occasions both in flaccid and erect states," with one erectile measurement "taken during automanipulation, and two measurements . . . initiated immediately upon withdrawal of the plateau-phase penis from active coition." Their findings showed that the smaller flaccid penises "increased by an average of 7.5–8 cm. at full . . . erection" and that the larger flaccid penises "increased by an average of 7–7.5 cm. in the fully erect . . . state." As the researchers point out, "Measurement of an erect penis was not attempted until the final engorgement of late plateau phase had been accomplished. Since full penile engorgement is a short-term process before ejaculation intervenes, measurement frequently was rushed and, therefore, additionally unreliable."[36] Although Masters and Johnson had accurate research data on penis size, Masters is quoted as saying, "[W]e purposely did not include information about the average size of penises. To some degree, we hoped that by not doing so, we would neutralize the concept that penis size is crucial to sexual response."[37]

The scientific interest in penis size, of course, did not end with Masters and Johnson. Of the many such studies following theirs, I will mention three. In the research by urologists Hunter Wessells, Tom F. Lue, and Jack W. McAninch, measurement of "flaccid and erect penile dimensions in 80 physically normal men" recorded more erect penile measurements in a range of shorter lengths than in the Kinsey data.[38]

Joseph Sparling reanalyzed the Kinsey data and presented new data, employing documentary photography as well as measurement of the penile erections of eighty-one research subjects to establish the shape, angle, and length of erections. A notable difference between the Kinsey data and Sparling's is also in the number of shorter lengths in the latter: Erections in the "range from 4.5 to 5.75 in. was occupied by 10% less of the Kinsey distribution (30.8%) than of the photo distribution (40.8%)." Sparling also found more downward curved erections, about 15 percent of the total, and "more erection angles in the lower ranges, with at least one fourth below the horizontal."[39]

Seeing opportunities for bias in the "self reported" data of the first Kinsey report and the "self selected" volunteer source of research subjects in both the Kinsey research and his own, Sparling notes that "the Wessells study found the average flaccid length to be 3.47 in. with a range from 1.97 to 6.10 in. Stretched length was very similar to erect length. And the average erect length was 5.07 in. with a range of 2.95 to 7.48 in." In Sparling's view, the full one inch shorter average length in the Wessells study "appears to provide a cautionary note regarding the average values for length found in the Sparling photo sample (6.05 in.) and the Kinsey self-reported sample (6.20 in.)." With regard to the male population in general, "The Wessells research feeds our suspicion that the mean, when it is finally measured, will be lower than the values determined in the Sparling article," Sparling observes. "In that eventual research the key methodological hurdle will be to draw a sample that will adequately reflect the general population of men."[40]

The real question is whether penis size matters as much as most men think it does. Based on statistics derived from their research data, Masters and Johnson suggest that both the "widely accepted 'phallic fallacy' . . . that the larger the penis the more effective the male as a partner in coital connection" and the related "'phallic fallacy' that the larger penis increases in size with full erection to a significantly greater degree than does the smaller penis" have no validity. Noting that a "constantly overlooked" factor in "theoretical discussions of penile effectiveness is the involuntary accommodative reactions of the vagina . . . under coital stimulation," Masters and Johnson conclude that the "delusion that penile size is related to sexual adequacy" is without foundation (Masters and Johnson, 193). This kind of scientific information may intellectually modify men's conscious views, but it is unlikely to change their irrational emotional responses rooted in primitive myth unless the unconscious source of these responses can be brought into consciousness and thus made accessible to analytic examination.

The significance of penis size in men's perception of themselves is addressed in a study by Harold Charles Winter, "An Examination of the Relationship between Penis Size, Genital Image, and Perception of Sexual

Competency in the Male." In this psychological study of ninety-six adult males aged twenty through fifty-nine, most of them college graduates, "The results revealed statistically significant positive correlations between circumference of flaccid and erect penis" with both body image and genital image. The correlations between length of flaccid and erect penis with both genital image and body image "were not statistically significant." The results, however, also revealed "statistically significant correlations between both circumference and length of flaccid and erect penis" and the men's perception of their sexual competency.[41] Clearly Masters and Johnson's exposing the "delusion that penile size is related to sexual adequacy" has had little effect. If perception rather than reality is all, then validity of perception rather than penis size per se may be the better focus for men's consideration.

Phallic veneration is such an essential theme in Lawrence's work that it would be simplistic to reduce it solely to a sexual fallacy. It is questionable whether penis size, as he employs it as a metaphor in relation to this theme, should be so labeled either. Phallic imagery in Lawrence's work evokes myth rather than reality. In the same passage from *John Thomas and Lady Jane* cited above, the narrator distinguishes between *penis* and *phallus:* "For this is the difference between the two: the penis is a mere member of the physiological body. But the phallus, in the old sense, has roots, the deepest roots of all, in the soul and the greater consciousness of man, and it is through the phallic roots that inspiration enters the soul" (233). Lawrence's distinction between the two is echoed in Jungian analyst and Episcopal priest Eugene Monick's definition of masculinity in terms of "phallos":

> To write of archetypal masculinity means to concentrate upon phallos, the erect penis, the emblem and standard of maleness. All images through which masculinity is defined have phallos as their point of reference. Sinew, determination, effectuality, penetration, straightforwardness, hardness, strength—all have phallos giving them effect. Phallos is the fundamental mark of maleness, its stamp, its impression. Erection points to a powerful inner reality at work in a man, not altogether in his control. This inner reality may be different from a man's conscious desires at a given time.[42]

Lawrence's mythic view of the phallus relates it to both sacral consciousness and the creative imagination. This places his conception of the phallus closer to Jung's and Monick's archetype of phallos than to Freud's theoretical formulations of castration anxiety and penis envy. Within this theme of phallic veneration, Lawrence's evocation of phallic spiritual power and sexual potency is sometimes expressed in metaphorical allusions to penis size or in linguistic terms relating to size. Although these allusions draw on the cultural fallacy and elicit in the reader preconscious traces of the popular equation of penis size with sexual effectiveness, penis size per se is not the central issue for Lawrence.

Female Pubic Hair Phobia

As a young man, Lawrence was ignorant of the fact that women, like men, have pubic hair. According to his friend George H. Neville, the only time Lawrence actually physically assaulted him, it was in response to Neville's taking a pencil and shading in underarm hair and pubic hair to make an idealized picture Lawrence had drawn of the female nude more realistic. "That," Neville told him, "is just the difference between your living, breathing woman, full of life and the statue I mentioned. That's HAIR!" Lawrence's response was to leap from his chair and attack Neville, gasping, "You dirty little devil. It's not true. It's *not* true, I tell you," all the while somewhat punily pummeling his athletic friend (Neville, 82). Lawrence's idealized picture of the female nude possibly derived from his youthful need to preserve a perception of his mother's purity. Years later, his youthful denial that women have pubic hair becomes the source of the gamekeeper's phobic response on his initial discovery that women do have pubic hair.

In *John Thomas and Lady Jane* (chap. 11), Parkin, as the gamekeeper is called in this second version of *Lady Chatterley's Lover*, describes to Connie his first sight of the female genitals when he was twenty-one and Bertha Coutts "lifted her clothes up an' showed me—you know what": "She wanted me to come an' feel. But I never knowed afore then as women had hair there. Black hair! An' I don't know why, it upset me an' made me hate the thoughts of women from that day." Connie ponders on this disclosure, then asks: "And you hated the thought of women because they have hair the same where men do?" Parkin answers: "Yes! I know now I was a fool. But that was it."[43] He had subsequently married Bertha, who was five years older than himself. But when Connie asks him, "And when you were married, didn't you mind any more about the black hair?" he hesitates, then replies with a suggestion that his feeling of revulsion and resulting fear of female genitalia had left him temporarily unable to function sexually: "Yes!" . . . "I couldn't touch it. I couldn't do nothing to her." Bertha had been understanding and supportive, but he had been too ashamed at first to tell her that the absence of female pubic hair was a necessary condition to his getting an erection: "She said, wait a bit. An' we waited. An' then she asked me about everything, an' I wouldn't tell her. But she never got mad with me, an' never threw it up at me. She seemed as if she wanted me to be all right. So in the end I told her: an' she cried.—She cried a' one night. Then in the morning, she said, if I shaved her. An' so I did, an' she laid there so still. An' then it come up in me, an' I wanted her—" (226).

Afterwards, Connie reflects on what the gamekeeper has told her: "His desire for sex intercourse, and his hatred of sex! His desire for woman, and his hatred of women! This made a gnawing soreness in her heart."[44] After a satisfying sexual experience, they sleep. Later when they wake up, the thought of what he has told her returns to her mind: "You don't think the hair on my body is nasty, do you? You don't wish it wasn't there?" As if in answer, "He put his face to her belly, and rubbed his nose among the sharp hair of her body, kissing her gently on the gentle mount of Venus, letting the little hairs brush his mouth, while his moustache brushed her body and made her laugh." "You don't want me shaved or anything, do you?" she asks. "'No-no!'" he replies, "in a low voice" (235–36).

In psychoanalytic theory, such "*phobic objects* and *situations* represent, unconsciously and usually symbolically, the underlying psychic conflict and the dangers involved." By means of the symbolic displacement, "the phobia serves to transform and disguise the unconscious psychological danger."[45] Although Lawrence, of course, cannot be unilaterally equated with Parkin, the gamekeeper's phobic reaction to Bertha's pubic hair echoes Lawrence's shocked disbelief in response to Neville's unwanted information. If the young Lawrence's idealized notion of the nude female body implies a willful ignorance on his part, what danger did he perceive in the more realistic view that Neville imposed upon him? Or to put it more specifically, in the unconscious fantasy behind his phobic response, what danger did the pubic hair conceal? Presumably, it would be something that he felt as a general threat to his absolute of male dominance, or a more specific threat of harm to the man's penis in sexual intercourse, or possibly both.

Lawrence was the son of a possessive mother who seductively took him as her fantasied son-lover in a family situation that prohibited any sexual response on his part. A reasonable psychoanalytic interpretation would be that what he saw as the masculine characteristic of pubic hair in a woman implies an unconscious fantasy that she also possesses a dangerous and powerful, if hidden, phallus. Marcia Ian, who has written extensively on this "poisonous stereotype," observes: "To my mind, the phallic mother represents the conflation, compaction, and concretion of all the most primitive fears and desires of hegemonic heterosexist white bourgeois patriarchy."[46] Hence, Parkin's shaving the woman's pubic hair is symbolically an act of castration that robs her of her fantasied power, restores her to the state that he deems appropriate for women, and establishes the condition necessary to his erectile function.

Lawrence's wariness of the phallic woman as a powerful adversary and rival and his animus against lesbians are well known. Two of Lawrence's female protagonists establish lesbian relationships—Ursula Brangwen with the independent and masculinized Winifred Inger in *The Rainbow,* and Ellen March with the dependent and clinging Jill Banford in *The Fox.* As Lawrence presents it, however, in the interest of full psychological and sexual growth, both of these protagonists must ultimately reject homosexuality and establish a clearly heterosexual identity. In *Lady Chatterley's Lover,* the gamekeeper, now called Mellors, rails against "the Lesbian sort" of woman, "the sort that puts you out before you really 'come,' and go on writhing their loins till they bring themselves off against your thighs." He declares: "When I'm with a woman who's really Lesbian, I fairly howl in my soul, wanting to kill her" (203).

Parkin's phobic response to female pubic hair was apparently overcome by means of gradual desensitization in repeated incremental experience of the situation that elicited his phobic anxiety. As presented in *John Thomas and Lady Jane,* Parkin's phobia has already been overcome, not by analytically resolving his anxieties, but behaviorally by means of satisfying, and repeated, sexual experiences with a supportive partner. In *Lady Chatterley's Lover,* Mellors shows no evidence of his earlier phobic response. Decorating Connie's body and his own body with flowers for the "marriage" of Lady Jane and John Thomas, he put a pink campion on her navel "and in her maidenhair were forget-me-nots and wood-ruff"; then he "wound a bit of creeping jenny around his penis" (228).

In the form in which this issue enters his fiction, Lawrence is not displaying the phobia, but laying the phobia to rest. In a late poem, "The Man of Tyre," female pubic hair arouses sexual attraction. As the woman wades ashore, the speaker's gaze moves from part to part of her body: "the dark hair piled up," "the full thighs slowly lifting," "the shoulders pallid with light," "both breasts dim and mysterious,"

> and the dim blotch of maidenhair like an indicator,
> giving a message to the man—
> [*Complete Poems,* 693]

Female pubic hair has become, as it is for most men, a source of arousal.

As an adolescent Lawrence pummeled his friend Neville for shading in the pubic hair on Lawrence's drawings of female nudes. The adult Lawrence had learned Neville's lesson so well that once his initial response was overcome, he insisted some years later on portraying both men and women with pubic hair in his paintings. When these paintings were exhibited in the Warren Galleries in London in June 1929, the resulting furor led to their impoundment in a police raid. Lawrence responded in verse with several poems in *More Pansies* and *Nettles,* including one entitled "13,000 People," which includes such verses as the following:

> And they stared and they stared, the half-witted lot
> at the spot where the fig-leaf just was not!
>
> But why, I ask you? Oh tell me why?
> Aren't they made quite the same, then, as you and I?
>
> Can it be they've been trimmed, so they've never seen
> the innocent member that a fig-leaf will screen?
> [*Complete Poems,* 578]

Vagina Dentata

Related to the female pubic hair phobia, Lawrence's most persistent and irrational form of castration anxiety is the fantasy that truly "clitoridal" women are possessed of the vagina dentata in the form of a powerful and dangerous clitoris, which poses a direct threat of injury to the man's penis in sexual intercourse.

What Lawrence fears in such women is made graphically clear in *The Rainbow* in the scene in which Ursula "destroys" Skrebensky with her "fierce, beaked, harpy's kiss" under the aegis of the flaring moon:

> Then there, in the great flare of light, she clinched hold of him, hard, as if suddenly she had the strength of destruction, she fastened her arms around him and tightened him in her grip, whilst her mouth sought his in a hard, rending, ever-increasing kiss, till his body was powerless in her grip, his heart melted in fear from the fierce, beaked, harpy's kiss. . . . She seemed unaware, she seemed to be pressing in her beaked mouth till she had the heart of him. Then, at last, she drew away and looked at him—looked at him. He knew what she wanted. . . . He felt as if the ordeal of proof was upon him, for life or death. . . .
>
> . . . She lay motionless with wide-open eyes looking at the moon. He came direct to her, without preliminaries. She held him pinned down at the chest, awful. The fight, the struggle for consummation was terrible. It lasted till it was agony to his soul, till he succumbed, till he gave way as if dead, and lay with his face buried partly in her hair partly in the sand, motionless, as if he would be motionless now for ever, hidden away in the dark, buried, only buried, he only wanted to be buried in the goodly darkness, only that, no more.[47]

The scene should be understood in context of the developmental process by which Ursula emerges as the first really modern woman in Lawrence's three-generational novel. In "the passionate struggle into conscious being," Ursula renounces the forms sexuality has taken in her relationships with Winifred Inger and Anton Skrebensky, as she had earlier rejected the marriage proposal of Anthony Schofield. In order to become herself, she must resist whatever would diminish her true self and prevent her from coming into her own being.

Lawrence, however, retained the metaphor of masculine injury by the willful woman's harpy's kiss. In *The Plumed Serpent,* he alludes to "the beak-like friction of Aphrodite of the foam" (422). And in "None of That!" Cuesta calls Ethel Cane a "cuttle-fish": "her gate is a beak. . . . She is all soft with cruelty towards a man's member."[48]

In *Lady Chatterley's Lover,* Mellors's ultimate complaint against Bertha Coutts is that she would not allow him to bring her to orgasm, but would spitefully wait him out no matter how long he delayed his ejaculation and then tear at his penis with beaklike ferocity to reach her own climax:

> " . . . She sort of got harder and harder to bring off, and she'd sort of tear at me down there, as if it was a beak tearing at me. By God, you think a woman's soft down there, like a fig. But I tell you the old rampers have beaks between their legs, and they tear at you with it till you're sick. Self! self! self! all self! tearing and shouting! They talk about men's sensual selfishness, but I doubt if it can ever touch a woman's blind beakishness, once she's gone that way. Like an old trull! And she couldn't help it. I told her about it, I told her how I hated it. And she'd even try. She'd try to lie still and let *me* work the business. She'd try. But it was no good. She got no feeling off it, from my working. She had to work the thing herself, grind her own coffee. And it came back on her like a raving necessity, she had to let herself go, and tear, tear, tear, as if she had no sensation in her except in the top of her beak, the very outside top tip, that rubbed and tore. That's how old whores used to be, so men used to say. It was a low kind of self-will in her, a raving sort of self-will: like in a woman who drinks. Well in the end I couldn't stand it. We slept apart. . . ." [202]

Not only is Bertha's capacity for orgasm entirely clitoral, but also, in her insistence on reserving the activity of sexual intercourse to herself, she reveals her clitoris to be, in his fantasy, a vaginal tooth or beak that poses the threat of harming his penis. Lawrence presents all such women as manipulative, despicable, castrating bitches like Bertha Coutts, who, in Mellors's inelegant phrase, preferred to "grind her own coffee" and did so by tearing at his penis with her dangerously powerful and phallic clitoris. It is hardly coincidental that Lawrence probably took the name Bertha Coutts from the real-life Bertha Cutts, who lived next door to the Lawrences in The Breach, East-wood,[49] thus linking the vagina dentata with the castration threat of the homonym "cuts" in association with his childhood home.

The myth of the vagina dentata, as an expression of the male's fear of the female genital, is well known in psychoanalysis. The dread that the vagina has teeth that may bite and injure the penis during sexual intercourse is some-times expressed in dreams in the form of entrances guarded by animals with teeth such as dogs or wild beasts. First described by Otto Rank as a conse-quence of birth anxiety, the fantasy of the vagina dentata, according to Sán-dor Ferenczi, derives from castration anxiety in regard to sexual intercourse: "Many neurotics unconsciously regard coitus as an activity which, either directly or subsequently, is calculated to injure life or limb, and in particular to damage the genital organ, *i.e.* an act in which are combined gratification and severe anxiety."[50]

Vaginal Orgasm vs. Clitoral Orgasm

Lawrence accepts unquestioningly the widespread theory of two kinds of orgasm in women and advocates female vaginal orgasms as superior to clitoral orgasms. The psychoanalytic distinction between the two derives from Sig-mund Freud's discussion of female sexuality in chapter 3 of *Three Essays on the Theory of Sexuality:* "The leading erotogenic zone in female children is located at the clitoris, and is thus homologous to the masculine genital zone of the glans penis. All my experience concerning masturbation in little girls has related to the clitoris and not to the regions of the external genitalia that are important in later sexual functioning" (*SE* 7:220).

Freud elaborates the implications of this theory in his lecture "The Sexual Life of Human Beings": "In her childhood, moreover, a girl's clitoris takes on the role of a penis entirely: it is characterized by special excitability and is the area in which auto-erotic satisfaction is obtained. The process of a girl's becom-ing a woman depends very much on the clitoris passing on this sensitivity to the vaginal orifice in good time and completely. In cases of what is known as sexual anaesthesia in women the clitoris has obstinately retained its sensitivity" (*SE* 16:318). Freud reiterates this theory more fully in "Femininity":

> We are entitled to keep to our view that in the phallic phase of girls the cli-
> toris is the leading erotogenic zone. But it is not, of course, going to remain
> so. With the change to femininity the clitoris should wholly or in part hand
> over its sensitivity, and at the same time its importance, to the vagina. This
> would be one of the two tasks which a woman has to perform in the course

of her development, whereas the more fortunate man has only to continue at the time of his sexual maturity the activity that he has previously carried out at the period of the early efflorescence of his sexuality. [*SE* 22:118]

In sum, Freud believes, little girls in the phallic stage learn to masturbate by stimulating the clitoris, but their later development of femininity in heterosexual intercourse requires that they transfer their sexual responses from the clitoris to the vagina. Those who fail to make the transfer, although they may retain the ability to achieve orgasm by clitoral stimulation, remain vaginally frigid.[51]

In reference to the passage from *Lady Chatterley's Lover* quoted above, Robert Scholes charges that Lawrence attempts to devalue the clitoris: "The supposed masculinity of Mrs. Mellors is what makes her so terrible—a masculinity expressed in her desire to take charge, to be in control of the sexual scene, but concentrated physically in her clitoral orientation, presented metaphorically as a predatory beak. . . . Exactly as Freud does, so Lawrence, too, orders the clitoris to cease and desist, orders women to be more 'feminine,' to become the perfect binary opposites that men require, and to become less sexual in the process."[52] To which Mark Spilka replies: "It is not so much Bertha's masculinity that makes her 'terrible'; . . . nor does her clitoris per se trouble Mellors: it is the willful, hardened, and perhaps 'common' way she uses her pelvis to reduce him to a mere instrument for her own sexual pleasure, a power game that men also play, as Lawrence had previously shown with the machismo industrialist Gerald Crich in *Women in Love*."[53]

These two critical statements, I think, are best understood in context. Scholes's charge that Lawrence, like Freud, attempted the erasure of the clitoris and the pejorative connotation of the quotation marks around the adjective "feminine" neatly pinpoint the purpose of the essay: the focus is not on human sexuality or even the female body, but on "The Female Body *as Text*" (my italics) in a politically based semiotic deconstruction of linguistic discourse. Spilka's defense that the real objection to Bertha Coutts is neither her masculinity nor her clitoris per se but her instrumentality places the issue firmly at the center of one of Lawrence's major literary and sexual themes. Spilka adds: "In asking Bertha to let him control their love-making, moreover, Mellors is opting for that mutual satisfaction through vaginal orgasm that Lawrence considered 'proper' in the 1920s" (Spilka, "Lawrence and the Clitoris," 184).

In Lawrence's work, the distinction between clitoral and vaginal orgasm leads to a fantasy model of sex, as Bernie Zilbergeld calls it, in which vaginal orgasms come in resplendent waves, as from the ocean depths, rather than in foam effervescence from surface sensation. Lawrence employs the familiar analogy to Botticelli's *The Birth of Venus*—"Aphrodite of the foam"—as a metaphor for clitoral orgasm, which he associates with the female will.

In *The Plumed Serpent*, Lawrence says of the Mexican peons: "But sex itself was a powerful, potent thing, not to be played with or paraded. The one mystery. And a mystery greater than the individual. The individual hardly counted" (152). After her marriage at age forty to Cipriano Viedma, Kate Leslie learns that this means giving up any will of her own in sex. In his description of the early marital relationship between Cipriano and Kate, Lawrence sets forth graphically, according to his fantasy model of female orgasm, the effect of Kate's transfer of sexual orgasm from clitoris to vagina:

> Her strange, seething feminine will and desire subsided in her and swept away, leaving her soft and powerfully potent, like the hot springs of water that gushed up so noiseless, so soft, yet so powerful, with a sort of secret potency.
>
> She realised, almost with wonder, the death in her of the Aphrodite of the foam: the seething, frictional, ecstatic Aphrodite. By a swift dark instinct, Cipriano drew away from this in her. When in their love, it came back on her, the seething electric female ecstasy, which knows such spasms of delirium, he recoiled from her. It was what she used to call her "satisfaction. . . ."
>
> But Cipriano would not. By a dark and powerful instinct he drew away from her as soon as this desire rose again in her, for the white ecstasy of frictional satisfaction, the throes of Aphrodite of the foam. She could see that to him, it was repulsive. He just removed himself, dark and unchangeable, away from her.
>
> And she, as she lay, would realise the worthlessness of this foam-effervescence, its strange externality to her. It seemed to come upon her from without, not from within. And succeeding the first moment of disappointment, when this sort of "satisfaction" was denied her, came the knowledge that she did not really want it, that it was really nauseous to her. [422]

As the passage continues, Cipriano introduces Kate to the contrasting fantasy model of the vaginal orgasm:

> And he, in his dark, hot silence would bring her back to the new, soft, heavy, hot flow, when she was like a fountain gushing noiseless and with urgent softness from the volcanic deeps. Then she was open to him soft and hot, yet gushing with a noiseless soft power. And there was no such thing as conscious "satisfaction." What happened was dark and untellable. So different from the beak-like friction of Aphrodite of the foam, the friction which flares out in circles of phosphorescent ecstasy, to the last wild spasm

which utters the involuntary cry, like a death-cry, the final love-cry. This she had known, and known to the end, with Joachim. And now this too was removed from her. What she had with Cipriano was curiously beyond her knowing: so deep and hot and flowing, as it were subterranean. She had to yield before *it*. She could not grip it into one final spasm of white ecstasy which was like sheer knowing. [422]

Lawrence's meaning is clear enough: vaginal orgasm in the woman is the sine qua non of the dominant male's success in sexual performance, but it is to be achieved only by the woman's renunciation of female will. What is not clear is why it also involves, at least in this instance, the woman's forgoing movement and, after such a volcanic eruption, even withholding vocalization. It is hard to avoid the suspicion that the reason may be the threat that Lawrence perceived in female desire.

H. M. Daleski argues that Cipriano's demand requires Kate's total sexual submission in voluntarily forgoing orgasm altogether.[54] It is noteworthy, however, that Kate's experience is described as "so deep and hot and flowing, as it were subterranean." The original typescript as revised by Lawrence is even more explicit: "And she was changed again to a soft, hot spring of inner waters, gushing noiselessly and beyond knowing in the dark" (*The Plumed Serpent*, ed. L. D. Clark, Textual Apparatus, p. 541: 422.35). The imagery in both the revised typescript and the published versions does not, in my view, support the reading that she withholds orgasm altogether, but rather that her orgasm has been transferred from what Lawrence now regards as the surface frictional sensation of the clitoris to a deeper vaginal source.

In their insistence that women forgo clitoral orgasm and cultivate the deeper satisfaction of vaginal orgasm, both Freud and Lawrence were culture-bound as creatures of their time. In the latter half of the twentieth century, both revisionist and counterrevisionist scientific views of the matter emerged.

Alfred C. Kinsey, in his scientific research on female sexual behavior, arranged for gynecological tests of the clitoris and other parts of the genitalia of approximately nine hundred women. The results showed that some "98 percent of the women could feel tactile stimulation of the clitoris (albeit with varying degrees of sensitivity), while only 14 percent had any touch sensation whatsoever in the vagina." In the extensive data on female sexual behavior that he had collected by sexual history interviews, Kinsey also found that in masturbation, "[i]nstead of focusing on the vagina, . . . the overwhelming majority of women relied upon labial and clitoral stimulation." On the basis of his exhaustive research, "Kinsey concluded that the vaginal orgasm was an anatomical impossibility."[55] In *Sexual Behavior of the Human Female* (1950), after reviewing the then-prescriptive view of psychoanalysis, Kinsey observes: "It is difficult, however, in the light of our present understanding of the anatomy and physiology of sexual response, to understand what can be meant by a 'vaginal orgasm.'"[56]

Masturbation and sexual intercourse are, of course, psychologically different, and for both men and women, whatever the means of achieving orgasm, there are unquestionably different qualities of orgastic experience at different times. But the difference for women, according to Masters and Johnson, cannot be attributed physiologically to a difference between clitoral and vaginal stimulation, since the clitoris is involved in *all* female orgasms, including those achieved by ordinary vaginal intercourse: "From an *anatomic* point of view, there is absolutely no difference in the response of the pelvic viscera to effective sexual stimulation, regardless of whether stimulation occurs as a result of clitoral-body or mons area manipulation, natural or artificial coition, or, for that matter, specific stimulation of any other erogenous area of the female body" (Masters and Johnson, 66). Although there may be variations in duration and intensity of orgasms, "the vagina and clitoris react in consistent physiologic patterns. Thus, clitoral and vaginal orgasms are not separate biologic entities" (67).

Masters and Johnson's extensive research on human sexual response was widely regarded as having exploded the previously accepted distinction between clitoral and vaginal orgasm. This revisionist theory has been partially challenged, however, by some like psychoanalyst Virginia Lawson Clower, who, while conceding that "Masters and Johnson have demonstrated no difference in the physiology of orgasm brought on by any effective stimulation,"[57] says that the question of difference in women's orgastic experience is still in dispute. On the basis of the experience of women in her own clinical practice, Clower comments as follows:

> Furthermore, they report that in masturbation as well as in coitus, there really are two kinds of orgasms. One type is felt as the relatively sudden spasm localized in and around the clitoris and the surface of the perineum. Its experience is very intense with a sharp rise and fall of excitement. The other is felt inside the body, by some women described specifically as high in the vagina and often accompanied by a spreading warmth throughout the pelvis, at times with what feels like vaginal contractions. The rise and fall of excitement in this experience is much more gradual.[58]

Clower declares, however, that "Freud's attempt to equate clitoral masturbation with a less mature level of development in contrast to vaginal dominance in women capable of orgastic experience in coitus is not substantiated by decades of clinical observation."[59] This view is reiterated in the entry on masturbation in Burness E. Moore and Bernard D. Fine's *Psychoanalytic Terms and Concepts* (1990): "Clitoral sexuality is no longer seen as masculine in character, and its repression is no longer seen as a necessary prelude to establishing vaginal supremacy or feminine identity."[60] Although there may be variations in duration and intensity of orgasms, "the vagina and clitoris react in consistent physiologic patterns. Thus, clitoral and vaginal orgasms are not separate biologic entities" (Masters and Johnson, 67).

Mutual Orgasm

Lawrence insists that mutual orgasm is necessary to sexual fulfillment. The difficulty of reaching simultaneous climax with his partner is what troubled Lawrence most in his early sexual relations with Frieda. He was concerned enough about it to discuss it with Compton Mackenzie at the time. According to Mackenzie, "What worried him particularly was his inability to attain consummation simultaneously with his wife, which according to him must mean that their marriage was still imperfect in spite of all they had both gone through. I insisted that such a happy coincidence was always rare, but he became more and more depressed about what *he* insisted was the only evidence of a perfect union."[61] Years later, in *Lady Chatterley's Lover*, in the sexual relationship of Connie and Michaelis, Lawrence presents the inability to achieve simultaneous orgasm as their main sexual problem, with a suggestion of premature ejaculation followed by a shrinking loss of erection on Michaelis's part, until Connie discovers that after his ejaculation, in what would normally be a refractory period for him, she can clip and hold his penis inside with her pelvic muscles in such a way as to keep it passively erect long enough for her to employ it as an instrument upon which to achieve her own independent orgasm:

> He roused in the woman a wild sort of compassion and yearning, and a wild, craving physical desire. The physical desire he did not satisfy in her; he was always come, and finished, so quickly: then shrinking down on her breast, and recovering somewhat his effrontery, while she lay dazed, disappointed, lost.
>
> But then she learnt soon to hold him, to keep him there inside her when his crisis was over. And there he was generous and curiously potent: he stayed firm inside her, given to her, while she was active, wildly, passionately active, coming to her own crisis. And as he felt the frenzy of her achieving her own orgiastic satisfaction from his hard, erect passivity, he had a curious sense of pride and satisfaction.

"Ah, how good!" she whispered tremulously: and she became quite still, clinging to him. And he lay there in his own isolation, but somehow proud. [29]

Despite his pride in the oxymoron of "his hard, erect passivity," Michaelis ultimately complains bitterly: "You keep on for hours after I've gone off—and I have to hang on with my teeth till you bring yourself off, by your own exertions." All women, he says, are like that: "I never had a woman yet who went off just at the same moment as I did" (54).

Simultaneous orgasm is also a central area of conflict in the relationship of Mellors and Bertha Coutts, whom he bitterly blames for the failure:

But when I had her, she'd never come-off when I did. Never! She'd just wait. If I kept back for half an hour, she'd keep back longer. And when I'd come and really finished, then she'd start on her own account, and I had to stop inside her till she brought herself off, wriggling and shouting. And when I'd gone little as anything, she'd clutch clutch with herself down there, an' then she'd come-off, fair in ecstasy. An' then she'd say: That was lovely! (201–2)

From his point of view, Bertha Coutts, rather than cooperating in arriving at a mutual and simultaneous orgasm, would spitefully wait him out, no matter how long he delayed his ejaculation, and then use his penis, already detumescent in what should have been the refractory stage for him, as a masturbatory instrument upon which to achieve her orgasm.

The contrasting experience of simultaneous orgasm is presented in the third sexual encounter of Mellors and Connie:

. . . She clung to him unconscious in passion, and he never quite slipped from her. And she felt the soft bud of him within her stirring and in strange rhythms flushing up into her, with a strange, rhythmic growing motion, swelling and swelling till it filled all her cleaving consciousness. And then began again the unspeakable motion that was not really motion, but pure deepening whirlpools of sensation, swirling deeper and deeper through all her tissue and consciousness, till she was one perfect concentric fluid of feeling. And she lay there crying in unconscious, inarticulate cries, the voice out of the uttermost night, the life—exclamation. And the man heard it beneath him with a kind of awe, as his life sprang out into her. And as it subsided he subsided too, and lay utterly still, unknowing, while her grip on him slowly relaxed, and she lay inert. [133–34]

Afterwards, when they discuss the experience, Mellors assumes a didactic stance.

> "We came-off together, that time," he said. . . .
> "It's good when it's like that. Most folks lives their lives through, and they never know it," he said, speaking rather dreamily. . . .
> "Don't people often come-off together?" she asked, with naïve curiosity.
> "A good many of 'em, never. You can see by the raw look of them." [134]

Consistency in orgastic experience, however, is difficult to maintain. In their fourth sexual encounter, Connie assumes an ironic spectator role during sexual intercourse so that although Mellors ejaculates, she does not reach an orgasm and the experience proves unsatisfying:

> Cold and derisive her queer female mind stood apart. And, though she lay perfectly still, her instinct was to heave her loins and throw the man out, escape his ugly grip and the butting over-riding of his absurd haunches. His body was a foolish, impudent, imperfect thing, a little disgusting in its unfinished clumsiness. For surely a complete evolution would eliminate this performance, this "function."
> And yet, when he had finished, soon over, and lay very, very still, receding into a silence and a strange motionless distance far, farther than the horizon of her awareness, her heart began to weep. She could feel him ebbing away, ebbing away, leaving her there like a stone on a shore. He was withdrawing. His spirit was leaving her. He knew.
> And in real grief, tormented by her own double consciousness and reaction, she began to weep. He took no notice: or did not even know. The storm of weeping swelled and shook her: and shook him.
> "Ay!" he said. "It was no good that time. You wasn't there."
> So he knew! Her sobs became violent. [172]

In this scene, as Connie watches derisively from an ironic distance "the butting over-riding of his absurd haunches," her sense of the ridiculous probably owes something to Compton Mackenzie's observation to Lawrence in 1920 that "except to the two people who are indulging in it the sexual act is a comic operation" (Mackenzie, 168)—only here it is one of the participants who recognizes the absurdity.

These instances illustrate two reasons for the powerful attraction of the mutual orgasm. The first two examples illustrate the man's motive to be in control of the situation and to demonstrate his control by bringing the woman to orgasm simultaneously with his own. In both cases, however, all the woman has to do to prevent his exercising that control is to delay her orgasm beyond his staying power, thus demonstrating her own control at the cost of frustration for both partners. In the fourth example, the man's deeper psychological motive is the desire for temporary union in sexual intercourse, but the fulfillment of this desire is prevented by the woman's distancing herself from the act sufficiently to withhold orgasm altogether. Lawrence's obsessive pursuit of the goal of mutual orgasm suggests that it had become for him exactly the kind of mentalized idea that in other areas he correctly saw as inimical to instinctual spontaneity.

Most couples regard mutual and simultaneous orgasm as a very satisfying experience when it occurs. The problem lies in reifying the idea as a goal to such an extent that obsessively pursuing it actually interferes with sexual fulfillment. Psychiatrist and sex therapist Helen Singer Kaplan says that "the myth of the mutual orgasm is extremely harmful and that as satisfying as the experience may be, mutual orgasm is not necessary to sexual fulfillment: "Actually, simultaneous coital orgasms are the exception rather than the rule." Usually when simultaneity does occur, Kaplan says, it is because the woman is so easily orgastic that she can produce an orgasm almost at will when she senses that her partner has arrived at his climax.[62]

The urologist Sherman J. Silber also comments on the "misunderstanding in the technique of lovemaking" that leads to

> the erroneous notion in our culture that mutual and simultaneous orgasm is the ultimate goal of sexual intercourse. This is a difficult goal to reach, and its quest can lead to a lot of anxiety and, again, inadequate lovemaking. If the husband is always concentrating on holding back his orgasm because he knows his wife will take somewhat longer to reach her climax, and if she is striving intellectually as hard as she can to try to reach her orgasm hurriedly for fear that she might be too late, sex becomes difficult to enjoy. Again, the result of this anxiety may be impotence.[63]

Other authorities on human sexuality whom I have consulted agree that simultaneous orgasm is not essential to sexual fulfillment and that its obsessive pursuit is counterproductive.[64]

The sexual model that Lawrence reflects is an idealized version of the reciprocal model. There are alternative nonreciprocal models, which many people learn to adapt to their own individual situations and needs. Lawrence rejected the nonreciprocal models of masturbation and nonsimultaneous orgasm, and spent a lot of frustrating effort in striving to achieve the idealized goal of mutual orgasm.

Conclusion

The attitudes expressed in the sexual myths that Lawrence believed in are best understood in terms of two different, though not mutually exclusive, sources from which they derive. Popular opinions that male dominance is essential in sex and in society, that the male is responsible for initiating and orchestrating the entire sexual encounter, that effectiveness of male sexual performance determines the quality of sexual relations, and that penis size is a crucial factor in sexual effectiveness were so general to the culture Lawrence grew up in that Lawrence's inability to transcend them is probably attributable more to cultural influences than to individual factors peculiar to himself. Two other fallacies, Lawrence's phobia about female pubic hair and the sexual anxiety expressed in the vagina dentata fantasy, though they were not unique to Lawrence, probably derive more from personal neuroses he struggled with, especially those relating to the threat of engulfment by the powerful, devouring mother, than from general cultural attitudes. Finally, Lawrence's denial of clitoral orgasm and advocacy of vaginal orgasm for women and his obsessive insistence on mutual and simultaneous orgasm seem both personal and cultural in origin. Both concepts reflect Lawrence's individual need to defend against the threat that female desire posed for him by asserting masculine control of the orgasm for both partners in sexual intercourse, but they also reflect the same cultural attitudes that shaped Freud's theory of female sexuality. Although some of Lawrence's sexual attitudes are still more or less current in our own society, the present struggle to redefine the sexual roles of both women and men may be seen as an attempt to effect a social and sexual realignment that will ultimately be satisfactory to both sexes, even if the extremes on either side remain unsatisfiable.

CHAPTER 7

Lawrence, Freud, and Masturbation

D. H. Lawrence thought of himself as a sexual liberator, and for several generations he was known as such, but he was a creature of his time in proclaiming the harmful consequences of masturbation. Sigmund Freud and others in the early psychoanalytic movement were also opposed to masturbation, although their views were not monolithic and were stated in scientific rather than moralistic terms. Lawrence saw masturbation as a personal and cultural vice that functionally hampered the development of dynamic, relational sexuality and that led to self-absorbed, mental analysis. Freud saw masturbation as a widespread childhood habit that, if not given up, became the etiology of neurasthenia as well as contributing to other pathological conditions. Their perspectives on the subject—Lawrence's cultural, Freud's scientific—intersect at a transitional point in social and cultural history when Victorian attitudes were changing but had not yet fully given way to modern ones. Taylor Stoehr comments that "Lawrence's attitude toward masturbation, although in one sense an attack on nineteenth-century practice, is also very much indebted to official Victorian opinion on the subject. It is not surprising therefore that Lawrence sometimes sounds like the generation of prigs he despised for their anti-sexuality."[1]

In this chapter, I will first examine Lawrence's discursive statements on masturbation in comparison with those of Freud and other early psychoanalytic theorists. Second, I will discuss Lawrence's own masturbatory experience and fantasies—insofar as these can be reconstructed from his poetic and discursive statements—in the light of Freud's theories of ego defenses and masochism.

~

For a writer who had endured so much censure for his sexual themes, Lawrence, in *Fantasia of the Unconscious,* is surprisingly moralistic in his recommendations on sex education: "After puberty, a child may as well be told the simple and necessary facts of sex," he says grudgingly. "As things stand, the parent may as well do it. But briefly, coldly, and with as cold a dismissal as possible." The stated purpose of this strategy is to avoid dragging the subject into consciousness, as if the urgency of the drive had not driven it there already. He recommends that the father tell the boy that the change he is experiencing means that the boy is "going to be a man" and later marry a woman and have children. "But in the meantime, leave yourself alone. . . . I know what is happening to you. And I know you get excited about it. But you needn't. Other men have all gone through it. So don't you go creeping off by yourself and doing things on the sly. It won't do you any good."[2] The strong implication is that it will do him considerable harm.

As Lawrence's model sex-education lecture continues, the father ostensibly encourages the boy's masculine identification with him, but in a manner so prohibitive and so lacking in empathic attunement that he emerges less as a viable role model than as an omniscient Old Testament God whose prohibition only makes the forbidden fruit more enticing:

> I know what you'll do, because we've all been through it. I know the thing will keep coming on you at night. But remember that I know. Remember. And remember that I want you to leave yourself alone. I know what it is, I tell you. I've been through it myself. You've got to go through these years, before you find a woman you want to marry, and whom you can marry. I went through them myself, and got myself worked up a good deal more than was good for me (146).

The uncharacteristically cold, judgmental attitude that the childless Lawrence recommends here, with its view of the child as a "sly," "secretive," and "unmanly" miscreant and the repeated formula "Remember that I know," is akin to the kind of "Poisonous Pedagogy" on masturbation that Alice Miller found to be so damaging to children in nineteenth-century Germany. Even so, Lawrence's proposed method of sex education gives the son greater access to the father than Freud's practice of sending his sons to another doctor for an explanation of the facts of life. Although morally Freud was more tolerant of masturbation than Lawrence was, medically he considered it a symptom. Thus, according to Paul Roazen, "when one of his adolescent sons [Oliver] came to him with worries about masturbation, Freud responded by warning the boy very much against it. An estrangement between father and son ensued."[3]

In Lawrence's warning, there is also an additional element in the father's direction to the son: "Always try to contain yourself, and be a man. That's the only thing. Always try and be manly, and quiet in yourself" (*Fantasia,* 146–47). Although on a conscious level this injunction refers to psychological mastery in the containment of impulses, its subtext suggests that behind Lawrence's negative judgment of masturbation is a view of semen as both the carrier and the symbolic equivalent of the life force or soul, and hence not to be wasted. This idea can be traced to the centuries-old semen conservation theory that semen comes from the brain and spinal cord, and hence its wastage leads to madness.

The cultural milieu in which Lawrence grew to manhood conditioned his negative attitude toward masturbation. This climate, of course, included the puritanical position of Robert S. S. Baden-Powell, founder of the Boy Scout movement. The section on masturbation in the Boy Scout Manual was headed "Conservation." Although he was not a Boy Scout, Lawrence's language in insisting that the boy be "manly" and "contain" himself until he is ready "to marry a woman later on, and get children" parallels the official Baden-Powell line in *Rovering to Success,* published in the same year as *Fantasia* (1922), that masturbation "just checks that semen getting its full chance of making you the strong manly man you would otherwise be. You are throwing away the seed that has been handed down to you as a trust instead of keeping it and ripening it for bringing a son to you later on." Nothing Lawrence says, however, carries the threat of Baden-Powell's warning: "The usual consequence is that you sap your health and brain just at the critical time when you would otherwise be gaining the height of manly health."[4]

Lawrence's view of the body has something of the Old Testament conception, in which, as Mary Douglas describes it, "the ideal of holiness was given an external, physical expression in the wholeness of the body seen as a perfect container."[5] In the New Testament, Jesus refers to his body as the temple to be destroyed and raised again in three days (John 2:19, 21); and Saint Paul declares: "If any man defile the temple of God, him shall God destroy; for the temple of God is holy, which *temple* ye are" (1 Corinthians 3:17). Lawrence conceived of the body as containing the soul and providing fuel for the soul's flame, burning between body and spirit in the triad of man's being.[6] It was important, therefore, to preserve the integrity of the body as container of the life force. Lawrence reinforces the lesson by repetition: "I've been as bad and probably worse than you. And the only thing I want of you is to be manly. Try and be manly, and quiet in yourself." He concludes: "That is about as much as a father can say to a boy, at puberty" (*Fantasia,* 147).

The issue for Lawrence is how the bodily fluid carrying the life force is to be emitted. For him, the sacramental significance of sexual intercourse lies in the emission of soul in union with the other. He might have agreed with Saint Thomas Aquinas's statement, "It is good for each person to attain his end, whereas it is bad for him to swerve away from his proper end," but not with Aquinas's definition of the "proper end" as procreation. According to Aquinas, "Every emission of semen, in such a way that generation cannot follow, is contrary to the good for man. And if this is done deliberately, it must be a sin."[7] To Lawrence, in contrast, the sexual act "is not for the depositing of seed. It is for leaping off into the unknown."[8] When Mellors ejaculates, in *Lady Chatterley's Lover*, "as his seed sprang in her, his soul sprang towards her too, in the creative act that is far more than procreative."[9] Lawrence presents Connie's subsequent pregnancy as incidental to the real creative process of expressing the soul, pressing it outward through ejaculation in sexual union with the unknown other: "There's the baby, but that is a side issue," Mellors says (300). One reason for Lawrence's opposition to masturbation, then, is that it habituates the known rather than "leaping off into the unknown."

In *Pornography and Obscenity*, Lawrence spells out his case against pornography by associating it with masturbation: The inevitable and "pernicious" effect of pornography, including the soft-core "pornography" of popular fiction and films, is "an invariable stimulant to the vice of self-abuse, onanism, masturbation." The strictures of the "grey ones" against sexual intercourse only encourage young men and women to masturbate separately, since the sex drive must have some outlet. Clergymen and teachers sometimes honestly "commend masturbation as the solution of an otherwise insoluble sex problem" (178). The same "moral guardians," while accepting the pornographic titillation of popular literature, hypocritically "censor all open and plain portrayal of sex."[10]

"Is masturbation so harmless, though?" Lawrence asks. The first reason he gives for answering *no* is that it produces shame: "[T]here is no boy or girl who masturbates without feeling a sense of shame, anger, and futility," which only "deepens as the years go on, into a suppressed rage." The second reason is that it is addictive: "The one thing that it seems impossible to escape from, once the habit is formed, is masturbation. It goes on and on, on into old age, in spite of marriage or love affairs or anything else" (179).

Lawrence's view that masturbation is a habit seemingly impossible to break unknowingly echoes an earlier analogous statement by Sigmund Freud in a letter to his friend Wilhelm Fliess (22 December 1897): "The insight has dawned on me that masturbation is the one major habit, the 'primary addiction,' and it is only as a substitute and replacement for it that the other addictions—to alcohol, morphine, tobacco, and the like—come into existence."[11] Three decades later, in "Dostoevsky and Parricide," Freud sees Dostoevsky's compulsive gambling as a replacement for the primary addiction of masturbation: "the emphasis laid upon the passionate activity of the hands betrays this derivation."[12]

Lawrence's view that masturbation leads to depletion of vitality and causes shame also directly parallels Freud's early theory (1898), causally linking masturbation to the "actual neurosis," neurasthenia. Freud warns, however, that "it has a harmful effect not only by producing neurasthenic symptoms, but also because it keeps the patients under the weight of what they feel to be a disgraceful secret" (*SE* 3:275). It follows that in treating neurasthenia, the physician has the responsibility of inducing the patient to give up the habit: "Left to himself, the masturbator is accustomed, whenever something happens that depresses him, to return to his convenient form of satisfaction. Medical treatment, in this instance, can have no other aim than to lead the neurasthenic, who has now recovered his strength, back to normal sexual intercourse. For sexual need, when once it has been aroused and has been satisfied for any length of time, can no longer be silenced; it can only be displaced along another path" (*SE* 3:275–76). Pressing his argument to its logical conclusion, Freud says: "If masturbation is the cause of neurasthenia in youth, and if, later on, it acquires aetiological significance for anxiety neurosis as well, by reason of the reduction of potency which it brings about, then the prevention of masturbation in both sexes is a task that deserves more attention than it has hitherto received." Freud maintains that "it is positively a matter of public interest that *men should enter upon sexual relations with full potency*" (*SE* 3:278).

Among the discussants in the Wednesday evening meetings in Vienna, Wilhelm Stekel was virtually alone in diverging from what quickly became the orthodox Freudian position on the harmful effects of masturbation in the etiology of neurasthenia. According to Leendert F. Groenendijk, the ensuing controversy ultimately led to Stekel's resignation from the Vienna Psychoanalytic Society.[13]

Lawrence's views on masturbation have greater affinities with the theories of several other early Freudian psychoanalysts. In his contribution to the 1912 discussions on masturbation in the Vienna Psychoanalytic Society,[14] Sándor Ferenczi presents a clear distinction between dynamic sex and masturbation as the kind of sex that Lawrence would call "sex in the head." Ferenczi theorizes that "normal coitus and masturbation are processes that are to be estimated differently not only psychologically, but also physiologically":

With onanism the normal fore-pleasure is absent, whereas the share taken by the phantasy is enormously increased. . . . When a satisfying sexual object is gazed at, touched, kissed, embraced, the optic, tactile, oral, and muscular erogenous zones are actively excited, and they automatically pass over a part of this excitation to the genital zone; . . . the phantasy is only secondarily drawn into sympathetic enjoyment. With onanism, however, all the sense organs are silent, and the conscious phantasy, together with the genital stimulation, have to procure the whole sum of excitation.[15]

The effect of this forcible retention of a mental picture "during a sexual act that normally is almost unconscious" is the fatigue and depletion symptomatic of neurasthenia. In sexual intercourse with a satisfying object, however, the pleasure radiates physiologically throughout the body rather than being localized mentally in a fantasy image:

> Through the stimulation of the erogenous zones in coitus a state of preparedness of the genital organ is aroused in the first place; in the friction that succeeds, the genito-spinal reflex then plays the chief part; it ends in a summation of genital stimuli, and finally—synchronously with ejaculation—in an explosive radiation of the excitation over the whole body . . . [with] the sensual pleasure . . . explosively radiating beyond the spinal centre into the whole sphere of feeling, thus into the cutaneous and sensorial centres as well. If this is the case, it is probably not a matter of indifference whether the wave of lust finds a sphere of feeling that is prepared by fore-pleasure, or one that is unexcited and, so to speak, cold. [Ferenczi, 189–90]

Since "with masturbation a part of the excitation cannot reach a proper level," the sexual tensions cannot be fully discharged. As the flow of libido is dammed up, the "amount of excitation remaining over" produces a "one-day neurasthenia" (190).

For Lawrence, as for Ferenczi, the mentalized sex of masturbation is a merely exhaustive activity, a wasteful spending of life force, leading to an emptying and debilitation of the vital self. Sexual intercourse, in contrast, is a regenerative activity, a vital interchange between self and other, leading to creative balance. Although Ferenczi attributes the effect of neurasthenic exhaustion in masturbation to the effort of maintaining the conscious mental picture of the fantasied object throughout the act, Lawrence attributes it to the absence of the reciprocal relationship between self and other experienced in sexual intercourse. Just as Freud sees masturbation as a principal cause of neurasthenia and the primary addiction from which other addictions derive, so Lawrence sees both masturbation and the habituated form of masturbatory consciousness as substitutes for vital relationship: "The great danger of masturbation lies in its merely exhaustive nature. In sexual intercourse, there is a give and take. A new stimulus enters as the native stimulus departs. Something quite new is added as the old surcharge is removed. And this is so in all sexual intercourse where two creatures are concerned, even in the homosexual intercourse. But in masturbation there is nothing but loss. There is no reciprocity. There is merely the spending away of a certain force, and no return. The body remains, in a sense, a corpse, after the act of self-abuse" (*Pornography and Obscenity*, 179).

When Lawrence calls masturbation "the deepest and most dangerous cancer of our civilization" and "the most dangerous sexual vice that a society can be afflicted with, in the long run," he generalizes the practice from an individual act of autoerotic gratification to a cultural vice. Although masturbation as a form of mentalized sex has the effect in some people of releasing mental energy, the intellectual activity thus generated always manifests itself either "in a vicious circle of analysis and impotent criticism, or else in a vicious circle of false and easy sympathy, sentimentalities. The sentimentalism and the niggling analysis, often self-analysis, of most of our modern literature, is a sign of self-abuse." Without an external object, the mentally masturbating author moves only "within the vicious circle of himself." The work of art so produced is "self-absorption made public." Lawrence's objection that "the outstanding feature of such consciousness is that there is no real object, there is only subject" (*Pornography and Obscenity*, 179–80) is accurate in the physical sense, although it should be noted that, psychologically, both in masturbation and in the masturbatory consciousness Lawrence describes, the object is always present in the accompanying fantasy and in the unconscious wishes behind it. Lawrence's concern is that the masturbatory object is not an independent subject and contributes nothing from a separate center of consciousness.[16]

Like individual masturbation, the masturbatory cultural process, Lawrence says, is purely exhaustive. In this respect, the "real masturbation of Englishmen began only in the nineteenth century. It has continued with an increasing emptying of the real vitality and the real *being* of men. . . ." The result might be described as cultural neurasthenia: "Most of the responses are dead, most of the awareness is dead, nearly all the constructive activity is dead, and all that remains is a sort of shell, a half-empty creature fatally self-preoccupied and incapable of either giving or taking . . . in the vital self. . . . But null or nothing as it may be, it still hangs on to the dirty little secret, which it must still secretly rub and inflame" (180). In Lawrence's view, the "vicious circle of masturbation" is at the root of modern self-consciousness, which is "never fully and openly conscious," but a nullity maintained by the "vast conspiracy of secrecy" among educators, the clergy, the family, the press; "at the same time, [there is] the endless tickling of the dirty little secret. The endless masturbation! and the endless purity!" (181)

Turning to the problem of how to get out of "the vicious circle," Lawrence proposes a solution: "No more secrecy! The only way to stop the terrible mental itch about sex is to come out quite simply and naturally into the open with it" (181). He proceeds, however, to attack the very people who were attempting to accomplish that end by educating the public on the scientific facts of human sexuality in order to correct widespread ignorance and misinformation about sex and thus to defuse its appeal as a "dirty little secret." In *Fantasia of the Unconscious* Lawrence had said, "To translate sex into mental ideas is vile, to make a scientific fact of it is death" (147). In *Pornography and Obscenity* he pointedly focuses his attack on a widely known author of sex-education and marriage manuals: "You can't do it by being wise and scientific about it, like Dr. Marie Stopes." Although preferable to the hypocrisy of "the grey ones," scientific seriousness tends only to disinfect "the dirty little secret" with scientific words, leaving a sanitized, "free and pure" "mentalized sex." "The danger is, that in killing the dirty little secret, you kill dynamic sex altogether, and leave only the scientific and deliberate mechanism" (182). Lawrence thought that demystifying sex would reduce it to a sterile idea of the physiological process and leave out of account the dynamic interaction involved in sexual response and satisfaction. He applies the same principle, in even greater proportion, to the ostensibly "emancipated bohemians." In attempting to kill the "dirty little secret" by sexually acting out in both speech and behavior, they had produced only emptiness, "dreariness and depression": "For sex is the fountain-head of our energetic life, and now the fountain ceases to flow" (182). The damming up of sexual energy in the masturbatory consciousness of the society, as Lawrence describes it, has led to the same neurasthenic symptoms that Freud found to be the result of individual masturbation.

In "Introduction to These Paintings," Lawrence sees the source of society's putative masturbatory consciousness as the mind-body split: "Any creative act occupies the whole consciousness of a man. . . . The whole consciousness is occupied, not merely the mind alone, or merely the body. The mind and spirit alone can never really grasp a work of art, though they may, in a masturbating fashion, provoke the body into an ecstasized response."[17] In such late works as "The Rocking-Horse Winner," masturbation, or its equivalent, became for Lawrence a metaphor for achieving mechanistic or materialistic ends by the conscious manipulation of vital instinctual forces that he thought were better left to the spontaneous expression of the unconscious.

~

Considering the question of Lawrence's own masturbatory experience in light of his adult disapproval of masturbation, William B. Ober, a medical doctor and pathologist, speculates that he probably masturbated in puberty and adolescence and that he "almost certainly masturbated when returning home after his

unsatisfactory assignations with Jessie Chambers." "We can reject as unlikely
the hypotheses that he never masturbated or was a compulsive masturbator; the
first is statistically improbable, the second out of keeping with his character."[18]
Although Ober cites no external evidence to support his speculation, Lawrence's
statement, "I know what it is, I tell you. I've been through it myself" (*Fantasia,*
146), indicates that masturbation was an area of conflict for him.

Masturbation has two components, physical (genital stimulation) and psychic (fantasy life). Both the physical masturbation and the accompanying fantasies may be either conscious or unconscious. As I will employ the term, the
masturbation fantasy also has two components: the usually conscious mental
imagery that accompanies the physical act, and behind this imagery, the
unconscious fantasies being gratified. A further consideration is the "central
masturbation fantasy," which contains the fantasied gratification, often in distorted or symbolic form, of unrelinquished infantile instinctual wishes. The
content of this "central masturbation fantasy" is usually unconscious in childhood, but with the maturation of the genitals in adolescence, it takes on new
and urgent meaning for the ego, involving as it does one's basic sexual organization and the expression of one's sexual role.[19] As a core theme, the central
masturbation fantasy is always present, with or without masturbation.

In "The State of Funk," Lawrence discloses: "I know, when I was a lad of
eighteen, I used to remember with shame and rage in the morning the sexual
thoughts and desires I had had the night before. Shame, and rage, and terror
lest anybody else should have to know. And I *hated* the self that I had been,
the night before."[20] Significantly, Lawrence associates his negative feelings of
"shame and rage" not with the physical act of masturbation, but with the "sexual thoughts and desires"—that is, the fantasies—that accompanied it. Since
the masturbatory fantasy emerges from unconscious wishes involving early
objects, it may be inferred that Lawrence's sense of shame and fear of being
found out are associated with the forbidden nature of the fantasied object
relation.

As Evelyn Shakir has noted, one can also find evidence of Lawrence's
"secret sin" encoded in his early verse. A revealing example here is "Virgin
Youth," which was originally titled "The Body Awake" and which was written when he was twenty or twenty-one and first published ten years later with
only slight revisions in *Amores* (1916). He subsequently rewrote the poem
extensively for his *Collected Poems* (1928, 1:18–20).[21] In both versions, the
poem centers on an autoerotic experience of masturbation. The pattern of
imagery of the 1916 version clearly expresses the intensity and power of the
sexual urge, following the flow of sexual arousal from the "flush" and "flame"
of the male breasts (nipple erection) in "urgent, passionate waves" to the lower
body, to the "soft, slumbering belly / Quivering awake with one impulse of

desire" (penile erection), with the "docile, fluent arms / Knotting themselves with wild strength / To clasp—what they have never clasped" (the fantasy object). As the autoerotic experience continues:

> Then I tremble, and go trembling
> Under the wild, strange tyranny of my body,
> Till it has spent itself.

The masturbatory climax offers only partial discharge and partial resolution of sexual tensions. The fantasy object has not been clasped in physical reality, and mental consciousness again intrudes upon the domain of blood consciousness:

> And the relentless nodality of my eyes reasserts itself,
> Till the bursten flood of life ebbs back to my eyes,
> Back from my beautiful, lonely body
> Tired and unsatisfied.

The 1916 version of "Virgin Youth," closer in time to the sexual strivings of late adolescence, is more spontaneous in feeling but less graphic in language than the 1928 version as rewritten for *Collected Poems*. Gail Porter Mandell points out the structural dialectic in the 1916 version between the blood consciousness communicated through the penis and the mental consciousness transmitted by the eye. In the 1928 version, "the two centers of consciousness confront each other" (Mandell, 53).

The 1928 version, almost three times as long as the earlier one, particularizes the state of arousal with graphic imagery of erection and places Lawrence's youthful sexual awakening in the context of his subsequent sexual philosophy, thus giving the young man's poem the perspective of the more experienced middle-aged man of forty-three:

> A lower me gets up and greets me;
> Homunculus stirs from his roots, and strives until,
> Risen up, he beats me.
>
> He stands, and I tremble before him. . . .
> —Who art thou? What hast
> Thou to do with me, thou lustrous one, iconoclast?—

Lawrence celebrates the iconography of the erect phallus in Old Testament religious imagery: "He stands, the column of fire by night. / And he knows from the depths. . . ." The poem repeats the dominant image of the phallus as sacral being in motifs that reiterate the upward thrust of male desire from its roots in darkness:

> He stands like a lighthouse, night churns
> Round his base, his dark light rolls
> Into darkness, and darkly returns.

In subsequent images, Lawrence addresses the phallus as "Traveller, column of fire," "Dark, ruddy pillar," and "tower."

In this retrospective on the aroused sexual desire of youth, although he

> Would so gladly lie
> In the womanly valley, and ply
> Thy twofold dance,

the young man confesses:

> I
> Am helplessly bound
> To the rock of virginity.

Continuing in the vocative mode, he rhetorically addresses the erect phallus as a dark deity: "Thou dark one, thou proud, curved beauty! I / Would worship thee, letting my buttocks prance." Then lamenting the strength of the prohibition—"But the hosts of men with one voice deny / Me the chance"— he concludes with an ambiguous reference to the futility of masturbation:

> I salute thee
> But to deflower thee. Thy tower impinges
> On nothingness. Pardon me!

In the 1928 "Virgin Youth," the narrative voice asks: "Does his steep / Curve sweep towards a woman's?" and imagines "letting my buttocks prance" in the "twofold dance." These are the impulses the middle-aged man attributes to the young man from the vantage point of an established adult sexual identity. In the 1916 version the sexual object to be clasped in the fantasy is vague and unspecified; even the 1928 version, narcissistically centered, is primarily an ithyphallic celebration of the erect penis. In both versions the speaker remains entranced with the phenomenology of the autoerotic experience.

~

In his reconstruction of the psychic state in early childhood of his patient the Wolf Man (Sergei Pankejeff), Freud explains: "The homosexual attitude which came into being . . . was of such overwhelming intensity that the little boy's ego found itself unable to cope with it and so defended itself against it by the process of repression. The narcissistic masculinity which attached to his genitals, being opposed to the homosexual attitude, was drawn in, in order to assist the ego in carrying out the task" (*SE* 17:110–11). Victor Tausk— another psychoanalytic contributor to the 1912 Vienna discussions on masturbation—provides a gloss on a striking element in the 1928 "Virgin Youth": "The individual gradually develops an enormous interest in his own genital. In some cases I have observed, this interest went so far that the genitals were completely personified, i.e., they were treated like real persons. Some masturbators carry on conversations with their genitals, call them 'the little one,' or 'the little son,' or 'the little friend,' and thank them for their loyalty, generosity, etc."[22] The speaker in the 1928 version of "Virgin Youth" directly addresses his erect penis in a phallic motif expressing a predominant sexual attitude of narcissistic masculinity. In *Lady Chatterley's Lover*, which was also published in 1928, Mellors, adopting the slang name for the male genital, personifies his penis as John Thomas and treats it throughout as a figure with a separate identity and a will of its own. Both he and Connie refer to the organ with the masculine personal pronoun, even playfully knighting "Sir John" for the marriage with "Lady Jane." In a memorable scene, Mellors addresses his phallus directly. Although the element of phallic narcissism would be hard to miss in *Lady Chatterley's Lover*, the prevailing issue is the struggle to establish an adult reciprocal heterosexual relationship.

Holly A. Laird comments on the sexual trend in "Virgin Youth": "In the 1928 version, he does not consider whether or not he has an external object. His object is himself."[23] I postulate, however, that internalized object representations of Lawrence's earliest parental objects were involved, either directly or indirectly, in the fantasy elements of this and other early poems. Ernest Jones demonstrates that "the individual recapitulates and expands in the second decennium of life the development he passed through during the first five years. . . . [T]he precise way in which a given person will pass through the necessary stages of development in adolescence is to a very great extent determined by the form of his infantile development."[24] Lawrence's symbiotic relationship with his mother from early childhood through late adolescence precluded his developing any significant relationship with another woman as long as his mother was alive. The depreciated position of his father in the family constellation, which was already in place when Lawrence was born, made the father unavailable for the positive masculine identification with the paternal figure that might have enabled Lawrence as a young boy to separate himself from the symbiotic merger with his mother and to achieve a greater measure of psychic autonomy. I posit that in Lawrence's development from the phallic stage to young manhood, in the absence of a viable paternal relationship, the penis itself came to represent the separation and differentiation from his mother that he could not yet otherwise establish.

Despite the young man's feeling of shame and disappointment with regard to masturbation, Lawrence's increased focus on the penis in the graphic phenomenology of erection in the 1928 "Virgin Youth" suggests that the experience was of greater significance than he had recognized at the time of original composition. Specifically, as Moses Laufer has argued, "in adolescence masturbation has the function of helping the ego reorganize itself around the supremacy of genitality. This is normally accomplished by using masturbation and masturbation fantasies as something equivalent to 'trial action,' that is, as an autoerotic activity which helps to integrate regressive fantasies as part of the effort to achieve genital dominance" (301). The genital supremacy that Lawrence's autoerotic experience in adolescence and later his heterosexual experience in young manhood helped him to achieve, despite the continued presence of regressive perverse fantasies, also enabled him to establish an independent, though not an untroubled, adult sexual identity.

∼

Having drawn the parallel between Lawrence's attitude toward masturbation and the early Freudian view of the subject, I want to turn now to an argument based on Freud's later theory of ego defenses. I argue that the extremity of Lawrence's negative judgment of masturbation represents a defense against the "shame and rage" he felt about the "sexual thoughts and desires" he had experienced in association with it. Although Lawrence does not specify their content in "The State of Funk," the nature of these fantasies may be inferred from several poems and scenes in his autobiographical fiction dating from his late adolescence. In the following discussion, I shall consider two types of sexual fantasy suggested by these sources, namely, those containing homoerotic and those containing sadomasochistic elements.

The idyllic adolescent bathing episode in chapter 8 of *The White Peacock* (222–23) and the recollection by Lawrence's friend George H. Neville of Lawrence's gaze of "rapt adoration" at the sight of his athletic friend's naked, muscular body (Neville, 78–80) suggest that the content of Lawrence's adolescent sexual fantasies was sometimes homoerotic. As John Worthen points out, "He certainly experienced homoerotic feelings, and he expressed them in his writing. But that is not the same as being a homosexual."[25]

I suggest that Lawrence's homoerotic attractions in late adolescence and young adulthood may also be related to early childhood developmental issues that were reactivated in what Peter Blos has called "the second individuation process" of adolescence. In Michael Black's précis of the nude male bathing scene in *The White Peacock,* "Cyril is taken with the nobility of George's body, and George, like a father, holds Cyril to him and rubs him dry." With regard to the inevitable interpretation that the scene is an example of latent homosexuality, Black insists that "the idea is too simple: George looks like a god and acts like a father, and Cyril's attitude to him is reverence without overtones of simple desire" (65). Most readers cannot so easily dismiss the homoerotic feeling tones of the scene, but psychologically Black's point has validity. For all the homoeroticism of the scene, the wish expressed in its fantasy elements is not a straightforward, undisguised, instinctive homosexual impulse but the sexualized need for the nurturing masculine paternal relationship that Lawrence felt he had never had. The homoerotic strivings that emerged in expression of this wish could be partially sublimated through idealization and his creative work and partially repressed in the interest of ego functioning in a primary heterosexual identity, but they tended to return whenever the longing for male nurturance reasserted itself, as it did especially in such crisis situations as the difficulties with governmental authorities and the persecutory feelings that Lawrence experienced in the Cornwall period during the First World War. If the body of the father or his surrogate could become the object of reverence that Cyril feels for George in the "Poem of Friendship" chapter, there is only a step further to the awe of the erect penis as sacral object that characterizes Lawrence's use of the phallus as a literary symbol.

Citing such early poems as "Discord in Childhood" and "Love on the Farm," Shakir argues persuasively that the sexual fantasy accompanying masturbation was sadomasochistic in character. As she sees it, in the first poem, the violent quarrel between mother and father became for Lawrence the prototypal pattern of male-female relationships. The second poem, which employs this pattern as a source of erotic imagery, "clearly reveals the sadomasochistic nature of Lawrence's sexual fantasies" (158–59).

Although I am unwilling to limit myself to early Freudian theory as the only basis for a psychoanalytic understanding of Lawrence, I think it useful to extend the Freudian focus in the present discussion. Since the driving elements of the fantasy are often unconscious, the more specific source of the feelings involved is not so easy to determine, but these early poems, as Shakir suggests, provide revealing clues. "Discord in Childhood" turns on a scene of family violence inside the house:

> a slender lash
> Whistling she-delirious rage, and the dreadful sound
> Of a male thong booming and bruising, until it had drowned
> The other voice in a silence of blood
>
> [*Complete Poems*, 36]

These angry sounds of the parents' voices are metaphorically correlated with the "terrible whips" of the ash tree, lashing and shrieking in the wind outside. In a parallel scene in *Sons and Lovers,* Lawrence gives realistic dimension to the impact of this family violence on the children when Paul is awakened at night by "the booming shouts of his father, come home nearly drunk, then the sharp replies of his mother." As the quarrel escalates, "the whole was drowned in a piercing medley of shrieks and cries from the great, wind-swept ash-tree." Fearful that the father may hit their mother again, the children wait in suspense, "their hearts in the grip of an intense anguish. . . . All the cords of the great harp hummed, whistled, and shrieked." Even more terrible is "the horror of the sudden silence: silence everywhere, outside, and downstairs. What was it?—was it a silence of blood? What had he done" (84–85). Although these questions resonate with the psychic conflicts of Paul's oedipal situation, the scene of childhood terror is not directly sexual.

"Cruelty and Love," which Jessie Chambers dates in early 1907, when Lawrence was twenty-one (Sagar, 66), was first published in *Love Poems and Others* (1913). Although Lawrence wrote to Edward Marsh (25 September 1915), saying that the poem "doesn't interest me a bit" (*Letters* 2:401), he included it in a revised version in his *Collected Poems* (1928) under the less revealing title "Love on the Farm." Lawrence's ambivalence is understandable. Speaking of this dramatic monologue and several other nominally "fictional" poems of the same period, Holly Laird says: "more compelling than any event in these poems are the emotional swings they register, between fierce energy and despondency. The Beulah-like laddishness of Lawrence's younger self is torn by discord, confusion, and fatigue" (186).

As Shakir suggests, the poem illustrates Lawrence's conversion of the imagery of violent parental conflict into a source of erotic stimulation. Although the figurative equation of orgasm and death (*la petite mort*) is traditional, the husband's throttling a rabbit caught in a snare is metaphorically associated with a vampiristic image of sexuality as he kisses his wife's throat like "a stoat / Who sniffs with joy before he drinks the blood," then kisses her mouth, and "so I drown / Within him, die, and find death good" (*Love Poems and Others,* vii). To the child observing it, Freud says, the sexual intercourse of the parents appears to be an act of violence (*SE* 5:584–86; 7:196). Lawrence's associations of marital relationship with struggle and conflict and of sex with cruelty suggest that a repressed element of the fantasy is the equation of the primal scene with violence. Although Lawrence consciously identified himself with his powerful mother and rejected any such identification with his devalued father, he assumes, in the narrative voice of "Love on the Farm," the feminine perspective and masochistic attitude of the farm wife, who, in the fantasy, takes erotic satisfaction in her passive submissive role in relation to the erotically sadistic husband. In the poem Lawrence corrects his childhood family situation by shifting the balance of power to the dominant male, but he also employs the preconscious fantasy elements to express his own "feminine" masochistic wishes.

The conflicting sadistic and masochistic impulses emerge in *Sons and Lovers* in Paul Morel's fight with Baxter Dawes, which is described in the same erotically evocative imagery of darkness, hardness, the unconscious, cleaving bodies, and passion, wherein the tension builds to a climax that Lawrence usually employs for sexual scenes between a man and a woman:

> His body, hard and wonderful in itself, cleaved against the struggling body of the other man. Not a muscle in him relaxed. He was quite unconscious. . . . He lay pressed hard against his adversary, his body adjusting itself to its one pure purpose of choking the other man, . . . silent, intent, unchanging, gradually pressing its knuckles deeper, feeling the struggles of the other body become wilder and more frenzied. Tighter and tighter grew his body, like a screw that is gradually increasing in pressure, till something breaks.
>
> Then suddenly he relaxed, full of wonder and misgiving. . . . He was all bewildered. Dawes' struggles suddenly renewed themselves in a furious spasm. [410]

With the emergence of Paul's oedipal guilt at the possible fulfillment of his wish to kill the father (85), he turns away from defeat of the surrogate father, the estranged husband of Clara Dawes, with whom Paul is involved in a sexual affair. Then bewildered by the emanation of tender feelings for the father, which he transfers to Dawes as their bodies cleave together, Paul is struck with wonder at his own feminine impulses and his pleasure in them. Assuming a submissive attitude toward the other man, Paul, instead of patricide, enacts the primal-scene fantasy of sex as violence, with himself in the fantasied woman's role. As Dawes kicks him into unconsciousness, "the whistle of the train shrieked two fields away" (410), echoing the shriek of the whips of family violence heard in the earlier ash tree scene and in "Discord in Childhood."

The repressed erotic content of the lash and whip imagery would return in another context that would reflect Lawrence's unconscious identification with the fantasied dominant sadistic father, anterior to his identification with the fantasied submissive masochistic mother. In his essay on Dana's *Two Years Before the Mast,* after paralleling the relationship of master and servant with that of male and female, Lawrence defends the captain's flogging the man Sam and another sailor on the vitalistic argument that the beating restores the circuit of "blood-reciprocity of master and servant," reestablishing the polarized current between them by means of the cat-o'-nine-tails (116). As Lawrence's description takes on the characteristics of sadomasochistic fantasy, the language becomes unmistakably sexual in tone:

> And the living nerves respond. They start to vibrate. They brace up. The blood begins to go quicker. The nerves begin to recover their vividness. It is their tonic. . . .
>
> There is a new equilibrium, and a fresh start. The *physical* intelligence of a Sam is restored, the turgidity is relieved from the veins of the Captain.
> It is a natural form of human coition, interchange. [118]

The fantasied equation between beating and the sex act could not be clearer.

Freud's analysis of how sadism becomes transformed into masochism helps to clarify the evolution of the child's terror-stricken response to parental violence in "Discord in Childhood" and *Sons and Lovers* into the fantasy of sadistic male dominance and masochistic female submission in "Love on the Farm." This pattern of thematic imagery then evolves into the homoerotically tinged sadomasochistic fantasy of being beaten by the father-surrogate in *Sons and Lovers* and finally into the sexualized equation of beating with coition in the Dana essay.

The two interpretations—that Lawrence's adolescent shame about his sexual fantasies derived in part from the homoerotic wishes they expressed, and that his sexual fantasies were sometimes sadomasochistic—are not mutually exclusive. According to Freud, in "'A Child Is Being Beaten,'" the beating fantasy is "invariably cathected with a high degree of pleasure and [has] its issue in an act of pleasurable auto-erotic satisfaction" (*SE* 17:180). "The boy, who has tried to escape from a homosexual object-choice, and who has not changed his sex, nevertheless feels like a woman in his conscious phantasies . . ." (*SE* 17:200). Applying the "rule that what belongs to the opposite sex is identical with the repressed" (*SE* 17:202), Freud observes that "with men, what is unconscious and repressed can be brought down to feminine instinctual impulses" (*SE* 17:201). In his analysis of the beating fantasies of men, Freud says: "The original phantasy, 'I am being beaten by my father,' corresponds, in the case of the boy, to a feminine attitude [that is, 'I am loved by my father'], and is therefore an expression of that part of his disposition which belongs to the opposite sex. . . . In the last resort, . . . both in male and female individuals masculine as well as feminine instinctual impulses are found, and . . . each can equally well undergo repression and so become unconscious" (*SE* 17:202). In "The Economic Problem of Masochism," Freud reiterates: "We now know that the wish, which so frequently appears in phantasies, to be beaten by the father stands very close to the other wish, to have a passive (feminine) sexual relation to him and is only a regressive distortion of it" (SE 19:169). Clinical experience in contemporary psychoanalysis confirms Freud's view. Leon Ferber reports the uncovering and reconstruction in analysis of an adult man's repressed beating fantasy: "The central meaning was a wish to be beaten by the father, which stood for a passive sexual yearning for him" (211).

The evolution of erotogenic masochism, as Freud traces the progress of the libido through the developmental phases from which it derives its changing psychic characteristics, is relevant for an understanding of several drive derivatives of Lawrence's early psychic experience. First, the "fear of being eaten up by the totem animal"—which Freud associates with the father, but which, as Judith Ruderman has persuasively demonstrated, Lawrence experienced as the devouring mother—"originates from the primitive oral organization." Next, the "wish to be beaten by the father"—which I have been tracing in the erotic beating fantasies in several of Lawrence's works—"comes from the sadistic-anal phase which follows" the oral phase. In turn, castration anxiety—which is demonstrably present in "The Thorn in the Flesh" in Bachmann's response to the barking voice and threatening, biting teeth of the sergeant, and in "The Prussian Officer" in Schöner's response to the captain's sadistically exercising control over every area of the orderly's life—"enters into the content of masochistic phantasies as a precipitate of the phallic stage or organization." Finally, "from the final genital organization there arises, of course, the situation of being copulated with and of giving birth, which are characteristic of femaleness" (*SE* 19:164–65). Derivatives of this repressed feminine attitude are located figuratively in the preconscious homoerotic fantasies that emerge in sublimated drive derivatives in such novels as *The White Peacock, Women in Love,* and *Aaron's Rod.*

Freud's comment that the buttocks "are the part of the body which is given erotogenic preference in the sadistic-anal phase, like the breast in the oral phase and the penis in the genital phase" (*SE* 19:165), is exemplified by Schöner's fascination with the captain's "amazing riding muscles" in "The Prussian Officer," and Lawrence's statement in the Dana essay: "As long as man has a bottom he must surely be whipped. It is as if the Lord intended it" (115). As Ferber explains, the wish to be beaten "arises in the anal phase, when beating and power struggles are the regular mode of object relations.

Because anal-phase concepts of object relations persist and are applied to the impulses of the phallic phase, the child forms a sadistic theory of adult intercourse, and it is through this sadistic theory of intercourse that the beating wish becomes sexualized" (212).

~

If Lawrence's sexual fantasies were sometimes homoerotic and sometimes sadomasochistic, does this mean that he was homosexual or sadomasochistic in his primary sexual organization? That is not what I intend to suggest. Such impulses may be partly accounted for, in Freudian terms, as the derivatives of component instincts. Freud writes to Oskar Pfister (9 October 1918): "But when it comes to sexual theory whatever makes you dispute the resolving of the sexual instinct into partial instincts to which our analysis compels us every day? . . . Don't you see that the multiplicity of instincts goes back to the multiplicity of erotogenic organs?" (qtd. in Jones, *Sigmund Freud* 2:506). The impulses, homoerotic or sadomasochistic, that emerged at times in Lawrence's late adolescence and young manhood can be understood in the context of Freud's concept, set forth in "Three Essays on the Theory of Sexuality" (*SE* 7:167–69), that polymorphous perverse component instincts are characteristic of human sexuality before it becomes organized around genital and reproductive aims and that these component instincts persist in subsequent sexual responses centered in the various nongenital erotogenic zones (see Nagera et al., 50–54, 61–66). Freud is speaking, of course, from the position of classical drive theory.

In mainstream psychoanalysis today, the concept of the masturbation fantasy is not limited to the particular fantasy image that Ferenczi describes as forcibly retained in the mind throughout the act of masturbation. Of greater significance than the conscious mental picture is the underlying fantasy, which remains largely unconscious and which—though it is correlated with the mental imagery during masturbation—is always present as a core fantasy: a powerful unconscious wish or longing that constitutes a motivating force in the personality, with or without masturbation.

In defining "the central masturbation fantasy," Moses Laufer explains its background and development as follows:

> The preoedipal child may have available a whole range of autoerotic activities, games, and fantasies which help to recreate and relive the relationship to the gratifying mother. After the resolution of the oedipus complex and the internalization of the superego, however, . . . all regressive satisfactions will be judged by the superego as being either acceptable or not.

Moreover, in terms of the future sexual orientation and the "final sexual organization" of the person, the *resolution of the oedipus complex fixes what can best be described as the "central masturbation fantasy"—the fantasy whose content contains the various regressive satisfactions and the main sexual identifications.* [300]

In this context, Laufer asserts two additional principles that establish the psychological significance of the concept and its relevance to the present discussion: (1) *"This central masturbation fantasy is . . . a universal phenomenon—* its existence or power does not depend on whether the child masturbates or not." (2) *"Although the content of this central masturbation fantasy does not normally alter during adolescence,* the fact that it is experienced within the context of physically mature genitals means that the defensive organization is under much greater stress," since "the incestuous wishes (which are contained within the masturbation fantasy) are now tested within a new context" (300–301).

In these terms, can one presume to say with any certainty what the young Lawrence's "central masturbation fantasy" was? My response at this point must be *no,* not if that means delineating this unconscious core fantasy in specific detail: conscious derivatives of the fantasy that sometimes emerged in Lawrence's personal relationships and correspondence and that informed some aspects of his literary work are all that one has to go on. What one can note is that the two elements I have discussed—the fantasies that accompanied the homoerotic impulses he experienced in late adolescence and young adulthood, and the sadomasochistic beating fantasies that emerged in several of his works—have essentially similar meaning: the wish to be loved and tenderly cared for by a powerful masculine paternal figure, often, though not always, a man of the working class. Sometimes this figure, in a wish-fulfilling righting of the balance, asserts a powerful male dominance in an erotically sadistic relationship with a passive, erotically masochistic woman. An example is the sadomasochistic relationship of the farm husband and wife in "Love on the Farm." The sadomasochistic imagery of erotic fantasies of this sort, and of the beating fantasies, suggests an unconscious wish to be beaten and penetrated by the rough, older male, as the mother was. Sometimes the masculine figure is a man whose physical form and bearing embody a certain nobility of soul even as, in the exigencies of his life circumstances and in relation to a woman with middle-class pretensions to refinement, he moves toward tragic ruin (George Saxton). At other times he is a man who, like Lawrence's father, has been tragically devalued and whom the Lawrence persona, in attempted reparation for his own part in the devaluation, attempts in fantasy to love and rescue (Baxter Dawes, as a stand-in for Walter Morel). In one instance, the paternal figure is arbitrarily brutal to the point of irrational

sadism, but Lawrence sees his violence as providing the reciprocal vital interchange needed for homeostatic balance (the ship's captain of Dana's *Two Years
Before the Mast*). In later novels, the masculine figure offers the means of psychic transformation into individual selfhood. He may provide love and tenderness in caring for the Lawrence persona in his despair and illness (Rawdon
Lilly in relation to Aaron Sisson in *Aaron's Rod*). Beyond a certain point, however, this figure's arbitrary political power and the danger of engulfment in his
merging embrace make him so unreliable as a paternal figure that he is to be
regarded with ambivalence and mistrust (Ben Cooley in *Kangaroo*). As a religious leader, the masculine figure is idealized as a "natural aristocrat," who
offers the way to dark godhead (Ramón Carrasco in *The Plumed Serpent*).
Ultimately, as the bearer of the regenerated and idealized phallus, this figure
becomes an object of identification (Mellors in *Lady Chatterley's Lover*, the
risen man in *The Escaped Cock*).

The preponderance of evidence shows compellingly that a loving relationship with the powerful masculine paternal figure was a major component of
Lawrence's early fantasy life. This longing derived, I believe, from the early
childhood deficit in such a relationship with his own father. This was not,
however, the only important part of Lawrence's psychic life. What Laufer
calls the "central masturbation fantasy" contains, by definition, one's unrelinquished infantile wishes, which can be gratified only in the symbolic or
distorted form of fantasy but which remain, usually unconsciously, as motivating forces within the personality. Lawrence's fantasy life, I believe, also
included at least one other major component, which I have not discussed here:
the wishes and fantasies deriving from his overgratifying but engulfing relationship with his mother. This issue is outside the scope of the present chapter, but I have discussed it in chapter 2 in terms of his having "loved her—
like a lover," which had kept him from loving Jessie, and of his awareness that
if his mother had lived, his symbiotic merger with her would have prevented
his being able to love Frieda: "She wouldn't have let me go" (See Frieda
Lawrence, *Not I, But the Wind*, 56).

~

Although Freud's psychology of drives has the appeal of offering a clear scientific explanation, contemporaneous with Lawrence, for manifestations of
homoerotic and sadomasochistic component instincts in his masturbatory
fantasies, I must reiterate that I am unwilling to limit myself to early Freudian
theory as the only basis for a psychoanalytic understanding of Lawrence.
Mainstream psychoanalysis today recognizes the adaptive and integrative
function of adolescent masturbation in assisting the transition from infantile

narcissism to object love. John J. Francis and Irwin M. Marcus emphasize this developmental function: "Masturbation in adolescence serves to assist the forward movement of the instinctual drives . . . , and to bring the pregenital drives under the regulation of the genital function. . . . Further development of object relatedness is facilitated by the masturbation fantasy, which brings the autoerotic experiences into contact with objects" (31). In addition, such post-Freudian psychoanalytic theories as object relations theory and self psychology provide alternative and for many, I think, potentially more satisfactory means of understanding the *relational* function for Lawrence of the polymorphously perverse elements of his sexual fantasies.

In the language of object relations theory, D. W. Winnicott says that "the capacity to be alone," which is "nearly synonymous with emotional maturity," depends on the individual's "ability to deal with the feelings aroused by the primal scene," whether observed or imagined. Unable as a child to incorporate such feelings "in the service of masturbation," understood in its developmental function, Lawrence in late adolescence remained unable to accept "the whole responsibility for the conscious and unconscious fantasy." According to Winnicott, "To be able to be alone in these circumstances implies a maturity of erotic development, . . . it implies fusion of the aggressive and erotic impulses and ideas, and it implies a tolerance of ambivalence; along with all this there would naturally be a capacity on the part of the individual to identify with each of the parents" (417).

Lawrence's primary sexual identity was consciously heterosexual. His sexual development in adolescence, however, rather than completing the phase-appropriate task of integrating aggressive and erotic impulses, was marked, I believe, by both "masculine" and "feminine" feelings and a confusing clamor of component instincts. Experienced as homoerotic as well as sadistic and masochistic impulses, these partial instincts were directed toward satisfying both aggressive and passive impulses in the dominant and submissive roles played out in fantasy. Rather than being characterized by an increasing tolerance of ambivalence, Lawrence's relationships in late adolescence and early adulthood were marked by the same wide emotional swings between love and hate that Holly Laird finds in his early poems. In *Sons and Lovers,* for example, Paul Morel's feelings about Miriam undergo a series of rapid and radical changes, in response to his mother's manipulation of his oedipal feelings, which in turn fuel the ensuing conflict with his father in which the two men nearly come to blows (249–54).

Rather than making a positive identification with both his parents, the young Lawrence could consciously identify himself only with his mother. His rejection of any such identification with his depreciated father consciously defined both the good and bad qualities of the father as outside the self. Even so, Lawrence, at the same time, unconsciously internalized, albeit in fragmented form, what he saw as the "masculine" qualities of the only male model he had. These qualities included not only the father's natural instinctuality, his vital sexuality, "dark ruddy life" and unconscious being, but also his irrationality, distrust of mental processes, impulse toward violence in response to family frustrations, and tendency to avoid conflict by seeking escape in drink at the public house (*Letters* 1:189–90)—just as Lawrence later saw his own world travels as "a form of running away from oneself and the great problems" (*Letters* 4:313). Actually there was no *whole* external masculine parental figure that Lawrence could identify with the internal idealized paternal imago. What was available for introjection was a part object, the penis, which, as in "Virgin Youth," could be idealized as both lustrous deity and iconoclast.

Employing Melanie Klein's concept of internal objects, often represented by introjected part objects, Winnicott says: "The capacity to be alone depends on the existence in the psychic reality of the individual of a good object. The good internal breast or penis or the good internal relationships are well enough set up and defended for the individual . . . to feel confident about the present and the future" (417). There is little question that despite the dangers of devourment and engulfment posed by the symbiotic merger with his mother, the imago of the nurturant and supportive mother was well established in Lawrence's internal representational world. His lifelong preoccupation with the image of the phallus, however, suggests, in object relational terms, a continued search for the father's penis as a part object that could substitute for the unavailable nurturant whole paternal imago that still could not be reliably established and stabilized in object constancy.

To return to the perspective of self psychology, one might note that Lawrence's early experience denied him the possibility of realizing, or even fully recognizing, the developmental need to identify himself with an idealized paternal figure. Consequently, in Heinz Kohut's terminology, the internal idealized paternal imago was shattered into pieces and the unmet need was subsequently sexualized and directed toward these fragments.[26] As a child, Lawrence's extreme disappointment in his father meant that the idealized paternal imago could find no validation in the external object. Thus, in self psychological terms, his late-adolescent homoerotic and sadomasochistic fantasies were an attempt to fill the deficit by means of a sexualized connection with the irrational, punitive, demeaning qualities of the omnipotent masculine parental imago. The drive was enlisted to effect a merger with the shattered fragments (represented variously by the erotically sadistic farm husband, the defeated and depressed Baxter Dawes, the irrationally arbitrary ship's captain of Dana's novel) in an attempt to repair the injury by magical means.

~

Lawrence's negative statements about masturbation may seem anachronistic in view of his reputation as a writer committed to freedom of sexual expression. This attitude, I believe, derived primarily from the shame he felt about the nature of his own masturbatory fantasies. It derived secondarily from his conscious response to the hypocrisy of official disapproval of masturbation, though hardly the private abstinence from it, in the society in which he matured from childhood through adolescence to young manhood. Lawrence's negative view of the practice, however, was also in keeping with much medical opinion of the time.[27] Although both Lawrence and Freud recognized that the public prohibitions against masturbation were widely ignored in individual practice, neither was able to transcend the official position that one should abstain from it. Yet Lawrence and Freud were also sexual liberators who challenged the sexual orthodoxy of their day and advocated a much greater sexual freedom in the interest of psychic health; hence their ideas on human sexuality had a liberalizing effect on all forms of sexual expression and behavior, including masturbation. My impression is that the liberalizing effect of their work, as conditioned by other external social and economic determinants, has contributed to a cultural change, in which the Victorian judgments that formed the context for both Lawrence's and Freud's views on masturbation have largely given way to social and sexual attitudes that characterize a more tolerant, laissez-faire position.

CHAPTER 8

The "Rocking-Horse Winner" as Self-State Tale

D. H. Lawrence's "The Rocking-Horse Winner," a short story presented in the frame of a fairy tale, employs fabular motifs and fantasy elements rather than relying on the imitation of reality and the use of realistic details for its effect. The opening sentence, "There was a woman who was beautiful, who started with all the advantages, yet she had no luck,"[1] is analogous to the conventional fairy tale opening, "Once upon a time. . . . " Paul's commanding the rocking horse, "Now, take me where there is luck," corresponds to such formulas as Belle's commanding the horse (in "Beauty and the Beast"), "Go, go, go where I'm going." In addition, various ritual and religious motifs suggest an element of magical thinking and wish fulfillment, rather than productions grounded in reality. Paul tells his mother that God has told him he is lucky, and the gardener, Bassett, who is as "serious as a church," adopts a "religious" stance in relation to Paul. These and other such elements support the fantasy mode of the story, which expresses a subjective psychic state rather than an objective external reality. Possibly the most frequently anthologized of Lawrence's stories, "The Rocking-Horse Winner" is among the most widely discussed works in critical studies of the author.

Almost everyone who has viewed the story in even marginally psychoanalytic terms has understood little Paul's driven, frenzied rocking to a climax, at which point he "knows" the name of the next winning horse at the track, as the symbolic equivalent of masturbation. The highly sexual tone of the description of the rocking suggests that this meaning was conscious on Lawrence's part: "[H]e would sit on his big rocking horse, charging madly into space, with a frenzy that made the little girls peer at him uneasily. Wildly the horse careered, the waving dark hair of the boy tossed, his eyes had a strange glare in them" (232). Lawrence had already condemned what he saw as the personally harmful effects of masturbation in *Fantasia of the Unconscious* (1922), and subsequently, in *Pornography and Obscenity* (1929) he would attack what he saw as its debilitating consequences for society. By the time he wrote "The Rocking-Horse Winner" (1926), Lawrence had begun employing masturbation as a metaphor for achieving mechanistic ends of the will by the conscious manipulation of vital instinctual forces that he thought were better left to the spontaneous expression of the unconscious.

For little Paul, the sexual equivalent of his rocking action remains unconscious until the climax of the story. Sensitively attuned to his mother's disappointment in life, he anxiously internalizes her unhappiness, which she attempts to assuage by her excessive concern with money and material acquisitions. His depressive anxiety in response to her dissatisfaction is projected as the lugubrious whispering that haunts the house: "*There must be more money! There must be more money!*" (230). In his concern to still the whispering, Paul repeatedly rides his rocking horse in masturbatory imitation of adult sexual activity in order to reach at the climax intuitive foreknowledge of the winning horse at the track in a vain effort to satisfy his mother's material, and psychological, demands by betting on the sure winner.

Psychoanalytically based criticism has generally focused on the masturbatory and uncanny elements of the story. The psychoanalyst Selma Fraiberg (1954) draws parallels between Paul's "rocking to win" and similar magical elements in tales of the discovery of the secret treasure, such as Aladdin's rubbing the lamp or the soldier's striking the tinderbox. In her view, "the recurrent theme of a magical act or discovery (masturbation), which serves as a means to the acquisition of great wealth, strongly suggests that these dreams of fortune belong to the masturbatory activity, we should say are masturbatory fantasies." A further element, in which the treasure thus acquired "now enables the hero . . . to overcome all obstacles between him and an inaccessible woman (the princess)," also "seems to belong to the masturbatory fantasy in which the inaccessible mother (princess) is sought."[2] In a subsequent essay, Fraiberg (1961) adds that the presentation of meaning through the symbol of rocking contributes to the success of the story. By keeping the "erotic undercurrent silent" while "making it present, it conceals and yet it is suggestive; a perfect symbol."[3]

Janice Hubbard Harris (1984) also sees the story as, on one level, the fairy tale of the brave boy's riding off "into a dreamland, where he struggles and succeeds at attaining secret knowledge," by which he "wins treasure houses of gold, giving all to his love." But undercutting this fairy tale, says Harris, "is another, which forms a grotesque nightmare counter to the wish fulfillment narrative. The 'true love' of the brave young boy is his cold-hearted mother." "Yearning for some response of affection from her," Paul equates "love" with "luck" and "lucre": "Quite simply, the tale concludes that these equations are deadly."[4]

Other critics have also read the story in psychoanalytic terms. The poet W. D. Snodgrass (1958), citing Lawrence's comments on masturbation in

Pornography and Obscenity as a gloss on the story, observes that "the rocking horse stands for the child's imitation of the sex act, for the riding which goes nowhere," and thus remains an unsatisfactory substitute that "can only famish the craving it is thought to ease."[5] James G. Hepburn (1959) relates the story briefly to Freud's concept of the uncanny in its evocation of the "unknown-known" and calls attention to the primitive thinking evidenced in the story's animism, omnipotence of thought, and fatalism.[6] Neil D. Isaacs (1965) comments that, unable to bear the "monstrous burden of guilt" for his oedipally involving his mother in his autoerotic act of love, Paul dies.[7] W. S. Marks III (1965-1966) relates "Paul's ability to make lucky predictions by riding himself into a trance on his totemic hobbyhorse" to Freud's concept in "The 'Uncanny,'" "where this phenomenon is defined as a product of narcissistic regression to a primitive belief in animism." Employing Freud's concept in "Beyond the Pleasure Principle," Marks sees Paul's obsessive and "self-destructive act of rocking" as a compulsion to repeat that overrides the pleasure principle and gives this aspect of his mind its demonic character.[8] Norman N. Holland (1968) considers "The Rocking-Horse Winner" "a tragedy of sublimation, of accepting more and more devious substitutes for one's real desires." In mythic terms, the boy is "trying to achieve a real relationship or union with the Great Mother by a devious Christian money-grubbing and money-charity." Ultimately, "The Rocking-Horse Winner" is "a story of desperate hunger, seemingly for money or luck, but actually for love, and there is no satisfaction of the hunger (unless we can see Paul's death as some kind of union with the ultimate mother)."[9]

In a psychoanalytic study employing both Lawrence's theories in *Fantasia of the Unconscious* (1922) and the object relations theories of D. W. Winnicott and M. Masud R. Khan, John F. Turner (1982) explores four related themes of play in "The Rocking-Horse Winner": "the nature and origin of the inability to play and the perversion of play," "its sexuality (playing with oneself)," "the cultural sickness both behind and within the individual (the play of gambling)," and "the tone in which Lawrence has told his tale (the free play of the author)."[10] Barbara Greenfield (1984) uses "The Rocking-Horse Winner" to show how psychoanalysis can enable the critic to make explicit the underlying feelings and dynamics that are only suggested in the story, without committing what she regards as the "fallacy of using the text to explain the author."[11] Cynthia R. Pfeffer (1988) discusses suicidal behaviors of young people in "The Rocking-Horse Winner" and Willa Cather's "Paul's Case."[12]

Norman Kiell (1975), citing Anna Freud's interpretation that "rocking is an autoerotic substitute for satisfactions originally provided by the mother, with the specific aim of re-establishing body contact with her," relates little Paul's efforts to satisfy his mother's perceived financial needs to the economic model of money on which the Victorian notion of semen was formed. As Kiell points out, "Up until the end of the nineteenth century, the chief English colloquial expression for the orgasm was 'to spend,' which bespeaks a complex shift to the contemporary 'to come.'"[13] In Lawrence's (1929) libidinal economy, masturbation is "the spending away of a certain force, and no return" (Kiell, 479). The semen conservation theory, a subtext in Lawrence's model sex education lecture in *Fantasia of the Unconscious* (1922), is not an organicist theory founded on plenitude but an economic theory founded on finitude. The notion that semen is allocated in a fixed amount rather than continually produced by the testicles underlies the common superstition that a man has only so many shots of semen and when all his supply has been expended, emptiness and impotence or death must inevitably follow. Isolating and literalizing the motif of masturbation, as several critics have done, affords the advantage of demonstrating, in terms of Freudian drive theory, the connection between Lawrence's sexual and economic themes. If carried to a logical conclusion, however, it leads to the untenable implication that little Paul, who is actually too young to ejaculate, though not too young to have orgasms, in effect dies of masturbation—as if he can never produce enough semen (here symbolically equated with money) to satisfy his mother.

Ben Stoltzfus (1996), in a Lacanian reading, frames the story within Freud's *Jokes and Their Relation to the Unconscious* and Jacques Lacan's "The Agency of the Letter in the Unconscious or Reason since Freud" in *Écrits*. Focusing on such linguistic elements as puns, rhymes, and word associations, Stoltzfus is less concerned with masturbation than with metonymy. Thus, Paul's word play on *luck* and *filthy lucre* is a signifier that emerges as the tip of the iceberg of the linguistically organized unconscious: In a slippage of metaphor, *lucre* echoes *lucker,* to which *filthy* then sticks, pointing to Paul as a *filthy lucker.* "In due course, the *f* of *filthy* slides over to replace the *l* of *lucker*" to reveal the little *lucker* as a little *fucker.* As Stoltzfus comments, "fucking is precisely the content of the story that is repressed but which is, nonetheless, manifest in the symptom 'little rocker.'"[14] The name of the last winning horse, Malabar, most immediately signifies something bad as in "Le Malin" (the devil): "Malabar wins, but winning his *Ma* is the *grand mal* that kills [Paul]—be it sin or the penalty for violating the Law" (Stoltzfus, 43)— an allusion to the incest taboo and to Lacan's Law of the Father.

~

At this point, I want to reconsider "The Rocking-Horse Winner" in terms of an alternative theoretical model, psychoanalytic self psychology. The story, for both the author and his protagonist, makes a statement about the condition of the self. Heinz Kohut (1977) defines a "self-state dream" as follows:

> The scrutiny of the manifest content of the dream and of the associative elaborations of the manifest content will then allow us to recognize that the healthy sectors of the . . . psyche are reacting with anxiety to a disturbing change in the condition of the self—manic overstimulation or a serious depressive drop in self-esteem—or to the threat of the dissolution of the self. I call these dreams "*self-state dreams*"; they are in certain respects similar to dreams of children . . . , to the dreams of traumatic neuroses . . . , and to the hallucinatory dreams occurring with toxic states or high fever.[15]

I argue that "The Rocking-Horse Winner," with its fairy-tale conventions and emotionally heightened, oneiric concentration, may be analogously considered as a "self-state tale" of an anxious boy of latency age who is experiencing a "serious drop in self-esteem," which he attempts to alleviate by the frenzied rocking to find a winner in an effort to make contact with his inaccessible mother. Although bright and articulate, Paul is in other respects developmentally delayed. He has not achieved adequate separation-individuation from the preoedipal mother, and is unable to resolve the oedipal conflicts of the phallic stage sufficiently to allow him to assume the developmental tasks of latency. Paul's age is not given, but he is big enough to ride with his "sturdy long legs straddling apart." His mother asks if he isn't "growing too big for a rocking-horse" and observes: "You're not a very little boy any longer, you know." Paul is delayed in his psychological development by failures in the emotional environment, specifically in the artificial "love" offered by his mother and in the unavailability of his ineffectual father as a viable model for masculine identification. Hester plays the public role of "such a good mother," one who "adores her children" (230); but privately she betrays her egocentric concern with her own acquisitive greed, bitterly telling the boy that they are poor because his father "has no luck" (231). The son is left in anxious isolation, desperately striving to satisfy his mother's unrealistic wishes and so "to compel her attention" and love (232).

The protagonist's name, Paul, and his obsession with his mother link "The Rocking-Horse Winner" with *Sons and Lovers* (1913), which Lawrence had published thirteen years earlier. As cited in chapter 2, Lawrence in later years said: "I would write a different 'Sons and Lovers' now; my mother was wrong, and I thought she was absolutely right."[16] In several late autobiographical pieces, Lawrence revises "his early history, and in particular the lives of his parents." John Worthen discusses ten such writings.[17] Although often unreliable objectively, these pieces provide psychoanalytically valuable subjective data on Lawrence's attempts to revise his earlier view of his parents. In the short auto-biographical works, he adopts a more critical, unsympathetic perspective on his mother and a more tolerant, sympathetic view of his father than in *Sons and Lovers*. These autobiographical revisions of Lawrence's earlier view of his parents suggest a corresponding attempt to modify the internal object repre-sentations on which some of his literary characterizations were founded. This working-through process continued throughout the last years of his life, and several of his later works were drawn into its service. In *Lady Chatterley's Lover* (1928), he idealizes the instinctual figure of Mellors, a working-class man who speaks in the broad Midlands dialect of Lawrence's father. A heroic mas-culine figure of vital sexuality, expressed through tenderness in a love rela-tionship, Mellors also denounces the same kind of materialistic values that little Paul's parents subscribe to in "The Rocking-Horse Winner."

Although not the imaginative transformation of autobiographical experi-ence that is characteristic of *Sons and Lovers*, "The Rocking-Horse Winner" is one of several late works in which Lawrence partially revises the emotional view of his parents that he had presented in that novel. Dissimilarities between the two works—in socioeconomic class, setting, characterization, genre, and style—suggest that the story is to be understood not as a realistic fictional representation of the actual familial and cultural milieu, but psycho-logically as the symbolic equivalent of the picture that currently prevailed in Lawrence's thinking about his childhood emotional situation in relation to his earliest objects.

The description of the stylish parents, who, in their vanity, live far beyond their means, bears little external resemblance to the parents of Lawrence's working-class childhood home: "The father, who was always very handsome and expensive in his tastes, seemed as if he never *would* be able to do anything worth doing. And the mother, who had a great belief in herself, did not suc-ceed any better, and her tastes were just as expensive" ("The Rocking-Horse Winner," 230). If this presentation of the fictional parents is understood as a description of particular aspects of object representations in the author's inter-nal representational world, however, the emotional correspondences emerge clearly in a pattern of contrasting characteristics: the father's handsome bear-ing and his limitations as a provider, the mother's outward self-confidence and her constant worries about money—attributes that are also characteristic of the parents in *Sons and Lovers*, but that are presented here from a new, more criti-cal perspective. Like the picture of Lawrence's own mother that emerges in the late autobiographical writings, Hester is presented as a class-conscious social climber, single-mindedly pursuing the consumer signifiers of "success." The father, however, has none of the instinctual qualities of the wish-fulfilling versions of idealizable manhood found in the paternal portraits of the short autobiographical pieces and in *Lady Chatterley's Lover*. The emotional environment of the story is permeated by upscale tastes coupled with a sense of financial failure, and behind that, an even more devastating failure in personal values. In this situation, the young son internalizes a pervasive sense of his father's worthlessness and his mother's anxiety, which he feels it incumbent upon himself to remedy.

Superficially, the cold, socially ambitious Hester would seem to have little in common, besides middle-class pretensions, money worries, and dissatisfaction, with Gertrude Morel, the collier's wife and mother of the novel. But the two characters share one crucial quality with Lawrence's possessive mother, Lydia Lawrence. Each of these mothers appropriates her young son's instinctual being and exploits it for her own needs, without regard for his developmental needs and possibly without full awareness of the consequences for him. Whatever his underlying anxieties about the relationship, little Paul's fervent wish that his mother should love him is expressed in the conscious assumption that she does. When Paul begs his uncle, Oscar Cresswell, not to tell his mother about his ability to gain foreknowledge of the winner because if she knew that he was "lucky" in that way she would stop him, his uncle replies skeptically, "I don't think she would" (238). The child may indulge in wishful thinking about his mother's love; his uncle knows better: that Hester is incapable of loving anybody, including her children, and has substituted in place of human relationship an endless greed for money in an effort to fill her own emptiness.

Little Paul is as closely bound to his mother as his namesake Paul Morel is in *Sons and Lovers*, but without the gratification in the merger with her that the earlier character receives. As in that novel, the most difficult problem confronting the boy is negotiating the passage through a separation-individuation process that would allow him ultimately to disengage from his mother and to give up his preoccupying idea that it is his responsibility to meet all her unrealistic needs. The difference between the novel and the story in the author's characterization of the mother bespeaks Lawrence's changed perspective on his own mother and the effect of his prolonged symbiotic relationship with her. The perversion of little Paul's instinctual life is the consequence of neither masturbation per se nor the symbolic equivalent of masturbatory activity in the rocking. It is rather the effect of the exploitation of his sexuality in a vain attempt to fill his mother's bottomless need, while his own developmental needs remain unmet. In the portrait of the narcissistic Hester as an unmirroring mother, wholly preoccupied with material greed, Lawrence corrects the impression he had consciously sought to convey thirteen years earlier in the picture of Gertrude Morel as the long-suffering middle-class wife of a sometimes brutish working-class man and as a dedicated mother who is the center of her children's lives. The ambivalence of Lawrence's presentation of the mother-son relationship in *Sons and Lovers* derives, I believe, from his growing awareness of the psychological effects of his having been exploited emotionally as a surrogate lover in place of his rejected father. Although he later objected to reducing the novel to a "mother complex,"[18] Lawrence at the time partially went along with Frieda's oedipal interpretation of the situation. As Judith Ruderman has pointed out, however, Lawrence, with few exceptions, presents the mother-son relationship in *Sons and Lovers* as a preoedipal dyad rather than as part of an oedipal triangle that includes the father.[19] As I have argued earlier in chapter 2, "The Two Analyses of D. H. Lawrence," the prevalence of preoedipal issues in the novel calls for some modification of the usual oedipal interpretation by reconsidering it in terms of separation-individuation issues and self structure.

In the subsequent story, by presenting little Paul as a lonely and unmirrored latency child whose instinctual life is exploited to meet his mother's unrealistic demands, Lawrence tacitly recognizes a truth that he had not consciously perceived before: that what he had received from his mother had not been the genuine mirroring he had consciously tried to represent in *Sons and Lovers,* but rather the possessive exploitation of his nascent self and instinctual being, which he had also conveyed as an undercurrent of meaning in the novel.

Similarly the weak, vacuous father of "The Rocking-Horse Winner" would appear to have little in common—except unavailability—with the instinctual, hard-drinking, semiliterate collier, Walter Morel, the father of *Sons and Lovers.* But the two characters share one crucial quality with Lawrence's depreciated working-class father, Arthur Lawrence. Each of these fathers abdicates his responsibility to foster his son's development, standing for freedom and independence as a model for identification in the son's need for separation-individuation from the engulfing preoedipal fusion with the mother. Instead, whereas the father in the novel seeks escape in drink and becomes brutish, abusive, and finally avoidant in defense against the depressive isolation of his position in the family, the father in the story is simply a cipher, a nonentity. Since neither father can effectively "stand up" to the overwhelming mother, either literally or figuratively, neither can provide his son with viable ideals to emulate nor stand as an idealizable masculine figure with whom the son can identify himself.

In terms of the bipolar structure of the self set forth in Heinz Kohut's theory, "The Rocking-Horse Winner," to the degree that it may be considered to refer indirectly to the author's own psychological situation, probably overstates the extent of the damage. According to Kohut, "the self will be seriously impaired only if, after one of the selfobjects of the child has failed to respond, the attempt to acquire compensatory structures via the adequate responses of another selfobject have also come to grief."[20] My impression is that from his mother, possessive and engulfing though she was, Lawrence received a selfobject response sufficient to enable him to survive without serious impairment, although not without narcissistic injury. In contrast, little Paul, in Kohutian terms, cannot find in his parents selfobject responses adequate to his needs either in the pole of his nuclear grandiose ambitions or in the pole of his nuclear ideals.

Paul's ambitions are directed, with wrenching depressive anxiety, toward meeting his mother's needs and thus silencing the whispering and gaining her attention and love. Hester, however, is too preoccupied with her own narcissistic greed to provide mirroring for her son. The prospect for a structure-building selfobject relationship is even bleaker where Paul's father is concerned. Ostensibly the man seems to have nothing to do with the exploitation of his son's instinctual being to meet his mother's perceived monetary needs. It must be recalled, however, that while all this is going on, the ineffectual and abdicating father is doing absolutely nothing to intervene on his son's behalf. It would be incongruous, if not impossible, to idealize a vacancy. For all his anxious love for his mother and her inadequate response to his need for her, Paul never turns to his father for help nor attempts to idealize him as an alternative selfobject.

To the extent that little Paul finds substitute selfobjects for his ambitions and ideals, he finds them only partially in the two men who become his partners in the gambling venture. It is notable that the boy turns first to the working-class Bassett, then to his uncle, Oscar Cresswell, for assistance with the adult activity of placing the bets and managing the money he wins. Through these men he gains a modicum of mirroring and, in the models of Bassett's scrupulous honesty and his uncle's knowledgeable financial management, a measure of ideals. But these gains are not enough to save him in the exploitative situation in which they, too, have a vested interest of financial profit.

In view of Lawrence's opposition to masturbation, which he considered both personally and socially harmful, it would be easy to read the story as the author's symbolic statement on the ill effects of the practice. A more accurate reading, I would argue, is that little Paul's obsessive masturbatory activity cannot fill the developmental deficits left by the inadequacy in maternal mirroring and by the impossibility of making an idealizing identification with his unavailable father. If those early developmental needs could be met effectively by other means, the house might stop its whispering. Although both his Uncle Oscar and Bassett function, within limits, as alternative selfobjects, Paul's developmental needs cannot really be met in a situation in which his instinctual being is exploited in the interest of the financial gain to be derived from his accurately predicting the winners.

Paul's madly frenzied rocking to a climax that will enable him to intuit the name of the winning horse only secondarily has the purpose of meeting a financial need. In self psychological terms, it has the purpose of maintaining his own self-cohesion by trying to fill his emotionally depriving mother's depressive emptiness and thus preserving his identification with her in a fantasied merger, in which the oedipal competition is now employed in the service of preoedipal aims. He tells Oscar Cresswell: "I started it for mother. She said she had *no* luck, because father is unlucky, so I thought if *I* was lucky, it might stop whispering." Further associations reveal that the narcissistic deficit Paul is seeking to fill is characterized by a sense of shame. He tells his uncle that when people send his mother writs for money she owes, "then the house whispers, like people laughing at you behind your back. It's awful, that is!" (237)

The repeated activity to which Paul resorts has neither the satisfaction of adult sexuality nor the joy associated with childhood play, and none of the healthy normative quality often found in childhood sexual exploration. As Kohut and Wolf (1978) point out, "Individuals whose nascent selves have been insufficiently responded to will use any available stimuli to create a pseudo-excitement in order to ward off the painful feeling of deadness that tends to overtake them." The two psychoanalysts comment further that "beneath the defensive façade" of adult self-stimulation, sexually in "addictive promiscuous activities and various perversions" and nonsexually in "such activities as gambling, drug, and alcohol-induced excitement," one "will invariably find empty depression." They add tellingly: "Prototypical is the compulsive masturbation of lonely 'un-mirrored' children. It is not healthy drive-pressure that leads to the endlessly repeated masturbation, but the attempt to substitute pleasurable sensations in *parts* of the body (erogenous zones) when the joy provided by the exhibition of the *total* self is unavailable."[21]

Freud, in "Dostoevsky and Parricide" (1928), locates the derivation of gambling in masturbation (*SE* 21:193). Both Lawrence's story and Kohut and Wolf's essay also link the two. The compulsive quality of Paul's rocking suggests not the pressure of the drive, but a repetition in a vain effort to master a nonsexual issue by sexual means. Specifically, Paul is attempting to neutralize the depressive affect and anxiety signaled each time by the house's whispering. But the masturbatory equivalent he employs, because it is based on magical thinking rather than insight, cannot realistically accomplish this end. The action of the story demonstrates clearly why this is true.

Paul believes that by manipulating his instinctual responses in order to become "lucky," he can supply the money that will control the whispering.

When Oscar Cresswell arranges to deposit £5,000 with the family lawyer to be sent to Hester anonymously, £1,000 at a time for five years on her birthday, she coldly demands the entire sum at once. With the mother's escalating and insatiable greed, the whispering, instead of abating, becomes even more insistent. The mother does not consciously know, and seemingly does not want to know, the source of the money. On a preconscious level, she does know. In the grip of "one of her rushes of anxiety about her boy," she leaves a big party to call home to inquire if he is all right. But she tells the nursery-governess, Miss Wilmot, not to check on her son, as if in tacit recognition that such an intrusion on his privacy would prevent his winning more money in the same way (241). For that matter, neither Bassett nor Cresswell knows the whole story: "He had a secret within a secret, something he had not divulged, even to Bassett or to his Uncle Oscar" (240). They accept as a given Paul's seemingly preternatural ability to gain foreknowledge of the winner, but they have no cognitive awareness of its secret source. The mother, however, "frozen with anxiety and fear," finally discovers what Paul is doing:

> The room was dark. Yet in the space near the window, she heard and saw something plunging to and fro. She gazed in fear and amazement.
> Then suddenly she switched on the light, and saw her son, in his green pyjamas, madly surging on his rocking-horse. The blaze of light suddenly lit him up, as he urged the wooden horse, and lit her up, as she stood, blonde, in her dress of pale green and crystal, in the doorway.
> "Paul!" she cried. "Whatever are you doing?"
> "It's Malabar!" he screamed in a powerful strange voice. "It's Malabar!"
> His eyes blazed at her for one strange and senseless second as he ceased urging his wooden horse. Then he fell with a crash to the ground, and she, all her tormented motherhood flooding upon her, rushed to gather him up. [242]

Since Paul has engaged repeatedly in the masturbatory sexual equivalent of riding the rocking horse to a climax, with a persistent determination to win by "getting there" but without apparent adverse physical effect, the question is why the frenzied activity results this time in his death. When Hester turns the light switch, the sudden "blaze of light" illuminates the two figures and imagistically unites them—Paul "in his green pyjamas, madly surging on his rocking-horse," and his mother, "blonde, in her dress of pale green and crystal, in the doorway." Her cry, "Whatever are you doing?" clearly indicates that she sees *him* and that his secret activity is out. But the more important recognition is that he sees *her*. A "pale green and crystal" vision, she stands revealed in the sudden light not only as the oedipal object of his sexual fantasy[22] but

more significantly as the preoedipal object of his longed-for psychic merger.[23]
"It's Malabar!" he cries. "It's Malabar!" As he falls with a crash to the floor,
Hester rushes to gather him up. The "heart-frozen mother" asks: "What does
he mean by Malabar?" (242) Oscar Cresswell identifies Malabar as the name
of a horse running in the Derby, and Bassett places the final bet "at fourteen
to one" and makes "a clean win" before Paul dies. Paul's agonized utterance of
the horse's name, however, encompasses both the oedipal and preoedipal
themes couched in the equations love = luck, and luck = money.

The Derby is the most prestigious of all the races, and Malabar suggests
the spices of the East Indies, sources of English riches, culminating in the
annexation of India, the "Jewel in the Crown" of Queen Victoria. On that
level, the Derby represents Paul's greatest chance of being perceived as "lucky"
and as of value to his emotionally distant mother. His "getting there and truly
knowing" and his mother's response are the final test of his value and selfhood. For Kohut, maternal mirroring serves as the basis for a sense of value
that is prerequisite to the development of the self.

On a more subliminal level, the name of the horse encodes Paul's overwhelming oedipal guilt (*mal*) for transgressing the barrier of the incest taboo
(*bar*)—as in the flare of light, he is suddenly flooded with the recognition that
his mother is the object of his, in part unconscious, masturbatory fantasy.

But what else might Paul have seen in his mother in her dress of pale green
and crystal as she stood in the doorway? As Hester approaches his door,
"There was a strange, heavy but not loud noise. Her heart stood still. It was a
soundless noise and powerful. Something huge in violent hushed motion. She
knew what it was but she could not place it. . . . She heard and saw something plunging to and fro." The markedly sexual imagery and its association
with violence and destruction can hardly be missed. As Hester enters Paul's
room with the sexual associations in her mind, she cries out: "Paul! Whatever
are you doing?" And Paul falls to the floor shouting in a powerful and strange
voice: "It's Malabar. It's Malabar" (242).

Paul may have been aware of a tone of disapproval in his mother's question.
If he is not, certainly the reader is. Earlier Paul was concerned about her dis-
approval when he said to his Uncle Oscar, "I shouldn't like mother to know.
She'd stop me."

If Paul saw his blonde, beautiful mother as the object of his oedipal strivings, might he not see her also from the perspective of his now frenzied, fragmented self as a distant, "heart frozen" ice princess? She did not ask, "Paul,
are you all right?" but rather "Whatever are you doing?" And she asks her
brother, Oscar, "What does he mean by Malabar?"

Paul is not the same now as at the beginning of the story. Through the
whispering voices, Lawrence has traced the fragmentation and dissolution of

Paul's fragile self, caught in an unyielding dilemma. The house's constant whispering had always reflected Paul's anxiety about his mother and his sense that his only chance to preserve a fragile self is to relieve her worry—to take the hardness and worry from her face. In a talk with his uncle, Paul had said, "I hate the house for whispering, I thought if I were lucky," and Uncle Oscar finishes: "You might stop it" (237–38).

After the settlement of five thousand pounds on his mother, Paul sits with her at breakfast, anxious to see how she reacts. As she looks at the letter, her mouth hardens and she hides the letter under other mail without saying a word. Later Oscar Cresswell explains that Hester has gone to the barrister to request the entire amount at once rather than receiving the annual stipend of one thousand pounds. When Paul is told that the response to the request is his decision, he says, "Oh, let her have it, then! We can get some more with the other" (239).

Afterwards, Paul notices that they live more luxuriously, but instead of stopping, "The voices in the house suddenly went mad, the voices simply trilled and screamed in a sort of ecstasy: 'There must be more money! Oh-h-h There must be more money! Oh, now, now-w! now-w-w! There must be more money! More than ever!'" (239). On an unconscious level, through the voices, Paul recognizes the anxiety of his being lucky. Each success requires more. The price of love and acceptance is always more money, the source of which he cannot reveal. He is also becoming more aware of the terrible price of being caught in that bind, as if to say: "She would love me for being lucky if she knew, but I can't tell her. It would mean disapproval, separation, and loss if I did."

Paul becomes more and more desperate. In some instances his rocking does not culminate with his "getting there," and he is unable to predict the winner accurately. "The Grand National had gone by: he had not 'known,' and had lost a hundred pounds." "He was in agony, for the Lincoln," but "he didn't 'know,'" and he lost fifty pounds." His anxiety had increased. "He became wild-eyed and strange, as if something were going to explode in him" (239). "I've got to know for the Derby!" he says, "his blue eyes blazing with a sort of madness" (239). Hester recognizes his agitation and wants to send him to the seashore. She threatens to send Bassett away if Paul does not stop talking about horse races. Paul says to Hester: "But you know you needn't worry, Mother, don't you?" Hester dismisses his statement. As the Derby approaches, Paul's anxiety builds to new heights. "He hardly heard what was spoken to him, he was very frail and his eyes were really uncanny." Paul persuades Hester that he must be in the house for the Derby. On that night she returns home. In the pivotal scene of the story, Paul in his fragmented state falls from the rocking-horse unconscious. During his three days of disorientation, he calls out Malabar's name, and on the third day he again speaks to his mother, still trying to make contact with her: "I never told you, mother, that if I can ride my horse and *get there,* then I'm absolutely sure—Oh absolutely! Mother, did I ever tell you? I *am* lucky." Hester replies: "No, you never did." Paul dies in the night.

Oscar Cresswell delivers a coda on the story: "My God, Hester, you're eighty-odd thousand to the good, and a poor devil of a son to the bad. But, poor devil, poor devil, he's best gone out of a life where he rides his rocking-horse to find a winner." On some level Oscar senses Paul's predicament and Hester's role in that drama.

This story throughout has been dyadic. It is about Paul and his mother and his inability to win her affection. It is concerned with separation-individuation and the development of self. Paul and his mother have apparently only one form of communication: to read each other's anxiety. But Hester is unable to translate this into caring attention, and Paul has become more aware of his inability to satisfy her emotional needs. Through Malabar, Paul gives Hester one last gift, but at the cost of fragmentation of a fragile self not strong enough to handle this level of anxiety or to comprehend the false equation of luck = money put forth by Hester.[23]

In his definition of the self-state dream, Kohut says that "the healthy sectors of the psyche are reacting with anxiety to a disturbing change in the condition of the self—manic overstimulation or a serious depressive drop in self-esteem—or to the threat of the dissolution of the self" (Kohut 1977, 109). This is the anxiety that we see developing in Paul, and as he dies, his self is extinguished completely. The formulations of self psychology help us to understand at a different level the life of little Paul and the conflicts he faces. There certainly is an oedipal component and it is distressing to Paul, but the story primarily traces the development and ultimate disintegration of a self whose goal is recognition and validation rather than sexual.

CHAPTER 9

The Fall of John Thomas

In "The Little Wowser" (composed 1928), one of the poems in *Pansies,* D. H. Lawrence, with his recent and continuing censorship battles in the background, satirizes official attitudes toward the penis, which society blames as the culprit responsible for practically everything since the Fall:

> There is a little wowser
> John Thomas by name,
> and for every bloomin', mortal thing
> that little blighter's to blame.[1]
> [lines 1–4, *Complete Poems,* 493]

Adopting ballad measure, dialect, and a mocking, Kiplingesque tone, Lawrence says that it's John Thomas who tempts you to sin, and "leads you by the nose / after a lot o' women" till someone marries you "to put him through 'is paces." But, he concludes,

> I think of all the little brutes
> as ever was invented
> that little cod's the holy worst.
> I've chucked him, I've repented.
> [lines 21–24, *Complete Poems,* 493]

Where his own life was concerned, Lawrence had neither "chucked" John Thomas exactly, nor "repented." Social satire aside, he was alluding with self-deprecating irony to his own present condition. Lawrence was, at the time, unable to function sexually.[2]

At this point a word about terminology may be useful. Throughout the following discussion, I will use the preferred medical term "erectile dysfunction," which accurately identifies the medical condition of Lawrence's sexual function, rather than the more general term "impotence," which, though employed by several older medical and critical sources cited here, has pejorative connotations. My purpose is to focus on the particular physical condition for which today there are a number of effective treatment options, and to state from the outset my own view that Lawrence was never impotent in the general sense. He was not impotent as a writer. On the contrary, as I hope this study demonstrates, his works in this period, including *Lady Chatterley's Lover* and *Last Poems,* are major contributions to modern English literature. He was not impotent as an artist. He mounted a major exhibition of his paintings at the Warren Galleries in a significant challenge to official censorship of art. He was not impotent as a human being. Writing against the clock, he continued to champion what he felt was most at risk, namely all that is organic and human about the human condition in opposition to the dehumanizing trend toward ever more robotic mechanization.

In this chapter, I first consider Lawrence's erectile dysfunction in his last years from medical and psychological perspectives. In discussing both the physiological and psychological issues, I will call on the authority of medical specialists in urology and psychiatry, whose scientific approach to human sexuality Lawrence would surely regard with the same reservations he had for the work of Marie Stopes and Sigmund Freud in his own day.[3] I will then turn to Lawrence's attempts to come to terms with his condition in two of his last literary works, *Lady Chatterley's Lover* (1928) and *Pansies* (1929). Lawrence was both a sensitive, self-aware man and an exceptionally articulate writer. These two qualities make his efforts to employ his writing in coping with one of the most frustrating medical problems seen by clinicians especially valuable for our understanding of how such a man experiences the condition and the strategies he follows in incorporating it psychologically. What makes Lawrence's work so instructive in this respect is that it illustrates, not merely the literary representation of a medical condition, but the literary adaptation of the personal experience of erectile dysfunction by the most prominent English literary writer on psychosexual issues in the twentieth century.

Derek Britton believes that "[t]he absolute impotence of Lawrence's last years may have been the final stage in a gradual decline in sexual capacity that afflicted him for much of his married life."[4] According to Britton, "Clinical studies of potency disorders of this type, characterized by a progressive and accelerated falling-off in sexual potency over a period of years, suggest that the origins of the condition typically lie in a combination of psychogenic and constitutional factors, with the latter often exerting a dominant influence."[5] William B. Ober, M.D., a medical pathologist, says that whether Lawrence's "alleged reduction of potentia was due to decreased libido, inability to achieve erection, or ejaculatio praecox, . . . [i]t is not unreasonable to infer that a

man suffering from far advanced pulmonary tuberculosis would be sufficiently debilitated to be unable to respond to sexual stimuli and unable to per-
form as satisfactorily or as frequently as before."[6] Britton also believes that
Lawrence's erectile dysfunction during his last five years was secondary to general metabolic disturbances related to his physical deterioration in the
advanced stages of pulmonary tuberculosis. However, he speculates as well on
a number of ancillary psychogenic factors in the etiology of Lawrence's condition: his hatred of willful women; "[t]he frailty of Lawrence's ego, his fears
of ridicule and rejection and his anxieties about his virility"; his having "often
been considered effeminate in his ways" in childhood and his continuing
struggle to incorporate his "feminine" traits; his possible fears about female
genitalia; his "latent homosexuality" and "repressed primary sexual preference
for men" (Britton, 46–51).[7] These psychogenic factors are related, I believe,
to both the deficit in paternal nurturance and the possessive if supportive
maternal relationship that characterized Lawrence's early self psychological
development.

Ober's and Britton's interpretation of the constitutional etiology of
Lawrence's condition may not be objectively verifiable, but medical studies of
the correlation between impaired pulmonary capacity and erectile function
bear out their view. According to psychiatrist Eric Wittkower, in an early
study of patients with tuberculosis, "A majority of tuberculous patients are in
a mood of mild (20 per cent), moderate or severe (34 per cent), overt or con-
cealed anxiety and depression."[8] In addition to the egocentricity and irritability typical of tuberculous patients, "[t]heir depressive and anxious thoughts
and feelings are either predominantly related to their physical condition or to
repercussions of the illness in social, occupational and economic spheres"
(Wittkower, 38). A close correlation between clinical condition and sexual
interest was established in a survey of 96 male sanatorium patients clinically
on the upgrade. The finding that sexual urge was diminished in 14 percent,
perturbed in 10 percent, and unchanged in 74 percent confirmed "that sexual interest diminishes while patients feel very ill and that it returns when
they are on the road to recovery" (Wittkower, 74, 76).

Although the deterioration of his physical condition—most notably in his
diminished pulmonary capacity—was the major factor, Lawrence's erectile
dysfunction, I believe, was also accompanied by psychological factors. The
dysfunction should be understood, however, in a wider context than oedipal
pathology, since its psychological component encompasses both earlier preoedipal issues and more immediate relational issues. As described by psychiatrist and sex therapist Helen Singer Kaplan, "Psychogenic impotence may be
associated with a general loss of libido and ejaculatory difficulty, but the
essential pathology is the impairment of the erectile reflex. Specifically, the

vascular reflex mechanism fails to pump sufficient blood into the cavernous sinuses of the penis to render it firm and erect."[9] As Kaplan observes, "Erectile function is impaired at the moment when the man becomes anxious" (256), which after an initial dysfunction may be whenever he approaches the sex act and feels anxious that the same thing may happen again. In the vicious cycle that often develops, erectile failure feeds on fear of failure.

Kaplan notes that in drive-centered classical psychoanalytic formulations, the psychogenesis of erectile dysfunction is usually attributed to "[u]nconscious intrapsychic conflicts" rooted in "unresolved oedipal problems, and concomitant feelings of fear and guilt with regard to sex." According to this hypothesis, "the preeminent cause of impotence is unconscious castration anxiety." As the Oedipus complex is elaborated, the boy, desiring to possess the mother and kill the father as a hated rival, is fearful "that detection of these incestuous impulses by his father will result in severe punishment, i.e., *castration*." Although repressed "in the interests of self-preservation," these "infantile sexual aims are . . . preserved in the unconscious," and "unresolved oedipal conflicts" are "re-evoked whenever sexual excitement is experienced and result in disturbances of potency. Thus impotence can be understood within this conceptual framework as a neurotic defense against the emergence of these unbearable affects" (259).

Is Lawrence's dysfunction to be interpreted in these terms? I do not think so. Unconscious intrapsychic conflicts originating in unresolved oedipal wishes may have been involved in his early masturbatory experience, about which he had felt considerable guilt and shame,[10] but behaviorally these issues had not prevented his functioning sexually before marriage and working out a satisfying sexual relationship with his wife. According to Kaplan, erectile dysfunction was formerly thought to be "always indicative of deep underlying psychopathology," but it is now recognized "that more immediate operating factors such as 'performance anxiety'" as well as "[u]nconscious intrapsychic and dyadic difficulties are also exceedingly important in the genesis of impotence, and often lie behind the more manifest stresses" (258–59). If there was a psychological component of Lawrence's sexual dysfunction in this period, it probably had more to do with immediate "dyadic difficulties" in the relationship than with oedipal issues. Although Frieda's latest love affair with Angelo Ravagli was not a direct cause of the problem, it could hardly have helped matters.[11] Lawrence had always found ways of rationalizing her infidelities with various lovers before, but his growing dependence on Frieda as his health deteriorated probably made her behavior less tolerable. According to Richard Aldington, Lawrence, coughing and hemorrhaging, was too ill to enjoy his month at Île de Port-Cros (15 October–17 November 1928): "Only then did I realise how frail and ill he was, how bitterly he suffered, what frightening envy and hatred of ordinary healthy humanity sometimes possessed him, how his old wit had become bitter malice, how lonely he was, how utterly he depended on Frieda, how insanely jealous of her he had become."[12] In my view, the early developmental issues that were being reactivated were anxieties and deficits of the preoedipal period, and the triadic oedipal rivalries of Lawrence's marital situation were in the service of these dyadic preoedipal issues.

This affective disorder recurred now during another time of loss. Lawrence's erectile dysfunction, largely constitutional in origin, became, I believe, an etiological source of his depression. Britton does not mention depression as a psychological factor, but it was nevertheless present, albeit in a diagnostically moderate form, insofar as Lawrence was not incapacitated by it but remained a productive artist to his last breath. Previously, Lawrence had experienced at least one episode of prolonged depression. That was during his "sick year" of mourning after his mother's long illness and death (9 December 1910), the ensuing collapse of his relationships with Jessie Chambers, Helen Corke, and Louisa Burrows, and his withdrawal into a state of "death in life." Lawrence, in Heinz Kohut's terms, experienced the loss of selfobjects as the threatened dissolution of the self and responded with disintegration anxiety at the anticipated loss of self-cohesion:[13] "I was twenty-five, and from the death of my mother the world began to dissolve around me, beautiful, irides- cent, but passing away substanceless. Till I almost dissolved away myself, and was very ill: when I was twenty-six" ("Foreword to Collected Poems," in Com- plete Poems, 851).

Lawrence's diminishing powers of physical health and his continuing cen- sorship battles were also ample causes for his depression. In this psychologi- cally vulnerable situation, the marital difficulties with Frieda must have posed the threat of possible loss of his most significant selfobject since his mother and thus the additional danger of annihilation of the self.

Mabel Dodge Luhan in 1923 wrote a poem for Lawrence entitled "Change," in which she first laments the effects of her menopause—"Scarlet days fading out to white"—then celebrates her discovery that, no longer sub- ject to the "ego-insistent flesh," she has become a new woman: "This is a happy time." Lawrence responded in a poem entitled "Change of Life" on the change that Mabel had experienced.[14] Partly by analogy to Mabel Dodge Luhan's menopause, Lawrence thought he recognized her complaint in the symptoms he was experiencing. He writes to Mabel (16 May 1927): "One changes—changes inside oneself—and then old interests die out. One has to change and accept it—and one's mentality becomes different along with the rest. I think men have perhaps a greater 'change of life' in the psyche, even than women. At least it seems happening so in myself. It's often unpleasant, but the only thing is to let it go on and accept the differences and let go the old."[15] In a subsequent letter to Mabel (28 May 1927), he writes: "You are right about that 'change of life' business. It's what ails me, as I said in my other letter. And partly why I lie so low here, is to let it happen, and not interfere with it, so it gets through as soon as possible. It's hell while it lasts—but I think I sort of see a glimpse of daylight through the other side. One emerges with a body, all right—but a different one, perhaps—not so mentalised" (*Letters* 6:73).

In a letter to Mark Gertler (23 December 1929), written a year after he completed the first version of *Pansies* and two and a half months before his death, Lawrence attributes his depression to the onset of a kind of male climacteric comparable to the female menopause: "it is very common with men when they pass forty—or when they draw near forty. Men seem to undergo a sort of *spiritual* change of life, with really painful depression and loss of energy. Even men whose physical health is quite good."[16] The symptoms Lawrence mentions, depression and loss of energy, are characteristic of a diminished testosterone level.

The problem in calling the syndrome a male change of life is partly one of definitions. Kaplan states the issue succinctly: "If the definition is an abrupt age-related change in the reproductive physiology, then there is no such thing as a male climacteric. . . . However, if the definition is a psychophysiologic constellation of reactions to declining sexuality which commonly are experienced by men of this age in our culture, then a case could be made for the existence of the male menopause" (Kaplan, 108). Among the physiological changes that may occur in various combinations in men between the ages of forty and fifty-five are reduction in sexual desire, with some decline in sexual potency experienced as difficulties in achieving or maintaining erections, a gradual decline in the force of ejaculation and other ejaculatory problems, reduction in fertility, and various urinary changes, such as difficulty in starting the urinary stream and urine retention, along with increasing frequency of urination, which often requires getting up at night for this purpose.

The syndrome, widely referred to as "andropause," inaccurately implying a condition parallel to the female menopause, is still being debated medically. Among the numerous medical studies on the subject, I will cite two informative review articles, which survey the medical literature in their respective fields. Urologists A. Morales, J. R. Heaton, and Culley C. Carson III see the term "andropause" as "a misnomer for a true clinical entity." They argue that a more appropriate designation for the syndrome is "androgen decline in the aging male" (acronym ADAM), "a clinical entity characterized biochemically by a decrease not only in serum androgen, but also in other hormones, such as growth hormone, melatonin and dehydroepiandrosterone. Clinical manifestations include fatigue, depression, decreased libido, erectile dysfunction, and alterations in mood and cognition." The decline in testosterone levels leading to these changes "can be corrected by manipulation of the androgen milieu," that is, by means of medically monitored testosterone replacement therapy.[17]

Psychiatrist H. Sternbach also points out that "testerone decline/deficiency is not a state strictly analogous to female menopause," and suggests that it "may exhibit considerable overlap with primary and other secondary psychiatric disorders": "Manifestations of testosterone deficiency have included depression, anxiety, irritability, insomnia, weakness, diminished libido, impotence, poor memory, reduced muscle and bone mass, and diminished sexual body hair."[18]

Like most medical authorities, Helen Singer Kaplan places the male syndrome in the fifties rather than, as Lawrence does, in the forties. But Kaplan, like Lawrence, sees it as both a physiological and a spiritual crisis: "Apart from his lowered androgen levels, in his mid-fifties a man also begins to face the idea of death and is confronted with his limitations. Further, he often finds it necessary to begin relinquishing whatever control he has gained over his environment" (108).

As an early proponent of the concept, Lawrence sets forth his theory of the male midlife change in terms that refer, at least obliquely, to his own diminished sexual function. His description of the depressive cycle is almost identical to the one he presents in what I will call the "loss of desire" sequence in *Pansies*. The condition, he says, often lasts for several years. "Then, in the end, you come out of it with a new sort of rhythm, a new psychic rhythm: a sort of re-birth." Meanwhile, one must tolerate the condition. Lawrence directly acknowledges his own depression—"I have had it too"—and attributes it primarily to his ill health, which "is enough to depress the Archangel Michael himself." But his refusal to label his illness tuberculosis even at this late day, when he had every medical reason to know better, is correlated with, and may have encoded, his natural reluctance to acknowledge his erectile dysfunction directly. "My bronchials are really awful," he explains deceptively. "It's not the lungs" (*Letters* 7:605).

Though in rationalizing responsibility for a physiological response over which he has no voluntary control, a man may prefer constitutional factors over psychogenic ones, the two are so interwoven in erectile dysfunction as to be virtually indistinguishable. Both finally must be dealt with together—psychological distress manifested in the physical symptom, the physical symptom incurring further psychological distress.[19]

~

With reference to the sexuality of the two major male characters in *Lady Chatterley's Lover*, Frieda Lawrence told Harry T. Moore that "[t]he terrible thing about Lady C. is that L. identified himself with both Clifford and Mellors; that took courage, that made me shiver, when I read it as he wrote it" (*Frieda Lawrence, The Memoirs and Correspondence*, 389). She is obviously correct. It seems patently true that in the creative process Lawrence split himself between the two major male characters. In Mellors he could project the phallic hero he would like to be; in Clifford he could cruelly berate himself for not being that hero.

Michael Squires points out that as "the gamekeeper is elevated" in the writing and revision of *Lady Chatterley's Lover* in three successive versions, "he slowly approximates Lawrence." Squires delineates the changes in character description by which Mellors comes to resemble Lawrence in appearance with his red mustache and blue eyes, his physical frailty, his "suffering and detachment," his isolation, his increase in intellectual power, his linguistic mastery of both standard English and Derbyshire dialect, which he, like Lawrence, uses as emotional armor. Squires suggests that in the third version he comes to embody Lawrence's final definition of manhood,[20] though that definition was modified in a later incarnation of manhood as the risen man in *The Escaped Cock*. In his sexuality, the gamekeeper also serves the author's wish-fulfillment fantasy.

In his sixth sexual encounter with Constance Chatterley, Mellors's arousal in penile erection is imagined as follows: "The quiver was going through the man's body, as the stream of consciousness again changed its direction, turning downwards. And he was helpless, as the penis in slow soft undulations filled and surged and rose up, and grew hard, standing there hard and overweening, in its curious towering fashion. The woman too trembled a little as she watched" (*Lady Chatterley's Lover*, 211).

Feminist critics of the novel have objected to the presentation of Mellors's sexual potency as the solution for all of Connie's problems.[21] They are not the only ones. Bernie Zilbergeld, a clinical psychologist and sex therapist, cites a scene from the novel—Connie's response to the "phallic hunt" on the "night of sensual passion"—as promulgating the fantasy model of sex. Real sexual activity, he points out, unlike the fantasy model, may be affected by any number of things, such as illness, medication, fatigue, depression, anxiety, or even temporary distractions that alter the conditions.[22]

In their fourth sexual encounter, when Connie assumes a spectator role during sexual intercourse and begins to view the act from a distanced, ironic perspective, the experience does not turn out well, and Mellors acknowledges and accepts that fact: "Ta'e th' thick wi' th' thin. This wor a bit o' thin, for once" (172). Recognizing that neither love nor sexual response can be forced, Mellors does not view the experience as "horrid" but as part of the ebb and flow of the relationship. This realistic attitude allows him and Connie to talk

about the situation rationally in an atmosphere free from blame. Their ensuing sexual experience that same night is satisfying for both partners and is
consummated for Connie in a powerful and regenerative orgasm: "She was
gone, she was not, and she was born: a woman" (208).[23] Although this experience is presented as crucial to Connie's emerging female sexuality, Zilbergeld's criticism (see note 22) that Lawrence's presentation of her ecstatic
orgasms derives from a male fantasy model of sex rather than from psychological reality reminds us that the scene is also the imaginative invention of a
writer who is defending himself psychologically against feelings attendant
upon his own erectile dysfunction.

Lawrence's presentation of Connie's temporary sexual problem seems credible in context. It is the male partner's performance that more nearly approximates the fantasy model of sexuality. Zilbergeld points out that the fantasy
penis is always exaggeratedly large, unbelievably hard as steel, throbbing and
pulsating, leaping out like a wild beast, lasting for hours with an infinite
capacity to satisfy, and "immediately regaining its hardness after ejaculation"
(Zilbergeld, *Male Sexuality*, 23–25; see also his *New Male Sexuality*, 49–51).
Although Lawrence does not exaggerate the gamekeeper's attributes to that
extent, there is not an instance in which Mellors, unlike the novelist who created the character, has the slightest difficulty in getting or keeping an erection,
maintaining perfect control, lasting with unflagging potency, and usually, after
the first couple of encounters, bringing Connie to resplendent waves of orgasm
simultaneously with his own orgasm and ejaculation. Heterosexual women
know that this picture does not invariably correspond to the reality of their
own experience. That is why, quite apart from feminist critics like Kate Millett (see Millett, 239), many women are put off by Connie's worshipping Mellors's lordly phallus (*Lady Chatterley's Lover*, 210). Mark Spilka correctly points
out, however, that the adoration is mutual: "his paean of praise to her vagina"
occurs "two chapters before her paean to his penis."[24]

These paeans are a reminder of the long tradition, in both Western and
Eastern cultures, of worship of the vulva as a transpersonal image of female
fertility and of the phallus as a transpersonal image of masculine spiritual
power.[25] The fantasy model modulates into, though it is not identical with,
the mythic model of sexuality. In *John Thomas and Lady Jane*, the second version of the novel, in Connie's meditation on the phallus as like a primitive
god, she sees it as "the third creature," risen between the two of them with
"erect, alert, overweening, utterly unhesitating" assertion. The narrator distinguishes between *penis* as "a mere member of the physiological body" and
phallus, which, "in the old sense, has roots, the deepest roots of all, in the soul
and the greater consciousness of man" (232–35). As Connie realizes, the modern preference for "the vulgar organ, the penis," reduces sex to "merely fuck-

ing, the functional orgasm, the momentary sensational thrill, the cheap and nasty excitation of a moment." She also understands that the mythic dimension is the reason that the modern world fears the phallus enough to trivialize and nullify it: "Fear of this alter ego, this homunculus, this little master which is inside a man, the phallus" (234). Lawrence's thematic point is consistent with the sexual philosophy he presents elsewhere in his work. In this instance, it is difficult to avoid the suspicion that his scornful view of the mechanics of sexual function and his fixation on the phallus, idealized as the organ of phallic consciousness, are being employed, in part, in rationalization and compensation for his own present erectile dysfunction.

There are suggestions in the novel that the reality has sometimes been other than mythic perfection. In *John Thomas and Lady Jane*, Parkin, as the gamekeeper is called in the first two versions, put off by the woman's pubic hair, had initially been unable to function sexually with his wife, Bertha Coutts. Connie's recognition that "this godhead in him had always been wounded, yet even now was not dead" (233) is echoed in Mellors's reference to "what a broken-backed snake that's been trodden on I was myself!" (*Lady Chatterley's Lover*, 206), which seemingly alludes to concerns about his sexual function in earlier relationships with women. As presented in the novel, however, Mellors does not have simply a penis that is usually normally functional, but a phallus, or phallos, that is endowed with mythic, even sacral, properties and that, in contrast to his creator's ups and downs, is ever potent and heroically hard. In his longstanding anxiety about his sexual performance, Lawrence creates in Mellors a middle-aged man in frail health and on the edge of despair, whose sexual wounds, largely from psychic blows to his masculine identity and self-esteem in a marital relationship characterized by anger, frustration, and disappointment, are so fully healed in a regenerative love relationship that his sexual performance equals or surpasses that of a man half his age and in his physical prime. Wayne Burns calls Mellors a "heroic" rather than a realistic, "Panzaic" character: "he is, in short, Lawrence's idealized self-image, a sensual Don Quixote with no Sancho Panza to challenge his sensual pretensions."[26]

On the other hand, in Lawrence's present erectile dysfunction and apparent anger at his own penis—Mellors's penis is, after all, personified as John Thomas and treated as a figure with a separate identity—he creates in the paraplegic Sir Clifford Chatterley another kind of alter ego, one who has not only an inert and flaccid penis but also unattractive personal qualities that Lawrence may have disliked in himself but attributes to his fictional character: Clifford, like Lawrence (and like Birkin in *Women in Love*), has a tendency toward abstract intellectualizing; a practice of exploiting his friends in spiteful personal portraits and stories (as in Lawrence's own satiric portraits of

Ottoline Morrell as Hermione in *Women in Love,* John Middleton Murry as Jimmy in "Jimmy and the Desperate Woman," Compton Mackenzie as Cameron Gee in "Two Blue Birds," and, of course, Osbert Sitwell as Clifford Chatterley); a never outgrown need for mothering, as seen in Clifford's relationship with Mrs. Bolton (and in Lawrence's increasing dependency, as his illness progressed, on Frieda); occasional class-conscious, elitist pride in aristocratic connections; and a forceful, opinionated will. Most of these autobiographical characteristics have been noted by Squires, who observes that as "Lawrence's attitude toward Clifford hardens with each rewriting," the narrator ridicules him and Connie indicts him more directly. More surprisingly, in each successive version, Clifford, like Mellors, "more clearly resembles Lawrence," and in all three versions he shares Lawrence's sexual dysfunction and the distress and "marital tensions" that go with it (Squires, 57). As Squires observes, "Critics have not recognized how forcefully Lawrence attacks himself in the novel, how ruthlessly self-analytical he is. The bullying 'will' that Connie and the narrator find repugnant in Clifford is precisely what Lawrence adds of himself to version 3." But Squires believes that "Lawrence found this layer of himself too unattractive to allow him to trace imaginatively its psychological roots—even with Clifford's background as a mask." As a result, the character is "psychologically motivated from the 'outside'" and remains "psychologically rootless" (58–59).

This two-dimensional characterization of the baronet makes the added complexity surprising when Clifford expresses something of Lawrence's own dubious hope—for renewed erectile function if not for procreation—when he tells Connie: "Of course *I* may have a child yet. I'm not really mutilated at all. The potency may easily come back, if even the muscles of the hips and legs are paralysed. And then the seed may be transferred" (*Lady Chatterley's Lover,* 147). This rationalization emerges, I believe, from the unrealistic hope to which Lawrence continued to cling, that his own erectile dysfunction derived not from irreversible organic deterioration of his health but from a temporary paralysis of sexual desire, which would spontaneously return. Both the fictional character and the writer seem to prefer this kind of vague fantasy to realistic medical assessment. In the novel, Sir Clifford Chatterley is never shown to consult a medical practitioner about his prospect for recovering erectile function, and there is no record that Lawrence himself ever did so.

Although medical options were limited in the 1920s, a paraplegic man in Sir Clifford's condition today would have access to several treatment modalities, including electrical stimulation of the hypogastric plexus or vibratory stimulation of the penis to induce ejaculation, possibly enabling him to father a child by artificial insemination. Although there have been some successes, the quality and motility of sperm in semen retrieved from men with spinal cord injuries in some cases has been low. Giles S. Brindley, who developed the former technique, is the same physiologist who pioneered research in the treatment of erectile dysfunction by intracavernous injection of the penis with vasoactive pharmacological agents to induce erection.[27] By the end of the twentieth century, intracavernous pharmacotherapy, employing drugs such as papavarine with phentolamine, or alprostadil (prostaglandin E1) injected into the corpus cavernosum of the penis, had become a widely used and effective treatment option for erectile dysfunction.[28] An external cylinder to be placed over the penis, with a vacuum pump to remove all air from the cylinder to induce erection and a tension ring to maintain it is also employed for this purpose. By the beginning of the twenty-first century, Viagra (sildenafil citrate), taken orally about an hour before intended sexual activity to direct increased blood flow to the penis, had become the first-line treatment of choice for most men, although it is contraindicated for heart patients and others taking nitrates.

In view of Lawrence's opposition to mechanistic control of spontaneous natural processes, it is difficult to imagine his availing himself of any of these recourses, even if they had been available to him. Lawrence's attitude is made clear in several poems in *Pansies*. In "Chastity," he writes:

> O leave me clean from mental fingering
> from the cold copulation of the will,
> from all the white, self-conscious lechery
> the modern mind calls love!
> [*Complete Poems*, 469]

One would assume that a sexually active man, if deprived of his erectile capacity, would be willing finally to set aside any feelings of embarrassment or shame and accept whatever medical intervention was needed, not as a mechanistic substitute but as a means to facilitate the natural process and thus to restore his sexual function. In fact, less than 10 percent of the estimated thirty to thirty-two million men in the United States suffering partial or chronic erectile dysfunction currently seek medical intervention. As the viable medical options for treatment increase, a corresponding change in attitude regarding this common medical condition will possibly diminish the intensity of erectile dysfunction as a modern illness metaphor. In that event, the theme of loss of erectile function in novels like *Lady Chatterley's Lover* and *The Sun Also Rises* may then be seen as dated representations of a bygone era.

In *Lady Chatterley's Lover,* both of the principal male characters incorporate Lawrence's sexual ambivalence, as measured against the gender stereotypes prevalent in his society. To Mellors he attributes his own "feminine" qualities of empathy and tenderness and his organicist critique of society; to Clifford he attributes his own "masculine" qualities, as transmuted into this character's intellectual wit, rational, mechanistic thought processes, and uncaring management policy that "industry comes before the individual" (215). Lawrence's approval of the former qualities and disapproval of the latter suggest his recognition that both sets of characteristics derive not from real differences in gender but from artificial differences in social stereotypes. With the splitting of his identity into both Mellors and Clifford, why did Lawrence need to incorporate further self-images into the novel? Why did he identify himself, at least in part, with other male characters and, arguably, with Connie as well? The answer, I presume, is that those two characters could not incorporate everything he felt about himself and his condition. Michaelis, Duncan Forbes, and Tommy Dukes, in their different ways, all represent aspects of both Mellors's and Clifford's characters, which, as I have suggested, derive from Lawrence's own character.

Michaelis, whom Lawrence added to the third version of the novel, was outwardly modeled on the Mayfair novelist Dikran Kouyoumdjian, who wrote under the nom de plume Michael Arlen. Michaelis is unable to achieve simultaneous orgasm with his partner, a matter that, as discussed in chapter 6, was of concern to Lawrence in the early years of his marriage. The ideal of simultaneous orgasm, obsessively pursued as a reified goal, is widely regarded by medical authorities today as actually destructive to spontaneity and genuine mutuality. The mutual orgasm was a popular sexual myth that Lawrence continued to believe in.

Duncan Forbes, whose sterile modern paintings Mellors objects to, sounds like Mellors (and Lawrence) when he comments on Mellors's situation: "It's the one thing they won't let you be, straight and open in your sex. You can be as dirty as you like. In fact the more dirt you do on sex, the better they like it. But if you believe in your own sex, and won't have it done dirt to: they'll down you" (*Lady Chatterley's Lover*, 264). But in his class, his intellectual cast of mind, his sterility, and his narrow aestheticism, Forbes resembles Clifford suitably enough to pose as Connie's corespondent in divorce proceedings.

Finally, Tommy Dukes often seems to speak for the author, as when he says, "Real knowledge comes out of the whole corpus of the consciousness, out of your belly and your penis as much as out of your brain and mind" (*Lady Chatterley's Lover*, 37), an idea echoed by Lawrence's statement in "Introduction to *Pansies*" that "a true thought . . . comes as much from the heart and the genitals as from the head" (*Complete Poems*, 417). When Dukes says, "I believe in having a good heart, a chirpy penis, a lively intelligence, and the courage to say shit! in front of a lady" (*Lady Chatterley's Lover*, 39), he is not really joking about what it would take to make him feel all right about himself. As Squires points out, the speech is echoed in Mellors's "I believe . . . in fucking with a warm heart" (206). Dukes, like Mellors, is a military officer, and both men cite the Protestant hymn "Blest Be the Tie That Binds" in a sensual context (Squires, 71–72). Yet what strikes one most about Dukes is how keenly he feels the loss of sexual desire. Is there a more despairing line in all Lawrence than his? After recalling Renoir's saying that "he painted his pictures with his penis," this army man confesses, "I wish I did something with mine. God, when one can only talk!" (*Lady Chatterley's Lover,* 40) Lawrence recognizes, however, that obsessive sexual activity is equally meaningless, and he finds abstinence that allows for "conscious realization of sex" preferable to that kind of compulsive repetition. In "A Propos of *Lady Chatterley's Lover,*" which is still the best commentary on the novel, Lawrence alludes indirectly to his own erectile dysfunction and describes "the real point of this book" as bringing about a change in thought, not action: "I want men and women to be able to *think* sex, fully, completely, honestly, and cleanly. Even if we can't *act* sexually to our complete satisfaction, let us at least think sexually, complete and clean" ("A Propos of *Lady Chatterley's Lover,*" in *Lady Chatterley's Lover,* 308). Appropriately, it is Tommy Dukes who, in *John Thomas and Lady Jane,* prophesies a "democracy of touch" as the next stage of civilization (58). But in the present, Dukes suffers the effects of inhibited sexual desire, which, by the sixth decade after the publication of *Lady Chatterley's Lover,* had become the most widespread sexual problem for both men and women.[29] If I read the biographical subtext of Dukes's statements correctly, Lawrence is saying that although temporarily he may be sexually dysfunctional, he can still be a "phallic" artist like Renoir while awaiting the resurrection in a society based on touch.

Basically, that is the theme that gives narrative unity to a sequence of poems in *Pansies.* Sandra M. Gilbert argues that "*Birds, Beasts and Flowers* is consciously or unconsciously organized and unified by a submerged narrative structure which gives it . . . dramatic coherence" by its subversive, revisionary synthesis of various myths of descent into darkness.[30] *Pansies,* a different and lesser poetic work, is patterned on a similarly subversive revisionist version of the myth of death and resurrection in the modern world. In this essay, I want to focus on what Gilbert elsewhere calls the "'desire' series," which might be more appropriately designated the "loss of desire" sequence; for in this cycle of poems, as Gilbert tactfully puts it, "the writer works through the crucial problem of the death of desire and by a process of 'continual, slightly modified repetition,' arrives at that rebirth which the man who died finds in the arms of the priestess of Isis."[31]

Without disagreeing with Gilbert's thesis, I would put the argument more directly: the submerged narrative structure is the story, first, of Lawrence's experience of erectile dysfunction, which he generalizes as the

universal condition of loss of sexual desire that, in both literal and meta-
physical senses, characterizes the modern world; second, of his hope for recovery in the continued evolution of the life cycle; and, third, of his evocation of
sexual healing in a subversive, revisionist reading of the biblical "resurrection
of the body" as the "resurrection of the flesh."

"Moon Memory," a prologue to the sequence, compares the cyclical
change of life to tides controlled by the moon: "When the moon falls on a
man's blood," Lawrence writes, "then the noisy, dirty day-world / exists no
more," and his soul becomes "dark ocean within him" (lines 1, 4–5, 9, *Complete Poems,* 453). This depressive imagery contrasts sharply with Lawrence's
use of the sea fifteen years earlier for sexual imagery in the autobiographical
myth of "Ballad of a Wilful Woman":

> The sea in the stones is singing,
> A woman binds her hair
> With yellow, frail sea-poppies,
> That shine as her fingers stir.
>
> While a naked man comes swiftly
> Like a spurt of white foam rent
> From the crest of a falling breaker,
> Over the poppies sent.
>> [lines 17–24, *Complete Poems,* 200]

"There Is Rain in Me," conversely, continues the depressive imagery as body
fluids turn inward: tears now fall internally, and the spurt of remembered
orgasm from the singing stones has become instead the source of "eternal salt
rage; angry is old ocean within a man" (line 10, *Complete Poems,* 454). In
"Desire Goes Down into the Sea" Lawrence clarifies his present condition:

> I have no desire any more
> towards woman or man, bird, beast or creature or thing.
>
> All day long I feel the tide rocking, rocking
> though it strikes no shore
> in me.
>
> Only mid-ocean.—
>> [lines 1–6, *Complete Poems,* 454]

This conception of the self as lost on a wide sea without moorings places
Lawrence's sexual dysfunction psychologically as, in part, related to a loss of
the ability to cathect, that is, to invest oneself emotionally in objects outside

the self, which is a characteristic of the depressive state of anhedonia, the inability to anticipate or respond to pleasurable reward. Peter C. Whybrow, Hagop S. Akiskal, and William T. McKinney Jr., medical and psychiatric authorities on the psychobiology of mood disorders, cite as an example of anhedonia Hamlet's "How weary, stale, flat, and unprofitable, / Seem to me all the uses of this world!" (1.2.133–34).[32] A comment by H. L. Newbold linking both depression and tuberculosis with the secondary symptom of erectile dysfunction is pertinent to Lawrence's situation: "When people are depressed, they are tired, they lose interest. . . . It is just a general loss of *joie de vivre*. They are withdrawn, they feel bad. Like, if you have tuberculosis and a temperature of 104° and you are coughing up blood, you are not too sexy."[33]

Another small group of poems urges the solution of a revival of masculine assertiveness. In "Fight! O My Young Men," erectile dysfunction becomes the metaphor for the ineffectuality of men robbed of their potential by a world that runs on "money, hypocrisy, greed, machines." Lawrence exhorts:

> Rise then, my young men, rise at them!
> Or if you can't rise, just think—
>
> Think of the world that you're stifling in,
> think what a world it might be!
> [lines 19–22, *Complete Poems,* 457]

In "Women Want Fighters for Their Lovers," Lawrence is even more satirically explicit about modern male sexual inadequacy. Women don't want

> mushy, pathetic young men
> struggling in doubtful embraces
> then trying again.
> [lines 2–4, *Complete Poems,* 457]

Tired of "Tomlets, Dicklets, Harrylets" (l. 7), women want a "fighting cock" (l. 9), Lawrence says, then asks pointedly:

> The fighting cock, the fighting cock—
> have you got one, little blighters?
> Let it crow then, like one o'clock!
> [lines 16–18, *Complete Poems,* 457]

There's certainly nothing wrong with this sentiment—if it feels like crowing! The real question, as Sam Julty suggests, is whether the meaning of the erection lies in giving and receiving pleasure or in proving one's masculinity by a performance test. "But if that erection is both a living confirmation of manhood and an indicator of the degree of manhood, then the dangers of the opposite must be true. Namely, that the failure to have an erection is a failure of manhood. In short, the state of our cocks defines our being" (Julty, 328–29). The subtext of "Women Want Fighters for Their Lovers" is the kind of "cultural demand for effectiveness of male sexual performance" that Lawrence himself must have felt as stressful. William H. Masters and Virginia E. Johnson see this demand as "the single constant etiological source of all forms of male sexual dysfunction": "The cultural concept that the male partner must accept full responsibility for establishing successful coital connection has placed upon every man the psychological burden for the coital process and has released every woman from any suggestion of similar responsibility for its success."[34] Zilbergeld, similarly, sheds realistic light on the fantasy-model myth that "The Man Must Take Charge of and Orchestrate Sex" (Zilbergeld, 38–40).

Lawrence's sexual attitude in this regard, complicated by a need to incorporate qualities that he considered feminine, is certainly conditioned by cultural attitudes. His demand that women renounce what he saw, in terms of the sexual theories of his day, as clitoral orgasm in the "frictional satisfaction" of "Aphrodite of the foam";[35] his repeated image of the sexually aggressive woman as tearing at the man's penis with her beaked vagina (*Lady Chatterley's Lover*, 202); and the scene in which Mellors subjugates Connie to a passive female catamite role in anal intercourse in *Lady Chatterley's Lover* (246–47), all suggest that Lawrence accepted the cultural stereotype of male dominance and female sexual passivity, even if Frieda did not. On the other hand, his sexual history was marked by terminating his relationship with a woman (Jessie Chambers), who took the kind of passive, or passive-aggressive, sexual role exemplified in *Sons and Lovers* by Miriam's Christlike, self-sacrificial approach to sexual relations with Paul. Although Lawrence did not choose that kind of woman as a life partner, internal evidence in his work suggests that he did not question the norm of a culturally conditioned demand that the male take full responsibility for successful coition. His erectile dysfunction may have encoded his resistance to society's demand, and his demand of himself, that he personally and sexually live out this kind of male myth. He continued to develop the theme of male dominance in *Lady Chatterley's Lover* and elsewhere. In *Pansies* the theme is reiterated in "It's Either You Fight or You Die" and "Don'ts," the latter sounding the first tentative strains of the resurrection theme.

"The Risen Lord" is a poetic treatment of the same kind of risen Christ figure that Lawrence treated fictionally in *The Escaped Cock*:

> The risen lord, the risen lord
> has risen in the flesh.
>
> [lines 1–2, *Complete Poems,* 459]

The risen man recognizes for the first time that people are not only spirit, but "substance" upon which the "flame of flesh" ripples with "moods, thoughts, desires, and deeds that chime" with its "fleshly change" (460). But he confesses to a new self-knowledge that echoes Lawrence's own present anxieties as a man whose spontaneous sexual responses have declined with his progressive illness, so that with hemorrhaging lungs he is afraid of becoming unable to breathe, and with a wounded sense of his sexuality he is concerned about what his inability to have erections may mean, even though he experiences a resurgence of both needs as basic to life:

> I have conquered the fear of death,
> but the fear of life is still here; I am brave
> yet I fear my own breath.
>
> [lines 38–40, *Complete Poems,* 460]

Being risen means accepting the needs of the flesh:

> What do you want, wild loins? and what
> do you want, warm heart?
>
> [lines 45–46, *Complete Poems,* 461]

These needs "must be answered" (l. 49):

> Lo! there is woman, and her way is a strange way,
> I must follow also her trend.
>
> [lines 51–52, *Complete Poems,* 461]

In the following poem, "The Secret Waters," Lawrence imagines the effect of the return of erectile function as a kind of sexual healing:

> What was lost is found
> what was wounded is sound,
> The key of life on the bodies of men
> unlocks the fountains of peace again.
>
> [lines 1–4, *Complete Poems,* 461]

In another small group of poems, Lawrence again criticizes "mentalized sex," but since he arrives at no new insights on the subject, one suspects that these verses function mainly to reinforce his own ego defense of intellectualization. In "Obscenity," he defends the body as clean; it is the mind that pollutes "the guts and the stones and the womb" (line 3, *Complete Poems*, 463). In the following poem, "Sex Isn't Sin," he declares, "Sex isn't sin, it's a delicate flow between women and men" (line 13, *Complete Poems*, 464), and in the next line refers obliquely to the interruption of the "delicate flow" between himself and Frieda: "and the sin is to damage the flow, force it or dirty it or suppress it again" (line 14, *Complete Poems*, 464). He sees the mind as a rapist who drags "the sensitive delicacy of your sex" from the "depths below" to

> . . . finger it and force it, and shatter the rhythm it keeps
> when it's left alone.
> [lines 23–24, *Complete Poems*, 464]

Without wishing to impose a reductive reading of the poetic metaphor by which Lawrence enlarges his personal experience, I think that on a literal level he has arrived at two significant conclusions: that genuine sexual response cannot be forced, even manually, and that any mental intervention, including medical management, is to be rejected on the hope that, left alone, his erectile dysfunction will undergo spontaneous remission in the cycle of time and he will be able to return to normal sexual activity.

This will mean, among other things, a redefinition of his relationship with women, beginning with reestablishing and strengthening the bond of trust with his wife. In "Sex and Trust," with Frieda's latest infidelities fresh in his mind, Lawrence suggests a way out of both mental exploitation of sex and the impasse of inhibited sexual desire:

> If you want to have sex, you've got to trust
> at the core of your heart, the other creature.
> The other creature, the other creature
> not merely the personal upstart;
> but the creature there, that has come to meet you;
> trust it you must, you must
> or the experience amounts to nothing,
> mere evacuation-lust.
> [lines 1–8, *Complete Poems*, 466]

The formula by which Lawrence tries to rationalize Frieda's behavior is a familiar one: it is the "personal upstart" who is unfaithful; it is the "creature" in all her otherness whom he must meet in married love. Stated simply in relational terms, he knows that establishing a relationship of mutual trust, not merely the urge to ejaculate, is the basis for a satisfying sexual experience.

The poems thus far in the sequence approach the issue of erectile dysfunction circuitously from a consciously idealistic or ideational perspective. What the condition requires psychologically, however, is the process of working through to which Gilbert refers. Lawrence begins, in "To Women, as Far as I'm Concerned," by renouncing any expression of counterfeit emotion:[36]

> The feelings I don't have I don't have.
> The feelings I don't have, I won't say I have.
> The feelings you say you have, you don't have.
> The feelings you would like us both to have, we neither of us have.
>   [lines 1–4, *Complete Poems*, 501]

The honest rhetoric of this poem gives it an emotional toughness that contrasts sharply with the chauvinistic concepts behind the earlier stereotypic imagery of fighting males and crowing cocks. In the following poem, "Blank," Lawrence, for the first time, somewhat prosaically but candidly describes the feeling of blankness that, after the initial "salt rage," constitutes the prevailing depressive response to the experience of sexual dysfunction:

> At present I am a blank, and I admit it.
> In feeling I am just a blank.
> My mind is fairly nimble, and is not blank.
> My body likes its dinner and the warm sun, but otherwise is blank.
>
> . . . .
>
> And I can't do anything about it, even there I am blank.
> So I am just going to go on being a blank, till something
>   nudges me from within,
> and makes me know I am not blank any longer.
>   [lines 1–4, 7–9, *Complete Poems*, 501]

These two poems are followed by a small group of poems, including "Elderly Discontented Women," "Old People," "The Grudge of the Old," and "Beautiful Old Age," in which Lawrence sees successful aging—by which I think he means living beyond the "change of life," which he places at about forty or so—as growing old without acquiescing in lies in order to appear satisfied. In both groups of poems, existential authenticity—accepting the actual condition, without pretense or lies—is seen as requisite to meaningful change. One must, Lawrence believes, wait patiently for change to emerge from within, rather than try to force it with pretended false feeling.

This unifying thread of emotional honesty is carried over into a further series of short poems in which "the core mood experience in depression, i.e., anhedonia" (Whybrow, Akiskal, and McKinney, 38), is expressed as loss of sexual desire. One of these that has the ring of poetic truth is "Desire Is Dead," which suggests that even so one can be creative:

> Desire may be dead
> and still a man can be
> a meeting place for sun and rain,
> wonder outwaiting pain
> as in a wintry tree.
> [lines 1–5, *Complete Poems*, 504]

"Man Reaches a Point" reiterates the theme of loss of desire in specific, personal terms:

> I cannot help but be alone
> for desire has died in me, silence has grown,
> and nothing now reaches out to draw
> other flesh to my own.
> [lines 1–4, *Complete Poems*, 507]

In "Grasshopper Is a Burden" Lawrence relates this personal condition to the biblical description of age in Ecclesiastes 12:5. And in "Basta!" he again expresses his feelings of powerlessness, withdrawal, and waiting:

> When a man can love no more
> and feel no more
> and desire has failed
> and the heart is numb
>
> then all he can do
> is to say: It is so!
> I've got to put up with it
> and wait.
>
> This is a pause, how long a pause I know not,
> in my very being.
> [lines 1–10, *Complete Poems*, 508]

Finally, in "Nullus," Lawrence frankly states his feeling of worthlessness: "I know I am nothing," he confesses, apparently because his erectile dysfunction and his general depression make him feel like a "nothing" (line 1, *Complete Poems,* 509). In a reference to his early morning depression, he says: "I am aware I feel nothing, even at dawn" (line 3, *Complete Poems,* 508). If this line is also an oblique allusion to the absence of early morning erections on awakening, it may lend support to the view that Lawrence's condition is mainly constitutional, but with ancillary psychogenic factors. But the psychogenic factors, perhaps more consequential than causal, are undeniably present. On the basis of numerous interviews with men who suffered the same complaint, Julty describes their universal feeling of worthlessness: ". . . the man without the erection sees himself as being less than a man, as an unworthy, as a fraud. It is as if the flag of his manhood must remain furled for lack of a mast. Thus the terror, the shame, the withdrawal spurred by the dysfunction far exceed the reaction to almost any other medical condition. . . ." (Julty, 15). The feelings of nullity and resignation that Lawrence describes certainly fit this pattern. He concludes:

> But I can do nothing about it,
> except admit it and leave it to the moon.
> [lines 10–11, *Complete Poems,* 510]

Leave it to the moon! As in "Moon Memory," he trusts to the tides. Hopefully regarding his condition as temporary, Lawrence maintained his faith, even in the face of sexual disability, that life moves in natural cycles:

> There are said to be creative pauses, pauses that are as good
>   as death, empty and dead as death itself.
> And in these awful pauses the evolutionary change takes
>   place.
> [lines 12–14, *Complete Poems,* 510]

In the next group of poems, beginning with "Dies Irae," "Dies Illa," and "Stop It," Lawrence generalizes his erectile dysfunction in terms of apocalyptic change. In "The Death of Our Era," he says that "the knell of our bald-headed consciousness" (line 10, *Complete Poems,* 512)—that is, the general impotence of our era—was rung by all of us. But at the end of the poem, he universalizes the recovery he anticipates in the new era by proclaiming: "the new word is Resurrection" (line 29, *Complete Poems,* 512). In the next poem, "The New Word," he specifies his meaning as "[t]he resurrection of the flesh" (line 4, *Complete Poems,* 513).

There can be little doubt that Lawrence's concern with the theme of resurrection during his last years—especially in *The Escaped Cock* and *Last Poems*—had its genesis in his erectile dysfunction, which, with some hope, he continued to regard as a "pause" in his very being from which he would recover, as in the climactic poem of the "loss of desire" sequence, "Sun in Me":

> A sun will rise in me.
> I shall slowly resurrect,
> already the whiteness of false dawn is on my inner ocean.
>   [lines 1–3, *Complete Poems*, 513]

The "salt rage" of the "inner ocean" in "There Is Rain in Me" has given way to the dawning whiteness presaging the rising sun, a symbol of sexual healing and a metaphor, as in *The Escaped Cock,* for both erection and resurrection. The situation, as Lawrence puts it in "At Last," may well have passed "beyond tragedy" (line 1, *Complete Poems*, 514). But accepting the condition realistically, without self-pity, he also refuses to be "The Optimist," who locks himself inside his sky-blue painted cell and calls it heaven (*Complete Poems*, 515). As he reiterates in "Be Still":

> The only thing to be done, now,
> now that the waves of our undoing have begun to strike on
>   us,
> is to contain ourselves.
> To keep still, and let the wreckage of ourselves go,
> let everything go. . . .
> . . . .
> For the word is Resurrection.
> And even the sea of seas will have to give up its dead.
>   [lines 1–5, 11–12, *Complete Poems*, 513–14]

This poem thematically anticipates the "Ship of Death" sequence in *Last Poems,* with its meditations on death, the ultimate impotence that all human beings face, and the tentative hope for continuing the energy of life in some form of rebirth. But in his present condition, Lawrence metaphorically equates erection with resurrection, in the hope that out of the quiescent pause in sexual function will emerge "the resurrection of the flesh" in the full potential of uninhibited sexual desire.

Did Lawrence regain full erectile function? In view of his deteriorating medical condition at the time, it is doubtful that he did. Sandra Gilbert, speaking literarily, suggests that "the writer works through the problem of the death of desire and . . . arrives at that rebirth which the man who died finds in the arms of the priestess of Isis" (Gilbert 1972, 257). In the scene in *The Escaped Cock* to which she refers, the man is no longer portrayed as the conventional phallic hero for whom the only acceptable male role is that of taking full responsibility for effecting coital connection and orchestrating sexual intercourse with a passive and available female. The woman no longer lies "quite still, in a sort of sleep," while the "activity, the orgasm [is] his, all his" (*Lady Chatterley's Lover*, 116), as in Connie's first sexual encounter with Mellors; nor does she become "a passive, consenting thing, like a slave, a physical slave" (247), as in the "night of sensual passion," though in context I find these two scenes both credible and mutual. Instead, both man and woman now accept her taking an active role in initiating and stimulating a mutual sexual experience, which can be a sacrament of sexual healing precisely because it is tender, caring, and shared.

When the man who had died, aroused again to full erection, proclaims, "I am risen!"[37] the scene has such artistic authenticity that one wants to believe it is validated, however partially or temporarily, by Lawrence's actual experience. But literary and literal, though they may meet, never quite merge and may in fact be far apart. One knows all that, but where this subject is concerned, to quote Hemingway's Jake Barnes, "Isn't it pretty to think so?" (Hemingway 1954, 247).

CHAPTER 10

Lawrence, the True Self, and Dying

Lawrence's *Last Poems* includes several poetic sequences that are psychological and spiritual exercises in preparation for his dying. Some of these poems are among the finest of modern poetic meditational works. The myths in which he had formerly centered his literary and personal thinking—the Wagnerian myths of *The Trespasser,* the Germanic *Blutbrüderschaft* of *Women in Love,* the pre-Columbian Aztec myths of *The Plumed Serpent*—do not meet the requirements of the task that now confronts him. Always one to seek the "poetry of the present" to express and the appropriate myth to structure his experience in every current of his life, Lawrence now turns to the Mediterranean myths encompassing the final journey, especially the ancient Etruscan rituals of the last voyage of the soul in the well-prepared ship of death. This chapter will focus on psychological, spiritual, and poetic strategies by which Lawrence sought to incorporate his experience in this last movement of his life.

Earlier in his canon, the struggles of the adolescent self with the preoedipal task of separation-individuation still preoccupied Lawrence in the oedipal situation of *Sons and Lovers.* The efforts of the self in young manhood creatively to incorporate homoerotic attractions and anxieties in relation to the commitments of a heterosexual marriage led to his effort to encompass "two kinds of love" in the structural balance of *Blutbrüderschaft* with a man and star polarity with a woman in *Women in Love.* The continuing struggle of the self with the unsatisfied need for idealization in early childhood emerged in the idealization of the leader (and in the leader's grandiosity) in *Aaron's Rod, Kangaroo,* and *The Plumed Serpent.* The struggle to free the self for the full range of sexual expression in the "forked flame" of heterosexual love in the context of his own primarily constitutional erectile dysfunction led to Lawrence's most controversial and ultimately his most widely read novel, *Lady Chatterley's Lover.* The self of *Last Poems* now faced a different issue: the need to live with integrity while dying.

If psychoanalysis offers limited assistance in either understanding or incorporating the inevitability of this vast unknown, it does offer a view of the task as requiring integrity rather than fragmentation. Erik Erikson discusses this idea in *Identity and the Life Cycle*. For D. W. Winnicott, the task is to accept the final reality rather than mounting the manic defense of denial against it: "The central fact denied in manic defence is death in the inner world, or a deadness over all; and the accent, in the manic defence, is on life, liveliness, denial of death as an ultimate fact of life."[1] The result is entrapment in a static defensive position characterized by denial, as elaborated in a paper Winnicott presented before the British Psycho-Analytical Society (1935), in which he discusses various forms of denial:

- Denial of inner reality.
- Flight to external reality from inner reality.
- Holding the people of the inner reality in 'suspended animation'.
- Denial of the *sensations* of depression—namely the heaviness, the sadness—by specifically opposite sensations, lightness, humorousness, etc.
- The employment of almost any opposites in the reassurance against death, chaos, mystery, etc., ideas that belong to the *fantasy content* of the depressive position.[2] (Winnicott's italics).

An example in Lawrence of denial as a manic defense is his refusal to label his illness as tuberculosis, as in his repeated insistence that his medical condition was in his "bronchials," not his lungs. By the autumn of 1929, however, he could no longer deny the reality of his situation and still remain sufficiently true to himself to see him through the ordeal that lay before him. He could, however, try to develop psychological and spiritual strategies for incorporating that reality in the last stage of his life and to find the experience as meaningful a part of the life cycle as the stages that had preceded it.

Winnicott argues that in infancy "the basis for ego establishment is the sufficiency of 'going on being', uncut by reactions to impingement." Fred Pine conjectures that "going on being" refers to "a not yet self-conscious forerunner of a subjective state of self. A period of being, of self experience."[3] "Maternal failures produce phases of reaction to impingement and these reactions interrupt the 'going on being' of the infant," says Winnicott. "An excess of this reacting produces not frustration but a *threat of annihilation*. This in my view is a very real primitive anxiety, long antedating any anxiety that includes the word death in its description."[4] It is probable that a man like Lawrence, who, as a preoedipal infant, must have experienced the outside demands of his needy mother and angry father as a threat of annihilation, may subsequently, as an adult in a physically weakened condition compromised by serious illness, find the threat of annihilation reactivated in the knowledge of impending death. The alternative to approaching death as the ultimate threat of annihilation is to approach it with integrity from a position of wholeness. As Winnicott writes: "There is no death except of a totality. Put the other way round, the wholeness of personal integration brings with it the *possibility* and indeed the *certainty of death;* and with the acceptance of death there can come a great relief, relief from fear of the alternatives, such as disintegration, or ghosts—that is the lingering on of spirit phenomena after the death of the somatic half of the psychosomatic partnership."[5]

~

In "Beware the Unhappy Dead," Lawrence states the dangers of death before integration:

> Beware the unhappy dead thrust out of life
> unready, unprepared, unwilling, unable
> to continue on the longest journey.
>
> . . . . . .
>
> Oh, now they moan and throng in anger, and press back
> through breaches in the walls of this our by-no-means impregnable
>   existence
> seeking their old haunts with cold, ghostly rage
> old haunts, old habitats, old hearths,
> old places of sweet life from which they are thrust out
> and can but haunt in disembodied rage.
>   [lines 1–3 and 9–14, *Complete Poems*, 722–23]

Acceptance of the task of dying with integrity derives from a sense of having been fully alive. In his notebook, Winnicott jotted the prayer: "Oh God! May I be alive when I die."[6] Lawrence touches on a related idea in the character of Mrs. Witt in *St. Mawr:* "I've come to the conclusion that hardly anybody in the world really lives, and so hardly anybody really dies. They may well say *Oh Death where is thy sting-a-ling-a-ling?* Even Death can't sting those that have never really lived.—I always used to want that—to die without death stinging me."[7]

At this point in her life, however, in a determination to feel real and to remain alive to experience, she turns to the alternative mode. "I want death to be real to me," Mrs. Witt tells her daughter, Lou Carrington. "I want it to hurt me, Louise. If it hurts me enough, I shall know I was alive" (*St. Mawr*, 92).

Lawrence's efforts to remain alive in dying are recorded faithfully in several sequences or clusters of poems. Each of these poetic sequences is centered in a single image or motif that is developed and redeveloped in successive poems in the sequence. I will briefly discuss the clusters of poems on the hands of God, the voyage and gods of the Greeks, modern mechanistic evil, the autumn calendar, doors, and the ship of death.

Lawrence's exploration of the major theme of "the hands of the living God" corresponds to Winnicott's (and Mrs. Witt's) need to be alive throughout the experience and to be in contact with a meaningful mythic or religious structure to encompass it. In approaching his death, which Lawrence now knows will come soon, the self must trust in "the hands of God." In reference to God's judgment, St. Paul writes:

> Vengeance belongeth unto me, I will recompense, saith the Lord,
> It is a fearful thing to fall into the hands of the living God.
> [Hebrews 10:30–31]

In "The Hands of God," Lawrence corrects this view of the deity as a punitive and vengeful God and presents his view of God as life affirmative:

> It is a fearful thing to fall into the hands of the living God.
> But it is a much more fearful thing to fall out of them.

His prayer is:

> Save me, O God, from falling into the ungodly knowledge
> of myself as I am without God.
>
> . . . . . .
>
> Save me from that, O God!
> Let me never know myself apart from the living God!
> [lines 1–2, 5–6, and 17–18, *Complete Poems*, 699]

The meditations in this sequence of poems repeatedly affirm this idea. In "Pax," Lawrence writes:

> All that matters is to be at one with the living God
> to be a creature in the house of the God of Life.
> [lines 1–2, *Complete Poems*, 700]

In "Abysmal Immortality," he continues:

> It is not easy to fall out of the hands of the living God:
> They are so large, and they cradle so much of a man.
>
>   .   .   .   .   .   .
>
> Even through the greatest blasphemies, the hands of the living God
>   still continue to cradle him.

Recalling the familiar concept of the Fall of man as a fall into knowledge, he adds a characteristically Lawrentian observation:

> And still through knowledge and will, he can break away,
> man can break away, and fall from the hands of God
> into himself alone, down the godless plunge of the abyss. . . .
>   [lines 1–2, 4, and 5–7, *Complete Poems*, 700]

If the Congregational chapel concept of God remembered from Lawrence's childhood reverberates in the poetic language of this sequence of poems, the identity of the living God remains unstated. According to Earl Brewster, although earlier Lawrence had said that "God was an exhausted concept," he now "wanted to establish a conscious relationship with God."[8]

David Ellis argues that "the God to which Lawrence pledges allegiance in all his poetry and prose of this period is never an anthropomorphic deity," but "akin to a pagan or animist creative force not simply 'manifest' in the universe but identical with it. Here 'God' is the word for that cycle of 'lapse and renewal' with which Lawrence movingly hopes to remain associated." In placing his trust entirely in this power, he remains open to the possibility of some kind of renewal beyond human experience (Ellis, 520).

This possibility is stated tentatively in several poems in *Last Poems*. In "The Ship of Death," after the little ship is gone, "It is the end, it is oblivion" (VIII, line 81):

> And yet out of eternity, a thread
> separates itself on the blackness,
> a horizontal thread
> that fumes a little with pallor upon the dark.
>   [IX, lines 82–85, *Complete Poems*, 719]

The poet questions: "Is it illusion?" But though the little ship drifts "beneath the deathly ashy grey / of a flood-dawn," there is "O chilled wan soul, a flush of rose": "A flush of rose and the whole thing starts again." (IX, lines 86, 92, 96, *Complete Poems,* 720). In the last section of the poem:

> The flood subsides, and the body, like a worn sea-shell
> emerges strange and lovely.
> And the little ship wings home, faltering and lapsing
> on the pink flood,
> and the frail soul steps out, into her house again
> filling the heart with peace.
>   [X, lines 97–102, *Complete Poems,* 720]

"Shadows" ends with the following lines:

> then I must know that still
> I am in the hands [of] the unknown God,
> he is breaking me down to his own oblivion
> to send me forth on a new morning, a new man.
>   ["Shadows," lines 29–32, *Complete Poems,* 727]

It would be easy to read such lines as these in a traditional Christian context as evidence of Lawrence's return to the fold of his Congregationalist child-hood. Ellis cautions against any such reductive view of Lawrence's position: "The overwhelming tendency in all Lawrence's last writings is to remain courageously agnostic on the issue . . . and to resist any consolation which was not physically grounded" (Ellis, 520).

Gail Porter Mandell cites another source for the deity in whose hands Lawrence places his trust, one that is related to the pagan creative force that Ellis suggests. This deity, according to Mandell, is the final version of the "demon" that Lawrence had ever relied upon as the unconscious instinctual force that kept him true to his essential self and thus as the creative source of his literary work. Mandell agrees with Aldous Huxley "that Lawrence's idea of the demon stems from the pre-Christian Greek concept of 'daimon,'" which probably came to Lawrence by way of English Romantic poets like Byron and Shelley.[9]

More significantly, I suggest, Huxley clarifies the connection between Lawrence's creative demon and his religious sense: "The daimon which pos-sessed him was, he felt, a divine thing, which he would never deny or explain away, never even ask to accept a compromise."[10] "To this strange force within him, to this power that created his works of art, there was nothing to do but submit. Lawrence submitted, completely and with reverence." As Huxley quotes Lawrence: "I often think one ought to be able to pray before one works—and then leave it to the Lord. Isn't it hard, hard work to come to real grips with one's imagination—throw everything overboard? I always feel as though I stood naked for the fire of Almighty God to go through me—and it's rather an awful feeling. One has to be so terribly religious to be an artist."[11]

Mandell also agrees with Baruch Hochman, who relates Lawrence's "demon" to the "dark gods" of his fiction, especially *Kangaroo* and *The Plumed Serpent*, where, Hochman writes, they "preserve individual identity."[12] In Mandell's view, this implies that "the demon becomes for Lawrence a 'true self,' but one that assumes the role of an 'anti-self' when viewed from the perspective of conventional social, moral, and artistic norms" (Mandell, 4). It follows, then, that the God in whom Lawrence places his trust in these poems is the means of preserving the true self even in the face of death.

Mandell does not further define her terms nor relate them to the "true self" and the "false self" as these concepts are set forth in the psychoanalytic object relations theory of D. W. Winnicott. Winnicott, like Lawrence, championed the true self. Winnicott also would have recognized the "conventional social, moral, and artistic norms" to which Mandell refers as the means by which the false self serves the "defensive function to hide and protect the True Self."[13]

According to Winnicott's formulation: "At the earliest stage the True Self is the theoretical position from which come the spontaneous gesture and the personal idea. The spontaneous gesture is the True Self in action. Only the True Self can be creative and only the True Self can feel real. Whereas a True Self feels real, the existence of a False Self results in a feeling unreal or a sense of futility" (*Maturational Processes*, 148). As he further elaborates: "The True Self comes from the aliveness of the body tissues and the working of body-functions, including the heart's action and breathing. It is closely linked with the idea of the Primary Process, and is, at the beginning, essentially not reactive to external stimuli, but primary" (148).

Quickly developing complexity, the true self "relates to external reality by natural processes, by such processes as develop in the individual infant in the course of time." Every new period of development "in which the True Self has not been interrupted" strengthens "the sense of being real" and "a growing capacity . . . to tolerate two sets of phenomena": "Breaks in continuity of True Self living," and "Reactive or False Self experiences, related to the environment on a basis of compliance" (148).

The true self, in sum, is "the 'inherited potential' that constitutes the 'kernel' of the child." Its development is facilitated by the "good enough mother," who provides a healthy environment, meaningful responsiveness to the child's sensorimotor self, and appropriate satisfaction of instinctual needs. "The true self evolves its idiom through a maternal care that supports the child's continuity of being, enabling the child to generate an expressive life from a core self

authorized by his or her sense of personal reality." It is the source of spontaneous expressions of one's real being.[14]

The false self is also a continuous and stable structure. Although some individuals suffer a false self disorder as in a schizoid personality, Winnicott
"repeatedly asserted that this partition of self into true and false is also normal. True and false thus refer not to a moral order, but to qualities in self-
other experiences that support spontaneous expression (true self) or reactive
living (false self)."[15]

D. H. Lawrence had made a similar point in his "carbon" letter to Edward
Garnett (5 June 1914): "that which is physic—non-human, in humanity, is
more interesting to me than the old-fashioned human element—which causes
one to conceive a character in a certain moral scheme and make him consistent.
The certain moral scheme is what I object to" (*Letters* 2:182). He continues:

> You mustn't look in my novel for the old stable ego of the character. There
> is another ego, according to whose action the individual is unrecognisable,
> and passes through, as it were, allotropic states which it needs a deeper
> sense than any we've been used to exercise, to discover are states of the
> same single radically-unchanged element. (Like as diamond and coal are
> the same pure single element of carbon. The ordinary novel would trace
> the history of the diamond—but I say, 'diamond, what! This is carbon.'
> And my diamond might be coal or soot, and my theme is carbon.) [*Letters*
> 2:183]

In this important letter, Lawrence, in several respects, prefigures Winnicott's
concept. The consistent "old stable ego of the character conceived in a certain
moral scheme" is the false self. The true self is what Lawrence calls "another
ego": "what the woman is—what she is, inhumanly, physiologically, materi-
ally." For Lawrence, it is the difference between either diamond or coal and
the essential element, carbon. Although presented as elaborations of ego theory, both Winnicott's concept of the true self and Lawrence's concept of
"another ego" are also defined by the self's ability to incorporate instinctual
forces of the id.

Lawrence's poems on death, oblivion, and the hands of God, are informed
by his effort to confront the difficult experience that lay before him with
integrity in his true self as informed by the natural cycles of death and rebirth
in the universe. These poems are marked by progression rather than completion, possibility rather than certainty, spontaneous feeling rather than a the-
ological absolute. This quality characterizes even Lawrence's attempt to
incorporate the idea of oblivion and tentatively to imagine in some sense the
possibility of rebirth.

The voyage motif is announced in the opening sequence evoking the
ancient Greeks. In "The Greeks Are Coming,"

> And every time, it is ships, it is ships,
> it is ships of Cnossos coming, out of the morning end of the sea,
> it is Aegean ships, and men with archaic pointed beards
> [lines 4–6, *Complete Poems,* 687]

In "The Argonauts,"

> Now the sea is the Argonauts' sea, and in the dawn
> Odysseus calls the commands, as he steers past those foamy islands
> [lines 8–9, *Complete Poems,* 687]

Here Lawrence introduces the motif of the ancient gods, who attend the
ships, and by extension, the dying poet himself, in their voyaging, accompanied by various manifestations of the living God in the form of the ancient
Mediterranean deities, appearing in the guise of a stranger. In "Middle of the
World,"

> and let the slim black ship of Dionysos come sailing in
> with grape-vines up the mast, and dolphins leaping.
>   .   .   .   .   .   .
> And the Minoan Gods, and the Gods of Tiryns
> are heard softly laughing and chatting, as ever;
> and Dionysos, young and a stranger
> leans listening on the gate, in all respect.
> [lines 4–5 and 17–20, *Complete Poems,* 688]

In "For the Heroes Are Dipped in Scarlet" the Greeks are described in the col-
ors of life:

> They are dancing! they return, as they went, dancing!
> For the thing that is done without the glowing as of god, vermilion,
> were best not done at all.
> How glistening red they are!
> [lines 17–20, *Complete Poems,* 689]

The living God is defined in bodily rather than in mental or spiritual terms.
In "Demiurge," Lawrence disputes the idea "that reality exists only in the
spirit"—"as if any Mind could have imagined a lobster":

Religion knows that Jesus was never Jesus
till he was born from a womb, and ate soup and bread
and grew up, and became, in the wonder of creation, Jesus,
with a body and with needs, and a lovely spirit.
[lines 13–16, Complete Poems, 689]

In "The Work of Creation,"

The mystery of creation is the divine urge of creation,
but it is a great, strange urge, it is not a Mind.
. . . . . .
God is a great urge, wonderful, mysterious, magnificent
but he knows nothing before-hand.
His urge takes shape in the flesh, and lo!
it is creation!
[lines 1–2, 8–11, Complete Poems, 690]

In "Bodiless God," Lawrence holds that "Everything that has beauty has a body, and is a body" (line 1):

And God?
Unless God has a body, how can he have a voice
and emotions, and desires, and strength, glory or honour?
[lines 4–6, Complete Poems, 691]

In "The Body of God," Lawrence suggests that God is a "great creative urge" incarnated in nature and in humanity:

God is the great urge that has not yet found a body
but urges towards incarnation with the great creative urge.
. . . . . .
There is no god
apart from poppies and the flying fish,
men singing songs, and women brushing their hair in the sun.
[lines 1–2 and lines 7–9, Complete Poems, 691]

In "Maximus," the ancient god again comes as a stranger:

But a naked man, a stranger, leaned on the gate
with his cloak over his arm, waiting to be asked in.
So I called him: Come in, if you will!—

He came in slowly, and sat down by the hearth.
I said to him: And what is your name?—
He looked at me without answer, but such a loveliness
entered me, I smiled to myself, saying: He is God!
So he said: *Hermes!*

God is older than the sun and moon
and the eye cannot behold him
nor the voice describe him:
and still, this is the god Hermes, sitting by my hearth.
                        [lines 4–15, *Complete Poems,* 692]

Hermes's appearance as a naked man with his cloak over his arm aptly
describes the impressive image of Hermes as an idealized male figure in divine
form in the Parian marble sculpture by Praxiteles in the Olympia Museum.
Mythologically associated more with mirth than with heroic exploits, Hermes
would have interested Lawrence as a phallic deity, known in ancient Athens
in the form of abbreviated statuary called "Hermeses" or "herms. " Consisting of a pillar, a head, and an erect phallus, on which Athenians conveniently
hung tributes in the form of cakes and flowers, these figures were vandalized
in the year A.D. 415.[16] The immediate reason for Hermes' appearance to
Lawrence is related to his status as a god of travelers, and in particular to his
role as a guide for the dead to the underworld. In this role, Hermes had led
the blind Oedipus to the place from which he would depart from life. At the
recurrence of spring, Hermes also guides Persephone back from the underworld to where her mother is waiting. His visiting Lawrence at this point in
the narrative line of *Last Poems* is consistent with his role as guide for the dead.
Significantly, Lawrence invites him in and asks his name.

   In another sequence of poems, Lawrence considers the question of evil,
which he defines as divisive and mechanistic. In "Walk Warily," he warns:

      Lo, we are in the midst of the Sunderers
      the Cleavers, that cleave us forever apart from one another
      and separate heart from heart, and cut away all caresses
                        [lines 15–17, *Complete Poems,* 707]

In "Kissing and Horrid Strife," "worsted by the evil world-soul of today" (line
2, *CP,* 709), he imagines the reconciliation of life's opposites in death:

      Life is for kissing and for horrid strife,
      the angels and the Sunderers.

And perhaps in unknown Death we perhaps shall know
Oneness and poised immunity.
> [lines 35–38, *Complete Poems,* 710]

In "Evil is Homeless," Lawrence associates evil with "men that sit in machines / among spinning wheels, in an apotheosis of wheels":

that is, they sit and are evil, in evil,
grey evil, which has no path, and shows neither light nor dark,
and has no home, no home anywhere.
> [lines 15–16 and 21–23, *Complete Poems,* 711–12]

In "The Evil World-Soul," Lawrence further defines evil in mechanistic terms:

But it is the soul of man only, and his machines
which has brought to pass the fearful thing called evil

.   .   .   .   .   .

And every man who has become a detached and self-activated ego
is evil, evil, part of the evil world-soul

.   .   .   .   .   .

The Robot is the unit of evil.
And the symbol of the Robot is the wheel revolving.
> [lines 2–3, 8–9, and 12–13, *Complete Poems,* 712–13]

As the title of another poem affirms: "Death Is Not Evil, Evil Is Mechanical." The danger is not the opposites that define mortal man's condition, but that in denying the human condition, he will "begin to spin around on the hub of the obscene ego" and become a totally false self, a robot, "a machine that in itself is nothing" (lines 21 and 23, *Complete Poems,* 714).

Finally, a significant organizing pattern in *Last Poems* is the calendar, in particular the Christian church calendar that Lawrence follows throughout the autumn of 1929. In *Bavarian Gentians,*

Not every man has gentians in his house
in soft September, at slow, sad Michaelmas.
> [lines 3–4, *Complete Poems,* 697]

The poem moves from the sadness of Michaelmas (the feast of St. Michael and All Angels, September 30) through a pattern of darkening imagery. The flowers are:

> Bavarian gentians, big and dark, only dark
> darkening the day-time, torch-like, with the smoking blueness of
>   Pluto's gloom
>
> > [lines 3–4, *Complete Poems*, 697]

With the call, "Reach me a gentian, give me a torch!" (line 11), the meaning and purpose of the gentians become clear: they will be used to guide the poet's descent into the darkness to come:

> let me guide myself with the blue, forked torch of this flower
> down the darker and darker stairs, where blue is darkened on blueness
> even where Persephone goes, just now, from the frosted September
> to the sightless realm where darkness is awake upon the dark
>
> > [lines 12–15, *Complete Poems*, 697]

Related to this progression is the image of the new moon as an opening door. In "Return of Returns," with the seven planets and the ancient Greek gods Hermes, Aphrodite, Ares, Kronos, and Zeus affirming their consent, the door will open, and the poet invites the awaited presence (a god welcomed as a stranger? death?) to "come then":

> When the moon from out of the darkness
> has come like a thread, like a door just opening
> opening, till the round white doorway of delight
> is half open.
>
> Come then!
> Then, when the door is half open.
> In a week!
> The ancient river week, the old one.
> Come then!
>
> > [lines 13–21, *Complete Poems*, 702]

In "Doors" Lawrence writes:

> There is a double sacredness of doors.
> Some you may sing through, and all men hear,
> but others, the dark doors, oh hush! hush!
> let nobody be about! slip in! go all unseen
>
> > [lines 12–15, *Complete Poems*, 711]

The calendar motif culminates in "The Ship of Death":

Now it is autumn and the falling fruit
and the long journey towards oblivion.

The apples falling like great drops of dew
to bruise themselves an exit from themselves.

And it is time to go, to bid farewell
to one's own self, and find an exit
from the fallen self.

[lines 1–7, *Complete Poems*, 716]

After this and a related poem, "Difficult Death," Lawrence turns in "All Soul's Day" (November 2) to those unable to complete the journey:

Be careful, then, and be gentle about death.
For it is hard to die, it is difficult to go through
the door, even when it opens.

[lines 1–3, *Complete Poems*, 721]

In "The Houseless Dead," as in "Beware the Unhappy Dead," Lawrence evokes the purpose of prayers on All Soul's Day for the souls in purgatory:

Oh pity the dead that are dead, but cannot take
the journey, still they moan and beat
against the silvery adamant walls of life's exclusive city.
.   .   .   .   .   .
The poor gaunt dead that cannot die
into the distance with receding oars,
but must roam like outcast dogs on the margins of life!
Oh think of them, and with the soul's deep sigh
set food for them, and encourage them to build
the bark of their deliverance from the dilemma
of non-existence to far oblivion.

[lines 1–3 and 9–15, *Complete Poems*, 722]

In "After All Saints' Day" (November 1):

Wrapped in the dark-red mantle of warm memories
the little, slender soul sits swiftly down, and takes the oars
and draws away, away, towards dark depths

[lines 1–3, *Complete Poems*, 723]

Keith Sagar argues that Lawrence's preferred final version of "The Ship of Death" is one published in an appendix both in the 1932 edition of *Last*

Poems, edited by Richard Aldington and Giuseppe Orioli, and in *The Complete Poems of D. H. Lawrence,* edited by Vivian de Sola Pinto and F. Warren Roberts (964–65). "If we can dismiss the familiar version of 'The Ship of Death' from our minds, this version will surely be seen to have all the characteristics of a finished poem—in fact, one of the most finished in the volume, with an unusual degree of formal control, coherence, and conciseness."[17] In this version of the poem, says Sagar, Lawrence "stripped it of the falling apples and the Hamlet posturings, dropped the attempt to describe the unknowable, leaving the journey only, 'so still / so beautiful over the last of seas.'"[18]

Whether or not one accepts the premise that this version is Lawrence's preferred text, Sagar's observations on its formal control are accurate. It is, however, precisely the finished quality of formality and control in this version of the poem that leads me to return to the more familiar version for the immediacy of what Lawrence, in his Introduction to the U. S. edition of *New Poems* (1918), calls "poetry of the present": "In its quivering momentaneity it surpasses the crystalline, pearl-hard jewels, the poems of the eternities." As in Whitman, "There must be the rapid momentaneous association of things which meet and pass on the forever incalculable journey of creation: everything left in its own rapid, fluid relationship with the rest of things" (*Complete Poems,* 183).

As Ginette Katz-Roy points out, Lawrence, in *Apocalypse,* "offers us what may be considered as the last version of his poetics in the guise of a comment on pre-Christian texts. He argues that the pagan thinker was necessarily a poet 'who starts with an image, sets the image in motion, allows it to achieve a certain course or circuit of its own, and then takes up another image.'" Lawrence refers to this as "The old pagan process of rotary image-thought."[19]

This way of thinking, according to Ellen Mahon, accounts for Lawrence's characteristic use of "clusters" of poems to develop a single theme. The method of "rotary image-thought" becomes the "unifying technique" by which Lawrence "shapes the growing resolve of his death-journeying persona." Mahon describes the "iterative abstraction until insight is gained" as a progression of "grappling through workaday poems until a lyric bursts through, and the topic, now understood, can be put aside for a new, usually associated, consideration."[20]

Lawrence's method, as Mahon describes it, of "grappling through" a cluster of related minor poems until the issue is resolved and lyrical insight is reached, though descriptive of Lawrence's concrete, pictographic poetic process, is in some respects analogous to the psychoanalytic concept of working through, which may be described as gradually overcoming resistance to an interpretation until insight emerges, leading to psychic growth, a process that is concretely experiential rather than merely persuasive in abstract reasoning.

According to Moore and Fine, "It is the goal of working through to make insight more effective, that is, to bring about significant and lasting changes . . . by altering the modes and aims of the instinctual drives." This may include repeating and elaborating one's responses to the interpretation, which often requires expansion and modification. "The process leads eventually to the inclusion in the personality of previously warded-off components as resistances are gradually relinquished."[21] As Laplanche and Pontalis observe, "Working-through permits the subject to pass from rejection or merely intellectual acceptance to a conviction based on lived experience . . . of the repressed instincts which 'are feeding the resistance.'"[22]

The familiar version of "The Ship of Death," adopted by Aldington and Orioli as well as Pinto and Roberts, is a symbolic record of Lawrence's working through his resistance to acceptance of his impending death in his effort to gain insight on the meaning of this experience. The poetic elements to which Sagar objects—"the falling apples and the Hamlet posturings" and "the attempt to describe the unknowable"—may be understood both as concrete examples of "rotary image-thought" and as associations in the process of working through. So may the "grim frost," the "smell of ashes," "the bruised body, the frightened soul," and "the cold / that blows upon it through the orifices." In context, the passing thought of maintaining one's control by putting an end to one's own life leads to the association with Hamlet: "And can a man his own quietus make / with a bare bodkin?" If in quoting from the third soliloquy Lawrence seems to be posturing, even histrionic, the allusion is appropriate to the matter at hand and consistent with Lawrence's long-standing interest in Hamlet, whose psychological struggles had provided a subtext for Paul Morel's in *Sons and Lovers*. It is also consistent with the kind of associations that might be brought forward by a literate person in the process of working through.

"The Ship of Death" is Lawrence's most significant meditation on the voyage, if you will, that engaged him in his preparation for dying. The more finished poem that Sagar considers the preferred final version, seemingly addressed to others who will come after, expresses neither the process of "rotary image-thought" nor the personal struggle of working through before arriving at the resolution conveyed after the fact in the formal control of the poem. Working through enabled Lawrence to incorporate the certainty of his approaching death and to confront it with the wholeness of life that both Winnicott and Erikson see as the major psychic attribute needed for this last stage of life.

After Lawrence's death (2 March 1930), Frieda wrote to their friends in New Mexico as follows: To Witter Bynner (12 March 1930): "You will know that Lorenzo is dead. Right up to the last he was alive, and we both made the best of our days; then he faced the end so splendidly, so like a *man,* and I could help him through, thank God. Dead, he looked proud and at peace and fulfilled."[23]

> To Mabel Dodge Luhan (undated):
>
> Yes, our Lorenzo is dead, but up to the end life never lost its glamour and its meaning. The courage, the courage with which he fought. I am so full of admiration that I can hardly feel much else. Dead, he looked so proud and so unconquered. I didn't know death could be *splendid;* it *was.* I didn't know anything about death, now I do. He opened a door into that place of the dead, and it's a great world too. He had given me a world here on this side, now he has given me the world of the dead. He was a great giver.
> [*Frieda Lawrence: The Memoirs and Correspondence,* 236]

Even allowing for her natural vulnerability at this time of mourning to feelings of loss, grief, and a need to idealize her lost husband, Frieda's statements attest to the integrity that characterized Lawrence's dying. Four months later in another letter to Mabel Dodge Luhan (3 July 1930), Frieda associates Lawrence's sense of life with the character of his dying: "He could never have written Lady C.—nor the 'Apocalypse' nor died so unflinchingly in utter belief if he hadn't known Taos and lived in it."[24] And in the following decade, she writes to screenwriter and director Dudley Nichols (undated [1944?]): "My Lorenzo (but the fact is he is not my Lorenzo but all the world's Lorenzo) is really a religious reformer. He wanted to put religion, that bond with all and everything, back into living and especially sex, that we don't live like a disturbed anthill" (*Frieda Lawrence: The Memoirs and Correspondence,* 292).

For Lawrence, integrity is established in the continuing creative search to make manifest the true self, often in the face of a hostile world. His final personal effort is perhaps the most courageous: the sharing of the self while confronting his own death.

In Erik H. Erikson's terms, the ego, in the last phase of the life cycle, emerges with a pervading sense of either integrity or despair. I want to conclude with Erikson's memorable description of the state of mind he characterizes as integrity:

> It is the acceptance of one's own and only life cycle and the people who have become significant to it as something that had to be and that, by necessity, permitted of no substitutions. It thus means a new different love of one's parents, free of the wish that they should have been different, and an acceptance of the fact that one's life is one's own responsibility. It is a sense of comradeship with men and women of distant times and of different pursuits,

who have created orders and objects and sayings conveying human dignity and love. Although aware of the relativity of all the various life styles which have given meaning to human striving, the possessor of integrity is ready to defend the dignity of his own life style against all physical and economic threats. For he knows that an individual life is the accidental coincidence of but one life cycle with but one segment of history; and that for him all human integrity stands and falls with the one style of integrity of which he partakes.[25]

Integrity is at the heart of Winnicott's prayer, "Oh God! May I be alive when I die." To which may I respond:

So let it be.

Glossary

actual neurosis (Freud): Somatic in origin, an actual neurosis was thought to be caused by faulty practices in contemporary sexual life. (From the German *aktual* with reference to the "present day.")

affects: Feeling states, especially pleasure or unpleasure, and physiological concomitants such as hormonal or somatic phenomena. Related to psychic energy, and the cognitive ideas and fantasies specific to the individual.

androgen deficiency: Serum testosterone level below normal range in males. Treated by monitored testosterone replacement therapy.

andropause: Nonscientific term for a syndrome of physiological and psychosexual changes in males between ages forty and fifty-five. Characterized by clinical symptoms variously including fatigue, depression, decreased libido, erectile dysfunction, and changes in mood and cognition. Misleading in suggesting analogy to female menopause, since no such abrupt change in reproductive physiology occurs in males.

anhedonia (Whybrow, Akiskal, and McKinney): Inability to anticipate or respond to pleasurable reward. Characteristic of depression, and marked by loss of the ability to cathect, that is, to invest oneself emotionally in objects outside the self.

awe: Overwhelming sense, sometimes tinged with fear or reverence, in response to beauty, majesty, power, or size. Psychoanalytic examples include the infant's response to the mother's breast and the child's phallic awe on witnessing the father's erect penis.

cathexis (n.), **cathect** (v.) (Freud): Term derived from Greek, introduced by translators of the Standard Edition, as English version of Freud's "Besetzung," denoting mental energy capable of increase or decrease, not quantitatively but in the sense of emotional investment in objects.

central masturbation fantasy (Laufer): The leading fantasy of gratification, often in symbolic form, of unrelinquished infantile instinctual wishes. Usually unconscious in childhood, it takes on urgent meaning for the ego with the maturation of the genitals, involving one's basic sexual organization and expression of one's sexual role.

component instincts (Freud): Sexual instinct "is made up of component instincts into which it may break up and which are only gradually united into well-defined organizations." Sources of component instincts are organs of the body, especially erotogenic zones, but contributions to libido come from all functional body processes. At first independent of each other, component instincts in time become more convergent. In the final stage, component instincts are organized under the primacy of the genitals, but some may remain in earlier stages, giving rise to "fixations." (See also "part objects" and "genital supremacy.")

conflict: Struggle between incompatible forces in the mind; e.g., in Freud's structural theory, the id desires, the superego prohibits, and the ego negotiates the resolution.

disintegration anxiety (Kohut): "The core of disintegration anxiety is the breakup of the self, not the fear of the drive." "It is the deepest anxiety man can experience." Also called "the dissolution of the self" (Kohut) and "annihilation of the self" (Winnicott).

empathy (Kohut): "Vicarious introspection, or . . . one person's attempt to experience the inner life of another while simultaneously retaining the stance of an objective observer." "Empathy is the operation that defines the field of psychoanalysis."

erectile dysfunction (Kaplan): "Impairment of the erectile reflex. Specifically, the vascular reflex mechanism fails to pump sufficient blood into the cavernous sinuses of the penis to render it firm and erect." "Erectile dysfunction," as an accurate, medically specific term, is now preferred to the older general term "impotence," which implies weakness and has pejorative connotations.

fantasy model of sex (Zilbergeld): The fantasy penis is "exaggeratedly large, hard as steel, . . . lasting for hours . . . and immediately regaining its hardness after ejaculation." Real sex, in contrast, may be affected by numerous things, such as illness, medication, fatigue, depression, anxiety, or even temporary distractions that alter the conditions.

gender role identity (Tyson and Tyson): A "gender-based patterning of conscious and unconscious interactions with other people." This "should not be confused with socially determined learned roles; rather it refers to an intrapsychic, interactional representation."

genital supremacy (Freud): "The third and final stage of organization is that in which the majority of the component instincts converge under the *primacy of the genital zones.*"

guilty man (Kohut): "Guilty man" and "tragic man" epitomize respectively the Freudian concept of man and that of self psychology. The pleasure-seeking "guilty man" is conceived in terms of Freud's structural theory as exemplified in the oedipal conflict between id and superego over incestuous wishes. (See also "tragic man.")

idealization (Kohut): Exaggeratedly high evaluation of the object's qualities. The idealizing selfobject relationship, usually with the father, one of the two major poles of the developing self. As the child gradually experiences the father's realistic flaws, the ideals can be transmuted and internalized as parts of self structure. See also "mirroring."

identification: Process of assimilating attributes of another, taken as model.

imago (Jung): Used instead of "image" to emphasize the subjective perception of the image in terms of the internal state, unconscious fantasies, and expectations of the perceiving subject. Also used in psychoanalysis to refer to a self or object representation.

masturbation: Pleasurable self-stimulation of the genitals, with or without orgasm. Freud saw it as the primary addiction from which other addictions (to alcohol, tobacco, drugs, gambling, etc.) derived. Since Freud also believed that masturbation caused neurasthenia, he insisted that analysts must prevail upon their patients to desist from the practice and redirect their sexual activities to sexual intercourse. (See "neurasthenia.")

masturbation fantasy: The fantasies associated with masturbation provide a psychoanalytic means of understanding mental activities, conscious and unconscious, expressing wish fulfillments. (See also "central masturbation fantasy.")

mirroring (Kohut): Confirmation of the self, its exhibition of achievements, its ambitions, and its need for approval. The mirroring selfobject relationship (usually with the mother) is one of the two major poles of the developing self. (See also "idealization.")

narcissistic injury: An insult to the self that creates a disturbance in self-esteem and equilibrium. Lawrence speaks of "wounds to the soul, to the deep emotional self."

neurasthenia (Freud, based on the concept of George Beard): An "actual neurosis," which Freud thought to be caused by masturbation, a sexual practice incapable of fully discharging sexual tensions. Characterized by such symptoms as fatigue, headaches, stomach and intestinal problems, paresthesias, and sexual weakness.

nuclear self (Kohut): The first organization of the self as a cohering structure, usually becoming evident during the second year of life.

object: In object relations theory, which presupposes an internal representational world, "object" refers to the intrapsychic representation of a person important to the subject.

object constancy (Piaget, Hartmann): In Piaget, object permanence is achieved when the representation of the need-satisfying object persists in the mind while the object in person is absent. In Hartmann, object constancy also requires a measure of neutralization of libidinal and aggressive drives.

optimal frustration (Kohut): Through a series of tolerable disappointments in the selfobject, the developing self experiences optimal frustration, which leads to gradual modification of expectations and to internalization of the selfobject's functions as self structure. Kohut recommends that analysis be conducted on basis of optimal frustration.

part objects (Klein): Often referring to parts of the body such as the breast or penis, or their symbolic equivalents, internalized part objects become the focus of component instincts, with no suggestion that the whole person has become a whole object.

penis envy (Freud): Discovery of the size of the penis in comparison to the girl's inconspicuous clitoris leads to the little girl's penis envy. Envy of the larger penis of another male also occurs in men.

phallos (Monick): The erect penis, the "emblem and standard of maleness," encompassing all the images that define masculinity: "sinew, determination, effectuality, penetration, straightforwardness, hardness, strength." "Erection points to a powerful inner reality in a man, not altogether in his control."

phobia (Freud): A symptomatic response characterized by avoidance of particular objects or situations, which, though not realistically dangerous, trigger phobic anxiety. (See "Analysis of a Phobia in a Five-Year Old Boy" [little Hans], *SE* 10:1–149).

phobic objects and situations (Freud): These represent, unconsciously and symbolically, the underlying conflict and the unconscious psychological dangers symbolically disguised.

selfobject (Kohut): "One's subjective experience of another person who provides a sustaining function to the self and the experience of selfhood by his or her presence or activity." Selfobjects help one maintain self-cohesion, in contradistinction from love objects that are instinctually cathected.

self-state dream (Kohut): Associations to the manifest content of this kind of dream reveal that "the healthy sectors of the self . . . are reacting with anxiety to a disturbing change in the condition of the self—manic overstimulation or a serious depressive drop in self-esteem—or to the threat of the dissolution of the self."

separation-individuation (Mahler): Two related processes in infant development, beginning at about six months and lasting for two years. In the first, the infant separates from the symbiotic fusion with the mother and forms a mental representation of her apart from the self. In the second, the child differentiates himself from the object and forms a series of intrapsychic self-representations as a separate self from the mother. Mahler divides the individuation phase into four subphases: differentiation, practicing, rapprochement, and on the way to object constancy.

structural deficit or defect (Kohut): If either of the major poles of the developing self does not meet the needs of the self, i.e. for mirroring and idealization, then the grandiosity fostered by the mirroring selfobject or the ideals attributed to the idealized selfobject will not be internalized and transmuted into self structure. Hence, a structural deficit occurs.

sublimation (Freud): Assuming the motivation of human activities by sexual instinct, in nonsexual activities such as intellectual study and artistic creation, instinct is said to be sublimated by diverting it to a nonsexual, socially valuable aim.

testosterone deficiency: (See androgen deficiency.)

tragic man (Kohut): Whereas "guilty man" epitomizes the Freudian view of man as primarily pleasure seeking, "tragic man" represents the concept of self psychology, which conceives of man in terms of self structure. Man seeks confirmation of the need for self-expression and creativity in the fulfillment of aims that are beyond the solely pleasurable. (See also "guilty man.")

transmuting internalization (Kohut): As the tolerable failures in responses of the mirroring selfobject or the realistic flaws of the idealized selfobject are gradually experienced and incorporated by the developing self, the qualities attributed to the selfobjects are internalized and transmuted into self structure.

true self and **false self** (Winnicott): As "the 'inherited potential' that constitutes the 'kernel' of the child," "the True Self is the theoretical position from which come the spontaneous gesture and the personal idea. Only the True Self can be creative and only the True Self can feel real." "False Self experiences, related to the environment on a basis of compliance," "[result] in a feeling unreal or a sense of futility." One function of the false self is to hide and protect the true self. Both true and false self are continuous, stable structures, and the distinction between them does not refer to the moral order.

unconscious fantasy (Arlow): One's fantasy life is idiosyncratic and specific to the individual, deriving from childhood experiences (object relations, traumatic events, unfulfilled wishes), which "are organized into a number of leading unconscious fantasies that persist throughout life," forming "a stream of mental representations and wishes," acting as "a constant source of inner stimulation of the mind" and "operating all the time we are awake and some of the time we are asleep."

working through: Gradually overcoming one's resistance to an interpretation until insight emerges, leading to psychic growth, "working through" is a psychoanalytic process that is concretely experiential rather than merely persuasive in intellectual terms. Repeating and elaborating one's responses to the interpretation leads to incorporation of previously rejected ideas as resistances are gradually given up and a conviction based on lived experience emerges.

Notes

Introduction

1. Charles M. T. Hanly, "Applied Psychoanalysis," in *Psychoanalysis: The Major Concepts,* ed. Burness E. Moore and Bernard D. Fine (New Haven, Conn.: Yale University Press, 1995), 555, 556, 558.

Chapter 1

1. Throughout this chapter, the brief summaries restating essential concepts and principles of each of these four schools of psychoanalytic thought are based on Fred Pine's seminal article "The Four Psychologies of Psychoanalysis and Their Place in Clinical Work," *Journal of the American Psychoanalytic Association* 36, no. 3 (1988): 571–96. For his fuller discussion with clinical case studies, see Fred Pine, *Drive, Ego, Object, and Self: A Synthesis for Clinical Work,* (New York: Basic Books, 1990).

2. Ivy Low Litvinov, qtd. in Edward Nehls, ed. *D. H. Lawrence: A Composite Biography,* 3 vols. (Madison: University of Wisconsin Press, 1957, 1958, 1959), 1:215.

3. Alfred Booth Kuttner, "*Sons and Lovers,*" *New Republic* 2 (10 April 1915): 255–57, and "*Sons and Lovers:* A Freudian Appreciation," *Psychoanalytic Review* 3 (July 1916): 295–317.

4. Joseph Sandler, Ethel Spector Person, Peter Fonagy, "Introduction," *Freud's "On Narcissism: An Introduction"* (New Haven, Conn.: Yale University Press, 1991), xi, xii–xiii.

5. Frederick J. Hoffman, "Lawrence's Quarrel with Freud," *Freudianism and the Literary Mind* (Baton Rouge: Louisiana State University Press, 1945), 149–80; 2nd rev. ed. (1957), 151–76.

6. Adrian Stephen, "The Science of the Unconscious," *The Nation and the Athenaeum,* 25 August 1923.

7. Philip Rieff, "The Therapeutic as Mythmaker: Lawrence's True Christian Philosophy," *The Triumph of the Therapeutic: Uses of Faith After Freud* (New York: Harper and Row, 1966), 189–231.

8. Daniel J. Schneider, *D. H. Lawrence: The Artist as Psychologist* (Lawrence: University Press of Kansas, 1984).

9. Arthur Efron, *Life-Energy Reading: Wilhelm Reich and Literature, Paunch,* nos. 67–68 (1997); "The Mind-Body Problem in Lawrence, Pepper, and Reich," *Journal of Mind and Behavior* 1 (fall 1980): 247–70; and *The Sexual Body: An Interdisciplinary Perspective, Journal of Mind and Behavior* 6, nos. 1–2 (winter-spring 1985).

10. Daniel A. Weiss, *Oedipus in Nottingham: D. H. Lawrence* (Seattle: University of

Washington Press, 1962), esp. chap. 3:13–37, and chap. 4:39–67.

11. Heinz Hartmann, Ernst Kris, and Rudolph Loewenstein, "Comments on the For-mation of Ego Structure," *The Psychoanalytic Study of the Child* 2 (1946): 11–38; and the Festschrift *Psychoanalysis—A General Psychology: Essays in Honor of Heinz Hartmann,* ed. Rudolph M. Loewenstein, Lottie M. Newman, Max Schur, and Albert J. Solnit (New York: International Universities Press, 1966).

12. Marguerite Beede Howe, *The Art of the Self in D. H. Lawrence* (Athens: Ohio Uni-versity Press, 1977), 1.

13. See Joseph Sandler, "The Concept of the Representational World," The *Psychoan-alytic Study of the Child* 17 (1962): 128–45.

14. Margaret Storch, *Sons and Adversaries: Women in William Blake and D. H. Lawrence* (Knoxville: University of Tennessee Press, 1991), esp. chap. 3:45–64; chap. 5:97–130; and chap. 7:157–78.

15. John Turner, "The Capacity to Be Alone and Its Failure in D. H. Lawrence's 'The Man Who Loved Islands,'" *D. H. Lawrence Review* 16, no. 3 (fall 1983): 259–89; and "The Perversion of Play in D. H. Lawrence's 'The Rocking-Horse Winner,'" *D. H. Lawrence Review* 15, no. 3 (fall 1982): 249–70.

16. David Holbrook, "The Fiery Hill—*Lady Chatterley's Lover,*" *The Quest for Love* (University: University of Alabama Press, 1965), 192–333. See also Holbrook, *Where D. H. Lawrence Was Wrong about Women* (Lewisburg, Pa.: Bucknell University Press, 1992).

17. Judith Ruderman, *D. H. Lawrence and the Devouring Mother: The Search for a Patri-archal Ideal of Leadership* (Durham, N.C.: Duke University Press, 1984), 8–9.

18. Daniel Dervin, *A "Strange Sapience": The Creative Imagination of D. H. Lawrence* (Amherst: University of Massachusetts Press, 1984); and "Michael Balint's Contribution to the Psychoanalysis of Literature," *Psychoanalytic Review* (1979–1980).

19. Kenneth Bragan, "Lawrence and Self Psychology." *Australian and New Zealand Journal of Psychiatry* 20, no. 1 (1986): 56–62.

20. Jeffrey Berman, "Echoes of Rejection in *Sons and Lovers,*" *Narcissism and the Novel* (New York: New York University Press, 1990); and Marshall W. Alcorn Jr., *Narcissism and the Literary Libido: Rhetoric, Text and Subjectivity* (New York: New York University Press, 1993).

21. "Healing," *The Complete Poems of D. H. Lawrence,* ed. Vivian de Sola Pinto and F. Warren Roberts (New York: Viking Press, Compass Books, 1971), 620, line 3.

22. Eugene Goodheart, *Desire and Its Discontents* (New York: Columbia University Press, 1992), 148.

23. Ben Stoltzfus, "D. H. Lawrence: *The Escaped Cock,*" *Lacan and Literature: Purloined Pretexts* (Albany: State University of New York Press, 1996), 2–3.

24. Earl G. Ingersoll, *D. H. Lawrence, Desire, and Narrative* (Gainesville: University Press of Florida, 2001).

25. Barbara Ann Schapiro, "'The Dread and Repulsiveness of the Wild': D. H. Lawrence and Shame," *Scenes of Shame: Psychoanalysis, Shame, and Writing,* ed. Joseph Adamson and Hilary Clark (Albany: State University of New York Press, 1999), 164–65n. 3.

26. Barbara Ann Schapiro, *D. H. Lawrence and the Paradoxes of Psychic Life* (Albany: State University of New York Press, 1999).

Notes to Chapter 2

1. Heinz Kohut, "The Two Analyses of Mr. Z," *International Journal of Psychoanaly-sis* 60 (1979): 3.

2. References to *Sons and Lovers* are cited in the text of this chapter in the version edited by Edward Garnett for the first edition (1913), reprinted with only minor corrections of a few misprints, as edited by Keith Sagar (1981), rather than in the expanded text, reinstating Garnett's editorial excisions, as edited by Helen Baron and Carl Baron for the Cambridge University Press edition (1992). It was, of course, the first edition text that Kuttner reviewed and that Schorer, Weiss, and other critics discussed here associated, although Schorer also had access to the manuscript. The extracts I cite are substantially the same in both texts, and the psychoanalytic meaning of material is not essentially altered by the elaboration of traditionally "realistic" details. It should also be noted that despite his reservations, Lawrence reviewed and approved Edward Garnett's "pruning" of the manuscript (*Letters* 1:517) and dedicated the novel to Garnett (*Letters* 1:477). See *The Letters of D. H. Lawrence*, vol. I: *September 1901–May 1913*, ed. James T. Boulton (Cambridge: Cambridge University Press, 1979).

3. See Edward Glover, "Eder as Psychoanalyst," *David Eder: Memoirs of a Modern Pioneer*, ed. J. B. Hobman (London: Victor Gollancz Ltd., 1945): 89–116.

4. Litvinov, in Nehls, *Composite Biography* 1:215.

5. See Otto Gross and Frieda Weekley, *The Otto Gross-Frieda Weekley Correspondence*, transcribed, translated, and annotated, by John Turner, with Cornelia Rumpf-Worthen and Ruth Jenkins. Published as a special issue of *D. H. Lawrence Review* 22, no. 2 (summer 1990): 137–227, the letters are printed both in English translation and in the original German. Turner's introduction, pp. 137–63, is indispensable. See also Sigmund Freud and C. G. Jung, *The Freud/Jung Letters: The Correspondence between Sigmund Freud and C. G. Jung*, ed. William McGuire, trans. Ralph Manheim and R. F. C. Hull (Princeton, N.J.: Princeton University Press, 1974), 141, 151, 152, 155–57. Freud, who recognized Gross's pathology, referred him for analytic treatment to Jung, who ultimately diagnosed his illness as *dementia praecox*. Ernest Jones, for whom Gross was his first instructor in the technique of psychoanalysis, concurs with that diagnosis. See Jones, *Sigmund Freud: Life and Work* (London: Hogarth Press, 1974), 2:33. For a contemporaneous monograph on this illness as it was understood at the time, see Adolf Meyer, Smith Ely Jelliffe, and August Hoch, *Dementia Praecox: A Monograph* (Boston: Richard G. Badger, 1911).

6. *Frieda Lawrence: The Memoirs and Correspondence*, ed. E. W. Tedlock Jr. (New York: Alfred A. Knopf, 1964), 171.

7. Ernest Jones founded the London Psycho-Analytical Society on 30 October 1913, with himself as president, Douglas Bryan as vice president, and David Eder as secretary. (*The Complete Correspondence of Sigmund Freud and Ernest Jones, 1908–1939*, p. 233.) Freud recognized Eder as "the first, and for a time the only," practitioner of psychoanalysis in England ("Foreword" to Hobman, p. [9]). After differences developed between Eder and Jones over Eder's expression of Jungian ideas, Jones wrote to Freud (27 January 1919) to ask his views about the "urgent . . . question of constituting a new society (purged of Eder, etc.)" (pp. 331–32). Freud replied (18 February 1919): "Your intention to purge the London society of the jungish members is excellent" (p. 335). The London Psycho-Analytical Society was dissolved and reconstituted accordingly. See also John Turner, "David Eder: Between Freud and Jung," *D. H. Lawrence Review* 27, nos. 2–3 (1997–1998): 289–309.

8. Kuttner, "*Sons and Lovers*: A Freudian Appreciation," 295–317.

9. Weiss, *Oedipus in Nottingham*.

10. *The Collected Letters of Jessie Chambers*, edited and with an introduction by George J. Zytaruk, *D. H. Lawrence Review* 12, nos. 1–2 (spring-summer 1979): 27 of the special issue of the Chambers letters, iii–xxxiii, 1–238.

11. Jessie Chambers [pseud. E. T.] (1935), *D. H. Lawrence: A Personal Record* (New York: Knight Publications, 1936), 202.

12. Frieda Lawrence (1934), *"Not I, But the Wind"* (Carbondale: Southern Illinois University Press, 1974), 56.

13. See Harry T. Moore, *The Priest of Love: A Life of D. H. Lawrence,* rev. ed. (New York: Farrar, Straus, and Giroux, 1974), 52; and Father Martin Jarrett-Kerr [pseud. Father William Tiverton], *D. H. Lawrence and Human Existence* (London: Rockliff, 1951), 25.

14. Mark Schorer, "Technique as Discovery," *Hudson Review* 1 (spring 1948), rpt. in Mark Schorer, *The World We Imagine: Selected Essays,* 3–23 (New York: Farrar, Straus, and Giroux, 1968), 11–12.

15. Alfred Booth Kuttner, "Report and Letter on 'The Wedding Ring'" (10 November 1914) in appendix III in D. H. Lawrence, *The Rainbow,* ed. Mark Kinkead-Weekes (Cambridge: Cambridge University Press, 1989), 483–85.

16. Pine, "The Four Psychologies of Psychoanalysis," 571–96. Pine's proposed questions concern the relative stability of "a sense of undifferentiated self-boundaries," the presence of "fantasies of merger, enactments of merger, or panics regarding loss of boundaries," the extent of "derealization or depersonalization" or of "discontinuity of the self-experience," the extent to which the individual experiences "himself or herself as the center of action in his or her own life," and "the ongoing sense of self-value, of esteem." Finally, he asks, "What pathological efforts to right imbalances in that subjective state of self are present—grandiosity, denial, flights into activity, disdain of others?" (582)

17. Ruderman, *D. H. Lawrence and the Devouring Mother,* 174–77.

18. Lawrence met Rachel Annand Taylor, a Scottish poet nine years older than himself, at a poets' supper party at Ernest Rhys's home in Hampstead in the spring of 1910, while Lawrence was teaching in Croydon. According to Majl Ewing, "Her cultural sophistication, her Pre-Raphaelite beauty, and her romantic poetry so strongly impressed Lawrence that when, in the autumn, he was asked to give a paper on a living poet before a Croydon literary group, he chose her as his subject." See Majl Ewing, "Foreword" to D. H. Lawrence, *Eight Letters by D. H. Lawrence to Rachel Annand Taylor,* [p. 1]. See also Lawrence's lecture "Rachel Annand Taylor." For further information on Rachel Annand Taylor, see also Nehls, *Composite Biography* 1:525.

19. Heinz Kohut, *How Does Analysis Cure?* ed. Arnold Goldberg with Paul Stepansky (Chicago: University of Chicago Press, 1984), 16–19.

20. Margaret S. Mahler, Fred Pine, and Anni Bergman, *The Psychological Birth of the Human Infant: Symbiosis and Individuation* (New York: Basic Books, 1975), 63.

21. Jessica Benjamin, "The Alienation of Desire: Women's Masochism and Ideal Love," *Psychoanalysis and Women,* ed. Judith L. Alpert (Hillsdale, N.J.: Analytic Press, 1986), 121–24.

22. In a brief discussion of an adolescent male patient, Peter Blos says: "only after the castration anxiety in relation to the archaic mother was recognized, could the phallic modality assert itself and counteract the passive submissive trend" (Blos, "The Second Individuation Process of Adolescence," *The Psychoanalytic Study of the Child* 22 [1967]: 165).

23. Heinz Kohut, *Restoration of the Self* (Madison, Conn.: International Universities Press, 1977, rpt. 1988), 217.

24. Geoffrey Cocks, introduction to *The Curve of Life: Correspondence of Heinz Kohut, 1923–1981,* ed. Geoffrey Cocks (Chicago: University of Chicago Press, 1992), 4–5.

25. Quoted in John Worthen, *D. H. Lawrence, The Early Years, 1985–1912* (Cambridge: Cambridge University Press, 1991), Appendix IV, 501.

Notes to Chapter 3

1. D. W. Winnicott, qtd. in Worthen, *D. H. Lawrence: The Early Years,* 76.
2. Nehls, *Composite Biography* 1:17.
3. Heinz Kohut, *The Analysis of the Self* (New York: International Universities Press, 1971, rpt. 1987), 244.
4. W. Ronald D. Fairbairn, *An Object-Relations Theory of the Personality* (New York: Basic Books, 1954), 41.
5. Lionel Ovesey, *Homosexuality and Pseudohomosexuality* (New York: Science House, 1969), 28.
6. Schapiro, "'The Dread and Repulsiveness of the Wild,'" 150–51.

Notes to Chapter 4

1. All references to *Women in Love* are to the Cambridge University Press edition, ed. David Farmer, Lindeth Vasey, and John Worthen, 1987.
2. Opposing viewpoints on this critical issue are presented by Michael Squires, "Dickens, Lawrence, and the English Novel," *The Challenge of D. H. Lawrence,* ed. Michael Squires and Keith Cushman (Madison: University of Wisconsin Press, 1990), 42–59; and George Donaldson, "'Men in Love'? D. H. Lawrence, Rupert Birkin, and Gerald Crich," *D. H. Lawrence: Centenary Essays,* ed. Mara Kalnins (Bristol, U.K.: Bristol Classical Press, 1986), 41–67. Squires places Birkin in a novelistic tradition of seducers and suggests that in earlier works his dalliance would have been with a woman (54).
3. Opposing views on the place and significance of the canceled "Prologue" are presented by Jeffrey Meyers, *Homosexuality and Literature: 1880–1930* (Montreal: McGill-Queen's University Press, 1977), 43; and Charles L. Ross, "Homoerotic Feeling in *Women in Love:* Lawrence's 'struggle for verbal consciousness' in the Manuscripts," *D. H. Lawrence: The Man Who Lived,* ed. Robert B. Partlow Jr. and Harry T. Moore (Carbondale: Southern Illinois University Press, 1980), 181. For Meyers, the "Prologue" clarifies such aspects of the novel as Birkin's destructive relationship with Hermione, his intimacy with Crich, and his repressed homosexual desires. For Ross, a study of the manuscripts clarifies Lawrence's artistic intentions in canceling the "Prologue" and leaving the *Blutbrüderschaft* theme submerged until chapter 16, "Man to Man."
4. Kohut, *Restoration of the Self,* 131.
5. *Sons and Lovers,* though autobiographical in fictional terms, cannot be taken literally at face value. Paul is more independent, less intellectual and educated, and more conventional and "ordinary" than Lawrence See Worthen, *D. H. Lawrence: The Early Years,* 52, 181, 317–18.
6. *The Standard Edition of the Complete Psychological Works of Sigmund Freud,* 24 vols., ed. and trans. James Strachey et al., (London: Hogarth Press and the Institute of Psycho-Analysis, 1962, rpt. 1975). Freud's work in the Standard Edition is cited throughout the text as *SE* followed by volume and page numbers.
7. Paul Delany, *D. H. Lawrence's Nightmare: The Writer and His Circle in the Years of the Great War* (New York: Basic Books, 1978), 227.
8. Lawrence's merger with his mother and hatred of his father are described with remarkable lucidity in his letter to Rachel Annand Taylor of 3 December 1910 (*Letters* 1:189–91).
9. See, for example, Meyers, *Homosexuality and Literature,* 130–61; and a contrasting

view by Delany, *D. H. Lawrence's Nightmare*, 222–26, 309–15. John Worthen (1991), in a biographical discussion of Lawrence's homoeroticism, concludes that Lawrence's experiencing homoerotic feelings and expressing them in his work is not the same as being a homosexual. I have no quarrel with this commonsense view, but I think that a clearer understanding of the psychological issues involved leads to a conclusion of greater complexity than the idea that Lawrence's occasional physical closeness with men was "uncomplicatedly happy" and his attractions to their beauty unthreatening (158). The text of the "Prologue" provides compelling evidence of the "despair," "deep misery," and "suffering" that these homoerotic feelings evoked in Birkin and the "long torture of struggle" against them (502–5). Although Birkin cannot be equated directly with Lawrence, one nonartistic reason for canceling the "Prologue" may have been that the description of Birkin's homoerotic attractions came too close for comfort to the author's real-life experience.

10. Compton Mackenzie, *My Life and Times, Octave Five: 1915–1923* (London: Chatto and Windus, 1966), 168.

11. Derek Britton, *Lady Chatterley: The Making of the Novel* (London: Unwin Hyman, 1988), 52.

12. C. J. Stevens, *Lawrence at Tregerthen* (Troy, N.Y.: Whitson, 1988), 32–33.

13. For Gross's early associations with psychoanalysis, see Freud's and Jung's correspondence about the brilliant but erratic young physician whom Freud referred to Jung for treatment and whose illness Jung ultimately diagnosed as *dementia praecox* (Freud and Jung, *The Freud/Jung Letters*, 141, 151, 152, 155–57).

14. Jeffrey Meyers, *D. H. Lawrence: A Biography* (New York: Alfred A. Knopf, 1990), 91.

15. John Middleton Murry, *Son of Woman: The Story of D. H. Lawrence* (London: Jonathan Cape, 1931), 119–21.

16. Frieda Lawrence, *Frieda Lawrence and Her Circle: Letters from, to and about Frieda Lawrence,* eds. H. T. Moore and D. B. Montague (Hamden, Conn.: Archon Books, 1981), 93.

17. F. Lawrence, *Frieda Lawrence: The Memoirs and Correspondence,* 360.

18. Birkin's judgmental view of himself, "It is the ultimate mark of my own deficiency, that I feel like this" (505), is analogous to the analytic interpretation that such feelings are an attempt to fill a structural deficit. Lawrence's early childhood developmental context is well known. The emotional situation is set forth clearly in Lawrence's letter to Rachel Annand Taylor of 3 December 1910 (*Letters* 1:189–91). See also G. H. Neville, *A Memoir of D. H. Lawrence (The Betrayal),* ed. Carl Baron (Cambridge: Cambridge University Press, 1981), 35–70; and memoirs collected in Nehls, *Composite Biography* 1:5–41. For biographical accounts with varying emphases, see those in Harry T. Moore (1954), *The Priest of Love: A Life of D. H. Lawrence,* rev. ed. (New York: Farrar, Straus, and Giroux, 1974), 7–31; Emile Delavenay, *D. H. Lawrence: The Man and His Work, The Formative Years, 1885–1919,* trans. Katharine M. Delavenay (Carbondale: Southern Illinois University Press, 1972), 3–14; and Worthen, *D. H. Lawrence: The Early Years,* 57–79.

19. Kohut, *Analysis of the Self,* 147.

20. Donaldson, "'Men in Love'?" 41–67; and Squires, "Dickens, Lawrence, and the English Novel," 42–59.

21. Meyers, *Homosexuality and Literature,* reads Birkin's homoerotic attractions in the "Prologue" as "homosexual affairs with working men" (143) and thinks that "the homosexuality in 'Gladiatorial' *is* overt" (148). The "Prologue," however, states clearly that Birkin's "reserve, which was as strong as a chain of iron in him, kept him from any demonstration" (502). "For he could never acquiesce to his own feelings, to his own passion" (504).

22. William B. Ober, "Lady Chatterley's What?" *Boswell's Clap and Other Essays: Medical Analyses of Literary Men's Afflictions* (Carbondale: Southern Illinois University Press, 1979), 109.

23. Ovesey, *Homosexuality and Pseudohomosexuality,* 31.

24. George Donaldson does question this idea and denies that "information provided by the 'Prologue' . . . can be applied directly to *Women in Love.*" See Donaldson, "'Men in Love'?" 60.

25. Ruderman, *D. H. Lawrence and the Devouring Mother,* 148.

26. Fairbairn, *An Object-Relations Theory,* 40.

27. W. Ronald D. Fairbairn, "A Revised Psychopathology of the Psychoses and Psychoneuroses," *International Journal of Psycho-Analysis* 22 (1941): Parts 3–4:262; also in *An Object Relations Theory,* 48.

28. Ernest Wolf, *Treating the Self: Elements of Clinical Self Psychology* (New York: Guilford Press, 1988), 186.

29. H. A. Bacal and K. M. Newman, *Theories of Object Relations: Bridges to Self Psychology* (New York: Columbia University Press, 1990), 249.

Notes to Chapter 5

1. Jacob A. Arlow, "Unconscious Fantasy," *Psychoanalysis: The Major Concepts,* 155–56.

2. Phyllis Tyson and Robert L. Tyson, *Psychoanalytic Theories of Development: An Integration* (New Haven, Conn.: Yale University Press, 1990), 282–83.

3. George H. Wiedeman, "Sexuality," *Psychoanalysis: The Major Concepts,* 337.

4. The psychoanalytic principles employed here are discussed more extensively in Burness E. Moore, "Narcissism," *Psychoanalysis: The Major Concepts,* 29–51.

5. Jay R. Greenberg and Stephen A. Mitchell, *Object Relations in Psychoanalytic Theory* (Cambridge, Mass.: Harvard University Press, 1983), 354–65.

6. Schapiro, *D. H. Lawrence and the Paradoxes of Psychic Life,* 50–51.

7. Kohut, *Restoration of the Self,* 56–58.

8. Kohut, *How Does Analysis Cure?* 197.

9. Neville, *Memoir,* 78–79. For further discussion of Neville's posing as a model for Lawrence, possibly for the Greiffenhagen copy and for life studies, see Baron's appendix B: "Lawrence, Neville and Greiffenhagen's 'Idyll'," in Neville, *Memoir,* 172–80; and Worthen, *D. H. Lawrence: The Early Years,* 552.

10. G. Atwood and R. Stolorow, qtd. in Stephen A. Mitchell, *Relational Concepts in Psychoanalysis: An Integration* (Cambridge, Mass.: Harvard University Press, 1988), 205.

11. Ruderman, *D. H. Lawrence and the Devouring Mother,* 174, 175.

Notes to Chapter 6

1. S. Freud, *Standard Edition,* 11:179–90.

2. Harry T. Moore, in his introduction to D. H. Lawrence, *Sex, Literature, and Censorship,* ed. Harry T. Moore (New York: Twayne Publishers, 1953), 9–32, briefly surveys censorship of Lawrence's work to 1953. For further details of the censorship of the novels I have cited, see the following editions of these Lawrence works: *The White Peacock,* ed. Andrew Robertson (Cambridge: Cambridge University Press, 1983), xxxiv–xxxv; *The Rainbow,* xlv–li; *Women in Love,* ed. Farmer et al., xxxix–lxi; and *Lady Chatterley's Lover, A Propos of "Lady Chatterley's Lover,"* ed. Michael Squires (Cambridge: Cambridge University

Press, 1993), xxviii–xl. Detailed accounts of the legal proceedings pursuant to charges of obscenity against *Lady Chatterley's Lover* are given, for the American trial, by the plaintiffs' attorney, Charles Rembar, in *The End of Obscenity: The Trial of "Lady Chatterley's Lover," "Tropic of Cancer," and "Fanny Hill"* (New York: Random House, 1968), 15–160; and for transcripts of the British trial, in H. Montgomery Hyde, ed., *The "Lady Chatterley's Lover" Trial (Regina v. Penguin Books Limited)* (London: Bodley Head, 1990).

3. The transcript of "Parliamentary Debates on Seizure of *Pansies* MSS" (28 February 1929) is reprinted in Nehls, *Composite Biography* 3:308–12. An account by Philip Trotter (husband of Dorothy Warren) of the seizure of Lawrence's paintings is published in Nehls, *Composite Biography* 3:342–57, 360, 362–75, 380–89, 399–400.

4. Neville, *Memoir,* 76.

5. D. H. Lawrence, "None of That!" in *The Woman Who Rode Away and Other Stories,* ed. Dieter Mehl and Christa Jansohn (Cambridge: Cambridge University Press, 1995), 720–21.

6. Sandra Eagleton, "One Feminist's Approach to Teaching D. H. Lawrence," *D. H. Lawrence Review* 19 (fall 1987): 326.

7. D. H. Lawrence, "The Woman Who Rode Away," in *The Woman Who Rode Away and Other Stories,* ed. Mehl and Jansohn, 61–62.

8. See Marian E. Dunn and Jan E. Trost, "Male Multiple Orgasms: A Descriptive Study," *Archives of Sexual Behavior* 18 (October 1989): 377–87.

9. William H. Masters and Virginia E. Johnson, *Human Sexual Response* (Boston: Little Brown, 1966), 213–14.

10. Beverly Whipple, Brent R. Myers, and Barry Komisaruk, "Male Multiple Ejaculatory Orgasms: A Case Study," *Journal of Sex Education and Therapy* 23, no. 2 (1998): 157–74.

11. Quoted in E. Delavenay, *D. H. Lawrence: The Man and His Work,* 155.

12. While it is always advisable to be cautious in drawing biographical inferences from works of fiction, the first two volumes of The Cambridge Biography of D. H. Lawrence offer a study in contrast on the biographical relevance of *Mr. Noon.* John Worthen, in *D. H. Lawrence: The Early Years 1885–1912,* writes: "*Mr. Noon* is a remarkable guide to much that happened to DHL and Frieda in 1912," and declares that "a biography of DHL which did not draw from it would be absurd." He adds, however, that "only occasionally shall I rely on it to supply something not confirmed by other sources: and I shall make very clear when I am using it as a source" (382 n) On the other hand, Mark Kinkead-Weekes, in *D. H. Lawrence: Triumph to Exile 1912–1922* (Cambridge: Cambridge University Press, 1996), warns against using "the poems in *Look! We Have Come Through!* (1917), let alone *Mr. Noon* (1920), as reliable biographical evidence" (18–19).

13. D. H. Lawrence, *Mr. Noon,* ed. Lindeth Vasey (Cambridge: Cambridge University Press, 1984), 145–46. I am indebted to Earl Ingersoll (personal communication, 1985) for pointing out that in the second part of *Mr. Noon,* Lawrence seems to confirm Alice Dax's assessment of his sexual capacity as a young man.

14. Keith Sagar, *D. H. Lawrence: A Calendar of His Works, with a Checklist of the Manuscripts of D. H. Lawrence* by Lindeth Vasey (Austin: University of Texas Press, 1979), 119.

15. D. H. Lawrence, *Complete Poems, 382.*

16. D. H. Lawrence, *The Plumed Serpent,* ed. L. D. Clark (Cambridge: Cambridge University Press, 1987), 422.

17. D. H. Lawrence, *Sons and Lovers,* eds. Helen Baron and Carl E. Baron (Cambridge: Cambridge University Press, 1992), 333.

18. D. H. Lawrence, *Lady Chatterley's Lover,* 53–55 and 172.

19. See Eugene Monick, *Phallos: Sacred Image of the Masculine* (Toronto, Canada: Inner City Books, 1987). See also two earlier studies: Richard Payne Knight, *A Discourse on the Worship of Priapus* (1786), and Thomas Wright, *The Worship of the Generative Powers during the Middle Ages of Western Europe* (1866), reprinted respectively as vols. 1 and 2 of *Sexual Symbolism: A History of Phallic Worship,* with original plates and with an introduction by Ashley Montagu (New York: Julian Press, 1957).

20. C. G. Jung, *Memories, Dreams, Reflections,* ed. Aniela Jaffé, trans. Richard and Clara Winston (New York: Pantheon Books, 1963), 12–13.

21. D. H. Lawrence, *John Thomas and Lady Jane* (New York: Viking Press, 1972), 232.

22. D. H. Lawrence, *The Letters of D. H. Lawrence,* vol. 5, ed. James T. Boulton and Lindeth Vasey (Cambridge: Cambridge University Press, 1989), 648.

23. Arnold M. Cooper, "On Metapsychology and Termination," in *On Freud's "Analysis Terminable and Interminable",* ed. Joseph Sandler (New Haven, Conn.: Yale University Press, 1991), 119.

24. D. H. Lawrence, "The Border-Line," in *The Woman Who Rode Away and Other Stories* (London: Martin Secker, 1928, rpt. 1930), 131, 133. This first edition text is reprinted in *The Complete Short Stories of D. H. Lawrence,* (New York: Viking Press, Compass Books, 1961), 3:603. In the Cambridge Edition, this portion of the first edition text is reproduced only in the textual apparatus. See *The Woman Who Rode Away and Other Stories,* eds. Mehl and Jansohn, 448.

25. Wiedeman, "Sexuality," 339.

26. Morris A. Sklansky, "The Pubescent Years: Eleven to Fourteen," in *Latency, Adolescence, and Youth,* vol. 2 of *The Course of Life: Psychoanalytic Contributions Toward Understanding Personality Development,* ed. S. J. Greenspan and G. H. Pollock (Adelphi, Md.: National Institute of Mental Health, 1980), 268.

27. Ovesey, *Homosexuality and Pseudohomosexuality,* 42–43.

28. Lawrence, "Sun," in *The Woman Who Rode Away and Other Stories,* eds. Mehl and Jansohn, 30.

29. Michael L. Ross, "Lawrence's Second 'Sun'," *D. H. Lawrence Review* 8, no. 1 (spring 1975): 15.

30. See Phyllis Greenacre, "Penis Awe and Its Relation to Penis Envy," *Drives, Affects, Behavior,* ed. R. M. Loewenstein (New York: International Universities Press, 1953), 176–90.

31. *My Secret Life* (New York: Grove Press, 1966), vol. 10, 2028.

32. Ibid., vol. 10, 2145. For an informed study of this erotic memoir, see Steven Marcus, *The Other Victorians: A Study of Sexuality and Pornography in Mid-Nineteenth-Century England* (New York: Basic Books, 1964, rpt. 1966), 77–196.

33. W. A. Schonfeld and G. W. Beebe, "Normal Growth and Variation in the Male Genitalia from Birth to Maturity," *Journal of Urology* 48 (1942): 759–77.

34. See Alfred C. Kinsey, Wardell B. Pomeroy, and Clyde E. Martin, *Sexual Behavior in the Human Male* (Philadelphia: W. B. Saunders, 1948).

35. See also the Kinsey survey of penis sizes, based on the researchers' accurate measurements of 3,500 college males. Available on the Internet as "Penis Size Survey Results."

36. Masters and Johnson, *Human Sexual Response,* 191–92.

37. Qtd. in Z. Wanderer and D. Radell. *How Big is Big? The Book of Sexual Measurements* (New York: Bell, 1982).

38. Hunter Wessells, Tom F. Lue, and Jack W. McAninch, "Penile Length in the Flaccid and Erect States: Guidelines for Penile Augmentation," *Journal of Urology* 156, no. 3 (September 1996): 995–97.

39. Joseph Sparling, "Penile Erections: Shape, Angle, and Length," *Journal of Sex and Marital Therapy* 23, no. 3 (fall 1997): 195–207, esp. 195, 204.

40. Joseph Sparling, "Erection Research," an Internet site based on the foregoing article, with additional discussion. See also his "Erection Photos" in a linked website featuring "galleries" of the black and white research photographs of the subjects employed in his study of shape, angle, and length of erections. In addition, this site includes full body portraits, outdoor photos, and studies of seniors. These are informative, explicit, nonpornographic erection and full body nude photographs of men between the ages of eighteen and seventy-six. http://www.erectionphotos.com.

41. Harold Charles Winter, "An Examination of the Relationships between Penis Size and Body Image, Genital Image, and Perception of Sexual Competence in the Male," *Dissertation Abstracts International,* 50, no. 5A (1989): 1225.

42. Monick, *Phallos,* 9.

43. See also David Ellis, "D. H. Lawrence and the Female Body," *Essays in Criticism* 46, no. 2 (April 1996): 136–52. Ellis's article, like mine, links the castration anxiety in response to female pubic hair in *John Thomas and Lady Jane* to Lawrence's idealized conception of the female body.

44. D. .H. Lawrence, *John Thomas and Lady Jane,* 232.

45. Burness E. Moore and Bernard D. Fine, eds., *Psychoanalytic Terms and Concepts* (New Haven, Conn.: The American Psychoanalytic Association and Yale University Press, 1990), 144.

46. Marcia Ian, *Remembering the Phallic Mother: Psychoanalysis, Modernism and the Fetish* (Ithaca, N.Y.: Cornell University Press, 1993), 7.

47. D. H. Lawrence, *The Rainbow,* 444–45.

48. D. H. Lawrence, "None of That!" 227–28.

49. Neville, *Memoir,* 158.

50. Sándor Ferenczi, "Psychoanalysis of Sexual Habits" (1925), in *The Theory and Technique of Psychoanalysis* (New York: Basic Books, 1926, rpt. 1960), 279.

51. Ruth and Edward Brecher, eds., *An Analysis of "Human Sexual Response"* (New York: Signet Books, 1966), 83.

52. Robert Scholes, "Uncoding Mama: The Female Body as Text," *Semiotics and Interpretation* (New Haven, Conn.: Yale University Press, 1982), 140.

53. Mark Spilka, "Lawrence and the Clitoris," in *The Challenge of D. H. Lawrence,* eds. Michael Squires and Keith Cushman (Madison: University of Wisconsin Press, 1990), 184.

54. H. M. Daleski, "Aphrodite of the Foam and *The Ladybird* Tales," *Unities: Studies in the English Novel* (Athens: University of Georgia Press, 1985), 211.

55. James H. Jones, *Alfred C. Kinsey: A Public/Private Life* (New York: W. W. Norton, 1997), 694–95.

56. Alfred C. Kinsey, *Sexual Behavior in the Human Female* (Philadelphia: W. B. Saunders Co.), 582.

57. Virginia L. Clower, "Significance of Masturbation in Female Sexual Development and Function," in *Masturbation: From Infancy to Senescence,* eds. Irwin M. Marcus and John J. Francis (New York: International Universities Press, 1975), 138.

58. Virginia L. Clower, in *Adult Masturbation: Clinical Perspectives* (American Psychoanalytic Association, 1979), audiotape, cassette II, side 3.

59. Ibid.

60. Moore and Fine, "Masturbation," *Psychoanalytic Terms and Concepts,* 117.

61. Mackenzie, *My Life and Times, Octave Five,* 167–68.

62. Helen Singer Kaplan, *The New Sex Therapy: Active Treatment of Sexual Dysfunctions* (New York: Brunner/Mazel Publication in cooperation with Quadrangle/*The New York Times,* 1974), 124. Dr. Kaplan was professor of psychiatry at Cornell University College of Medicine and head of the Sex Therapy and Education Program at the Payne Whitney Clinic of New York Hospital.

63. Sherman J. Silber, *The Male: From Infancy to Old Age* (New York: Charles Scribner's Sons, 1981), 76.

64. See Bernie Zilbergeld, *Male Sexuality: A Guide to Sexual Fulfillment* (Boston: Little Brown, 1978), 170–71.

Notes to Chapter 7

1. Taylor Stoehr, "'Mentalized Sex' in D. H. Lawrence," *Novel: A Forum on Fiction* 8 (1975), 111.

2. D. H. Lawrence, *Fantasia of the Unconscious,* in *Psychoanalysis and the Unconscious* and *Fantasia of the Unconscious* (New York: Viking Press, Compass Books, 1960), 146.

3. Paul Roazen, *Brother Animal: The Story of Freud and Tausk* (New York: Alfred A. Knopf, 1969), 41.

4. Robert S. S. Baden-Powell, qtd. in Robert H. MacDonald, "The Frightful Consequences of Onanism: Notes on the History of a Delusion," *Journal of the History of Ideas* 28 (1967): 431n. 35.

5. Mary Douglas, qtd. in Murray S. Davis, *Smut: Erotic Reality/Obscene Ideology* (Chicago: University of Chicago Press, 1983), 123.

6. D. H. Lawrence, "'Man is essentially a soul . . . ,'" in *Reflections on the Death of a Porcupine and Other Essays,* ed. Michael Herbert (Cambridge: Cambridge University Press, 1988), 389.

7. Thomas Aquinas, qtd. in Davis, *Smut,* 168.

8. D. H. Lawrence, *Study of Thomas Hardy and Other Essays,* ed. Bruce Steele. Cambridge: Cambridge University Press, 1985), 53.

9. D. H. Lawrence, *Lady Chatterley's Lover,* 279.

10. D. H. Lawrence, "Pornography and Obscenity," in *Phoenix: The Posthumous Papers of D. H. Lawrence* (1936), ed. Edward D. McDonald (New York: Viking Press, 1968), 178, 179.

11. Sigmund Freud, *The Complete Letters of Sigmund Freud to Wilhelm Fliess, 1887 to 1904,* trans. and ed. Jeffrey Moussaieff Masson (Cambridge, Mass.: Harvard University Press, 1985), 287.

12. S. Freud, *Standard Edition,* 21:193.

13. The controversy between Freud and Stekel is discussed by Leendert F. Groenendijk, in "Masturbation and Neurasthenia: Freud and Stekel in Debate on the Harmful Effects of Autoerotism," *Journal of Psychology and Human Sexuality* 9, no. 1 (1997): 71–94.

14. These discussions were originally published as *Die Onanie: Vierzehn Betrage zu einer Diskussion der "Wiener Psychoanalytischen Vereinigung,"* with contributions by B. Dattner, Paul Federn, Sándor Ferenczi, Sigmund Freud, Josef K. Friedjung, Edward Hitschmann, Otto Rank, Rudolf Reitler, Gaston Rosenstein, Hanns Sachs, J[=Isador] [Isaak] Sadger, Maximilian Steiner, Wilhelm Stekel, and Viktor Tausk (Wiesbaden: J. F. Bergmann, 1912). Although the volume has not been published in an English language edition, several of the contributions have been published in English translation.

15. Sándor Ferenczi, "On Onanism," 1912, in *The Selected Papers of Sándor Ferenczi,*

M.D., vol. I: *Sex in Psychoanalysis,* trans. Ernest Jones (New York: Basic Books, 1950), 188–89.

16. As Marcio de F. Giovannetti, in "The Scene and Its Reverse: Considerations on a Chain of Associations in Freud," in *On Freud's "A Child Is Being Beaten,"* ed. Ethel Spector Person (New Haven, Conn.: Yale University Press, 1997), comments: "The field of masturbation . . . presupposes not only the possession but also the creation of the object by the ego," so that "sexual enjoyment of the object and its possession are confused, . . . there being no clear distinction between ego and object, between I and the outside world, between I and the other, between father and mother" (106).

17. D. H. Lawrence, "Introduction to These Paintings," in *Phoenix: The Posthumous Papers of D. H. Lawrence,* 1936, ed. Edward D. McDonald (New York: Viking Press, 1968), 573–74.

18. Ober, "Lady Chatterley's What?" 108.

19. Moses Laufer, "The Central Masturbation Fantasy, the Final Sexual Organization, and Adolescence," *The Psychoanalytic Study of the Child* 31 (1976): 300–301.

20. D. H. Lawrence, "The State of Funk," *Phoenix II: Uncollected, Unpublished, and Other Prose Works by D. H. Lawrence,* eds. Warren Roberts and Harry T. Moore (New York: Viking Press, 1968), 568.

21. Keith M. Sagar, *D. H. Lawrence: A Calendar of His Works, with A Checklist of the Manuscripts of D. H. Lawrence* by Lindeth Vasey (Austin: University of Texas Press, 1979), approximates the date of the poem as 1905–1906 (3). An early manuscript version entitled "The Body Awake" survives in MS. E317 at the University of Nottingham. "Virgin Youth," as the revised version in MS. E320.2 is called, was published as a poem of twenty-two lines in *Amores* (1916) (see *Complete Poems,* 896). A later version, prepared for *The Collected Poems of D. H. Lawrence* (1928, 18–20), is expanded to sixty-two lines (see *Complete Poems,* 38–40). These three versions are printed together in Gail Porter Mandell, *The Phoenix Paradox: A Study of Renewal through Change in the "Collected Poems" and "Last Poems" of D. H. Lawrence* (Carbondale: Southern Illinois University Press, 1984), appendix F, 181–83.

22. Victor Tausk, "On Masturbation," trans. William G. Niederland, *The Psychoanalytic Study of the Child* 6 (1951): 75.

23. Holly A. Laird, *Self and Sequence: The Poetry of D. H. Lawrence* (Charlottesville: University Press of Virginia, 1988), 168.

24. Ernest Jones, "Some Problems of Adolescence," 1922, *Papers on Psycho-Analysis,* 5th ed. (London: Baillière, 1948), 398–99.

25. Worthen, *D. H. Lawrence: The Early Years,* 158.

26. Kohut, *Restoration of the Self,* 127–28.

27. Medical opinion on the subject has markedly changed since Lawrence's time. Some urologists today recommend frequent ejaculation, either by sexual activity with a partner or by masturbation, to maintain healthy functioning of the prostate gland and the male urogenital system. See, for example, I. Yavascaoglu, B. Oktay, U. Simsek, and M. Ozyurt, "Role of Ejaculation in the Treatment of Chronic Non-Bacterial Prostatitis," *International Journal of Urology* 6, no. 3 (March 1999): 130–34.

Notes to Chapter 8

1. D. H. Lawrence, "The Rocking-Horse Winner," in *The Woman Who Rode Away and Other Stories,* eds. Mehl and Jansohn, 230.

2. Selma Fraiberg, "Tales of the Discovery of the Secret Treasure," *The Psychoanalytic Study of the Child* 9 (1954): 240.

3. Selma Fraiberg, "Two Modern Incest Heroes," *Partisan Review* 28 (1961): 650.

4. Janice Hubbard Harris, *The Short Fiction of D. H. Lawrence* (New Brunswick, N.J.: Rutgers University Press, 1984), 225.

5. W. D. Snodgrass (1958), "A Rocking Horse: The Symbol, the Pattern, the Way to Live," *Hudson Review* 11 (summer 1958): 191–200, rpt. in *D. H. Lawrence: A Collection of Critical Essays,* ed. Mark Spilka (Englewood Cliffs, N.J.: Prentice-Hall, 1963), 122.

6. James G. Hepburn, "Disarming and Uncanny Visions: Freud's 'The Uncanny' with Regard to Form and Content in Stories by Sherwood Anderson and D. H. Lawrence," *Literature and Psychology* 9 (winter 1959): 9–12.

7. Neil D. Isaacs, "The Autoerotic Metaphor in Joyce, Sterne, Lawrence, Stevens, and Whitman," *Literature and Psychology* 15 (spring 1965): 92–106.

8. W. S. Marks III, "The Psychology of The Uncanny in Lawrence's 'The Rocking-Horse Winner,'" *Modern Fiction Studies* 11, no. 4 (1965–1966): 384.

9. Norman N. Holland, *The Dynamics of Literary Response* (New York: Oxford University Press, 1968), 257.

10. Turner, "The Perversion of Play," 250–51.

11. Barbara Greenfield, "In Support of Psychoanalyzing Literary Characters," *Journal of the American Academy of Psychoanalysis* 12, no. 1 (1984): 127–38.

12. Cynthia R. Pfeffer, "In Remembrance of Things Past: Prospects for the Future," *Understanding and Preventing Suicide: Plenary Papers of the First Combined Meeting of the AAS and IASP,* ed. Ronald Maris (New York: Guilford Press, 1988), 127–38.

13. Norman Kiell, "'Ay, there's the Rub': Masturbation in Literature," *Masturbation: From Infancy to Senescence,* ed. Irwin M. Marcus and John J. Francis (New York: International Universities Press, 1975), 469.

14. Ben Stoltzfus, "D. H. Lawrence: 'The Rocking-Horse Winner,'" *Lacan and Literature: Purloined Pretexts* (Albany: State University of New York Press, 1996), 38–39.

15. Kohut, *Restoration of the Self,* 109.

16. F. Lawrence, (1934), *"Not I, But the Wind,"* 56.

17. Worthen, *D. H. Lawrence: The Early Years,* 500–503.

18. D. H. Lawrence, *The Letters of D. H. Lawrence,* vol. II: *June 1913–October 1916,* eds. George J. Zytaruk and James T. Boulton (Cambridge: Cambridge University Press, 1981), 655.

19. Ruderman, *D. H. Lawrence and the Devouring Mother,* 8–9.

20. Kohut, *How Does Analysis Cure?* 505–6.

21. Heinz Kohut and Ernest S. Wolf, "The Disorders of the Self and Their Treatment: An Outline," *International Journal of Psycho-Analysis* 59 (1978): 418.

22. I am indebted to psychoanalyst Burton R. Hutto, M.D., for his suggestion that in the climactic scene, Paul suddenly recognizes his mother as the oedipal object of his heretofore unconscious masturbatory fantasy (personal communication).

23. I am indebted to my wife, Judith R. Cowan, M.D., a psychiatrist, for her contribution in this understanding and retracing of Paul's growing disintegration anxiety, culminating in his fragmentation and death.

Notes to Chapter 9

1. Pinto and Roberts identify *wowser* (from the *Oxford English Dictionary*) as an Australian slang word meaning "Puritanical enthusiast or fanatic," "one who wants to compel

everybody else . . . to do whatever he thinks right, and abstain from everything he thinks wrong" (*Complete Poems,* 1046). The earliest manuscript version of this poem recorded by Lindeth Vasey is the holograph manuscript, then entitled "An old acquaintance," which Lawrence sent to Charles Wilson on 28 December 1928. See Vasey, "A Checklist of the Manuscripts of D. H. Lawrence," in Sagar, *D. H. Lawrence: A Calendar of His Works,* 241–42.

2. Robert Lucas says that Frieda revealed "that towards the end of 1926 [Lawrence] had become sexually impotent" (238). Richard Aldington says that *Lady Chatterley's Lover* was "a case of 'sex in the head' . . . (such as he was always denouncing in others), since there is every reason to suppose that when he wrote the book he was already virtually if not completely impotent" (335).

3. For Lawrence's comments that you cannot dispel the view of sex as a "dirty little secret" by "being wise and scientific about it like Dr. Marie Stopes," see D. H. Lawrence, "Pornography and Obscenity," in *Phoenix,* 182. For his even more satirical comments on the Freudian interpretation of sexual repression, inhibition, sexual complexes, and "incest craving," see D. H. Lawrence, *Psychoanalysis and the Unconscious,* 5–7.

4. The date of onset is difficult to establish. Lawrence's early marital concern about simultaneous orgasm indicates that he was not sexually dysfunctional at that time. Cecil Gray's statement that in the Cornwall period (1916–1918), "It might not be true to say that Lawrence was literally and absolutely impotent . . . but I am certain that he was not very far removed from it" (138) cannot be taken at face value, since Gray, who was one of Frieda's probable lovers, was hardly an objective commentator.

5. Britton, *"Lady Chatterley": The Making of the Novel,* 45.

6. Ober, "Lady Chatterley's What?" 108.

7. I do not think that the failure of Lawrence's alleged sex-in-the-head encounter with Dorothy Brett, to whom he was not attracted sexually, proves anything, and I believe that his so-called latent homosexuality derived from nonsexual self psychological issues rather than from a "repressed primary sexual preference for men." Otherwise, Britton's discussion of Lawrence's sexual dysfunction, both in medical terms and with reference to *Lady Chatterley's Lover,* seems to me among the best available on the subject. Literary dimensions of Lawrence's experience are perceptively explored by Mark Spilka in "Lawrence versus Peeperkorn on Abdication, or *What Happens to a Pagan Vitalist When the Juice Runs Out?*" in *D. H. Lawrence: The Man Who Lived,* ed. Robert B. Partlow Jr. and Harry T. Moore (Carbondale: Southern Illinois University Press, 1980), 105–20.

8. Eric Wittkower, *A Psychiatrist Looks at Tuberculosis* (London: National Association for the Prevention of Tuberculosis, Tavistock House North, 1949), 24.

9. Kaplan, *The New Sex Therapy,* 256.

10. D. H. Lawrence, "The State of Funk," 568.

11. According to Frieda Lawrence's biographer, Robert Lucas, the Lawrences rented the Villa Bernarda in Spotorno, Italy (19 November 1925 to 20 April 1926), from Angelo Ravagli, an officer in the *bersaglieri* stationed in Gradisca. Ravagli had become Frieda's lover by 1928 when she visited him in Trieste, possibly earlier, and ultimately became her third husband, 31 October 1950 (Lucas, 218, 242, 279). For an informative discussion of the matter, see Raymond T. Caffrey, "D. H. Lawrence's Impotence and Frieda Lawrence's Affair with Angelo Ravagli: Fact and Tradition," *Journal of the D. H. Lawrence Society* (Nottingham), (1998): 96–121.

12. Richard Aldington, *Portrait of a Genius, But . . . (The Life of D. H. Lawrence, 1885–1930)* (London: William Heinemann, 1950), 337.

198   Notes

13. Kohut's concept of the *selfobject* is defined as "one's subjective experience of another person who provides a sustaining function to the self within the relationship, evoking and maintaining the self and the experience of selfhood by his or her presence or activity." See Moore and Fine, *Psychoanalytic Terms and Concepts,* 178. For Kohut's discussion of *disintegration anxiety* as the anticipated breakup of the self, see Kohut, *How Does Analysis Cure?* 16–19.

14. Lois Palken Rudnick discusses Luhan's poem in *Mabel Dodge Luhan: New Woman, New Worlds* (Albuquerque: University of New Mexico Press, 1984), 195–96. Luhan's poem "Change" was published in *Palms* 2, no. 5 (1923). Lawrence's poem "Change of Life," published posthumously in *Fire and Other Poems,* is reprinted in *Complete Poems,* 766–71.

15. D. H. Lawrence, *The Letters of D. H. Lawrence,* vol. VI: *March 1927–November 1928,* eds. James T. Boulton and Margaret H. Boulton, with Gerald M. Lacy. (Cambridge: Cambridge University Press, 1991), 58.

16. D. H. Lawrence, *The Letters of D. H. Lawrence,* vol. VII: *November 1928–February 1930,* eds. Keith Sagar and James T. Boulton (Cambridge: Cambridge University Press, 1993), 605.

17. A. Morales, J. P. Heaton, and Culley C. Carson III, "Andropause, A Misnomer for a True Clinical Entity," *Journal of Urology* 163, no. 3 (March 2000): 705–12.

18. H. Sternbach, "Age-associated Testosterone Decline in Men: Clinical Issues for Psychiatry," *American Journal of Psychiatry* 155, no. 10 (October 1998): 1310–18.

19. In an interview with Sam Julty, Harold Lear, a professor in the Human Sexuality Program, Mount Sinai School of Medicine, New York, sees the distinction between physical and psychological etiology in sexual dysfunction as an "artificial dichotomy." He cites the example "that when men are under great stress their testosterone level changes and they lose their libido. . . . Conversely, we also know that if a man is impotent for physical reasons, it certainly has psychological implications." Qtd. in Sam Julty, *Male Sexual Performance* (New York: Grosset and Dunlap, 1975), 262.

20. Michael Squires, *The Creation of "Lady Chatterley's Lover"* (Baltimore, Md.: Johns Hopkins University Press, 1983), 64, 68, 71.

21. See Kate Millett, *Sexual Politics* (Garden City, N.Y.: Doubleday and Co., 1970), 238–40. For a balanced view of how various women have seen the novel, see Lydia Blanchard, "Women Look at *Lady Chatterley:* Feminine Views of the Novel," *D. H. Lawrence Review* 11 (fall 1978): 246–59. Charles Rossman, "'You are the call and I am the answer': D. H. Lawrence and Women," *D. H. Lawrence Review* 8 (fall 1975): 255–328, persuasively modifies Millett's reading, with special insight on *Lady Chatterley's Lover* (306–16). Carol Dix, in *D. H. Lawrence and Women* (Totowa, N.J.: Rowman and Littlefield, 1980) refutes what she sees as Millett's "misreading" of *Lady Chatterley's Lover* and her "misrepresentation" of Lawrence's ideas on sexuality and women (81–92). Peter Balbert, in *D. H. Lawrence and the Phallic Imagination: Essays on Sexual Identity and Feminist Misreading* (New York: St. Martin's Press, 1989), gives a more detailed refutation of the feminist ideological reading of Lawrence, including *Lady Chatterley's Lover* (133–87). Finally, Carol Siegel, in *Lawrence among the Women: Wavering Boundaries in Women's Literary Tradition* (Charlottesville: University Press of Virginia, 1991), challenges what has become the standard representation of Lawrence in feminist criticism and places his work firmly within the women's literary tradition.

22. Zilbergeld, *Male Sexuality,* 27–28, 67–68. See also Zilbergeld's expansion of his themes and materials in *The New Male Sexuality* (New York: Bantam Books, 1992), esp. 57, 98–99. Bernie Zilbergeld, Ph.D., formerly head of the Men's Program and codirector

of Clinical Training of the Human Sexuality Program, University of California, San Francisco, entered private practice in San Francisco and Oakland. It is precisely the "element of adolescent fantasy" in Lawrence that critic Anne Smith challenges in "A New Adam and a New Eve—Lawrence and Women: A Biographical Overview," *Lawrence and Women*, ed. Anne Smith (London: Vision Press, 1978), 45.

23. This passage is discussed astutely in literary terms by Mark Kinkead-Weekes, in "Eros and Metaphor: Sexual Relationship in the Fiction of Lawrence," in Smith, *Lawrence and Women,* 115–16.

24. Mark Spilka, "Lawrence's Hostility to Wilful Women: The Chatterley Solution," in Smith, *Lawrence and Women,* 205.

25. For an informed discussion by a Jungian analyst of the archetype of phallos (i.e., the erect phallus) in sacral tradition, see Eugene Monick, *Phallos: Sacred Image of the Masculine.* See also two earlier studies: Knight, *A Discourse on the Worship of Priapus,* and Wright, *The Worship of the Generative Powers.*

26. Wayne Burns, *Journey Through the Dark Woods* (Seattle: Howe Street Press, 1982), 182.

27. See two articles by Giles S. Brindley: "Sexual and Reproductive Problems of Paraplegic Men," *Oxford Reviews of Reproductive Biology* 8 (1986): 214–22; and "Pilot Experiments on the Actions of Drugs Injected into the Human Corpus Cavernosum Penis," *British Journal of Pharmacology* 87 (March 1986): 495–500; and an article coauthored by G. S. Brindley, D. Sauerwein, and W. F. Hendry: "Hypogastric Plexus Stimulators for Obtaining Semen from Paraplegic Men," *British Journal of Urology* 64, no. 1 (July 1989): 72–77. Giles S. Brindley was a physiologist in the Institute of Psychiatry, London.

28. For an authoritative review of available drug treatment options for erectile dysfunction at the beginning of the twenty-first century, see Tom F. Lue, "Drug Therapy: Erectile Dysfunction," *New England Journal of Medicine* 342, no. 24 (15 June 2000): 1802–13. An authoritative medical text on the etiology and all forms of treatment for erectile dysfunction is *Textbook of Erectile Dysfunction,* eds. Culley C. Carson III, Roger S. Kirby, and Irwin Goldstein (Oxford: Isis Medical Media; Herndon, VA: Books International, 1999). For a very readable account by a sixty-seven-year-old man of his own successful treatment for erectile dysfunction, see Robert Stock, "How One Man Confronted and Conquered Impotence," *New York Times,* 6 February 1997.

29. See [Paul Fleming], "Lack of Sexual Desire in Men," *Sex Over Forty* 5 (March 1987): 1–4: "In a survey done at the University of Pittsburgh, 35 percent of women and 16 percent of men reported inhibited sexual desire" (p. 1). The term refers not simply to the normal physical slowing in sexual response in the aging process but to loss of interest in sex. In *Sex Over Forty* 4 (October 1986) a similar article examines loss of sexual desire in women.

30. Sandra Gilbert, "D. H. Lawrence's Uncommon Prayers," *D. H. Lawrence: The Man Who Lived,* eds. Robert B. Partlow Jr. and Harry T. Moore (Carbondale: Southern Illinois University Press, 1980), 78.

31. Sandra Gilbert, *Acts of Attention: The Poems of D. H. Lawrence* (Ithaca, N.Y.: Cornell University Press, 1972), 257.

32. Peter C. Whybrow, Hagop S. Akiskal, and William T. McKinney Jr., *Mood Disorders: Toward a New Psychobiology* (New York: Plenum Press, 1984), 16–17.

33. Qtd. in Julty, *Male Sexual Performance,* 271.

34. William H. Masters and Virginia E. Johnson, *Human Sexual Inadequacy* (Boston: Little Brown, 1970), 159.

35. D. H. Lawrence, *The Plumed Serpent,* 422.

36. For Lawrence's insightful discussion of "counterfeit emotion," see "A Propos of *Lady Chatterley's Lover*," in *Lady Chatterley's Lover*, 411–14.

37. D. H. Lawrence, *The Escaped Cock*, ed. Gerald M. Lacy (Los Angeles: Black Sparrow Press, 1973), 57.

Notes to Chapter 10

1. D. W. Winnicott, *Human Nature* (New York: Schocken Books, 1988), 87.

2. D. W. Winnicott, *Collected Papers: Through Paediatrics to Psycho-Analysis* (London: Tavistock Publications, 1958), 129–44, especially 132–35.

3. Fred Pine, *Drive, Ego, Object and Self: A Synthesis for Clinical Work* (New York: Basic Books, 1990), 10.

4. Winnicott, *Collected Papers*, 303.

5. D. W. Winnicott, *Home Is Where We Start From: Essays by a Psychoanalyst*, comp. Clare Winnicott, Ray Shepherd, and Madeline Davis (New York and London: W. W. Norton and Co., 1986), 61–62.

6. Winnicott, quoted. in Anne Clancier and Jeannine Kalmanovitch, *Winnicott and Paradox from Birth to Creation* (London and New York: Tavistock Publications, 1987), 103.

7. D. H. Lawrence, *St. Mawr and Other Stories*, ed. Brian Finney (Cambridge: Cambridge University Press, 1983), 92.

8. Cited in David Ellis, *D. H. Lawrence: Dying Game* (Cambridge: Cambridge University Press, 1998), 520.

9. Gail Porter Mandell, *The Phoenix Paradox: A Study of Renewal Through Change in the "Collected Poems" and "Last Poems" of D. H. Lawrence* (Carbondale and Edwardsville: Southern Illinois University Press, 1984), 3.

10. Aldous Huxley, "Introduction," *Letters of D. H. Lawrence*, ed. Huxley (New York: Viking Press, 1932, rpt. 1936), xv.

11. Quoted in Ibid., x.

12. Baruch Hochman, *Another Ego: The Changing View of the Self and Society in the Work of D. H. Lawrence* (Columbia: University of South Carolina Press, 1970), 188.

13. D. W. Winnicott, "Ego Distortion in Terms of True and False Self" (1960). *The Maturational Processes and the Facilitating Environment* (New York: International Universities Press; London: Hogarth Press and the Institute of Psycho-Analysis, 1965), 142. Hereafter cited in the text as *Maturational Processes*.

14. Burness E. Moore and Bernard D. Fine, eds. *Psychoanalytic Terms and Concepts* (New Haven, Conn., and London: The American Psychoanalytic Association and Yale University Press, 1990), 209.

15. Ibid., 209.

16. James Davidson, Review of Simon Goldhill, *Foucault's Virginity. London Review of Books* (October 1995).

17. Keith Sagar, "Which 'Ship of Death'?" *D. H. Lawrence Review* 19, no. 2 (1987): 181.

18. Ibid., 184.

19. Ginette Katz-Roy, "The Process of Rotary Image-Thought in D. H. Lawrence's *Last Poems*," *Études Lawrenciennes* 7 (1992): 129.

20. See Ellen MacLeod Mahon, "Behind the Dancing: D. H. Lawrence's 'Apocalypse' and 'Last Poems,'" *Dissertation Abstracts International*, 49, no. 09A (1988): 2669.

21. Moore and Fine, *Psychoanalytic Terms and Concepts,* 210.

22. J. Laplanche and J.-B. Pontalis. *The Language of Psychoanalysis,* trans. Donald Nicholson-Smith. (New York and London: W. W. Norton & Co., 1973), 488.

23. *Frieda Lawrence: The Memoirs and Correspondence,* ed. E. W. Tedlock, Jr. (New York: Alfred A. Knopf, 1964), 235.

24. Frieda Lawrence, qtd. in Lois P. Rudnick, "D. H. Lawrence's New World Heroine, Mabel Dodge Luhan," *D. H. Lawrence Review* 14, no. 1 (Spring 1981): 108.

25. Erik Erikson, *Identity and the Life Cycle* (New York: International Universities Press, 1959), 98.

Bibliography

Works by D. H. Lawrence

Aaron's Rod. Ed. Mara Kalnins. Cambridge: Cambridge University Press, 1988.

Apocalypse and the Writings on Revelation. Ed. Mara Kalnins. Cambridge: Cambridge University Press, 1980.

The Complete Poems of D. H. Lawrence. Eds. Vivian de Sola Pinto and F. Warren Roberts. New York: Viking Press, Compass Book, 1971.

Eight Letters by D. H. Lawrence to Rachel Annand Taylor. Foreword by Majl Ewing. Pasadena, Calif.: Grant Dahlstrom at the Castle Press, 1956.

The Escaped Cock. Ed. Gerald M. Lacy. Los Angeles: Black Sparrow Press, 1973.

"Fantasia of the Unconscious," in *Psychoanalysis and the Unconscious* and *Fantasia of the Unconscious.* Introduction by Philip Rieff. New York: Viking Press, Compass Books, 1960.

"Foreword to *Collected Poems*" (1928). Rpt. in *The Complete Poems of D. H. Lawrence,* eds. Vivian de Sola Pinto and F. Warren Roberts, 849–52. New York: Viking Press, 1971.

"Introduction to These Paintings." *Phoenix: The Posthumous Papers of D. H. Lawrence* (1936). Ed. Edward D. McDonald, 551–84. New York: Viking, 1968.

John Thomas and Lady Jane. New York: Viking Press, 1972.

Kangaroo. Ed. Bruce Steele. Cambridge: Cambridge University Press, 1994.

Lady Chatterley's Lover, A Propos of "Lady Chatterley's Lover." Ed. Michael Squires. Cambridge: Cambridge University Press, 1993.

Last Poems. Eds. Richard Aldington and Giuseppe Orioli. Florence: Giuseppe Orioli, 1932.

The Letters of D. H. Lawrence. Ed. and with an introduction by Aldous Huxley. 3rd printing. New York: Viking Press, 1932, rpt. 1936. [Cited as *Letters,* ed. Huxley]

The Letters of D. H. Lawrence, Vol. I: *September 1901–May 1913.* Ed. James T. Boulton. Cambridge: Cambridge University Press, 1979. [Cited as *Letters* 1, followed by page numbers.]

The Letters of D. H. Lawrence, Vol. II: *June 1913–October 1916.* Eds. George J. Zytaruk and James T. Boulton. Cambridge: Cambridge University Press, 1981. [Cited as *Letters* 2, followed by page numbers.]

The Letters of D. H. Lawrence, Vol. III: *October 1916–June 1921.* Eds. James T. Boulton and Andrew Robertson. Cambridge: Cambridge University Press, 1981. [Cited as *Letters* 3, followed by page numbers.]

The Letters of D. H. Lawrence, Vol. IV: *June 1921–March 1924.* Eds. Warren Roberts, James T. Boulton, and Elizabeth Mansfield. Cambridge: Cambridge University Press, 1987. [Cited as *Letters* 4, followed by page numbers.]

The Letters of D. H. Lawrence, Vol. V: *March 1924–March 1927.* Eds. James T. Boulton and Lindeth Vasey. Cambridge: Cambridge University Press, 1989. [Cited as *Letters* 5, followed by page numbers.]

The Letters of D. H. Lawrence, Vol. VI: *March 1927–November 1928.* Eds. James T. Boulton and Margaret H. Boulton, with Gerald M. Lacy. Cambridge: Cambridge University Press, 1991. [Cited as *Letters* 6, followed by page numbers.]

The Letters of D. H. Lawrence, Vol. VII: *November 1928–February 1930.* Eds. Keith Sagar and James T. Boulton. Cambridge: Cambridge University Press, 1993. [Cited as *Letters* 7, followed by page numbers.]

Love Poems and Others. New York: Mitchell Kennerley, 1915.

"'Man is essentially a soul . . . ,'" *Reflections on the Death of a Porcupine and Other Essays.* Ed. Michael Herbert, 389–90. Cambridge: Cambridge University Press, 1988.

Mr. Noon. Ed. Lindeth Vasey. Cambridge: Cambridge University Press, 1984.

Phoenix: The Posthumous Papers of D. H. Lawrence (1936). Ed. Edward D. McDonald. New York: Viking, 1968.

Phoenix II: Uncollected, Unpublished, and Other Prose Works by D. H. Lawrence. Eds. Warren Roberts and Harry T. Moore, 217–20. New York: Viking Press, 1968.

The Plumed Serpent. Ed. L. D. Clark. Cambridge: Cambridge University Press, 1987.

"Pornography and Obscenity," *Phoenix: The Posthumous Papers of D. H. Lawrence* (1936). Ed. Edward D. McDonald, 170–87. New York: Viking, 1968.

Psychoanalysis and the Unconscious. New York: Thomas Seltzer, 1921.

Psychoanalysis and the Unconscious and *Fantasia of the Unconscious.* Introduction by Philip Rieff. New York: Viking, 1960.

"Rachel Annand Taylor." *Young Lorenzo: Early Life of D. H. Lawrence Containing Hitherto Unpublished Letters, Articles and Reproductions of Pictures,* by Ada Lawrence and G. Stuart Gelder, 249–68. Florence: Giuseppe Orioli, 1931. Rpt. in *Phoenix II: Uncollected, Unpublished, and Other Prose Works by D. H. Lawrence,* eds. Warren Roberts and Harry T. Moore, 217–20. New York: Viking Press, 1968.

The Rainbow. Ed. and with an introduction by Mark Kinkead-Weekes. Cambridge: Cambridge University Press, 1989.

Reflections on the Death of a Porcupine and Other Essays. Ed. Michael Herbert. Cambridge: Cambridge University Press, 1988.

St. Mawr and Other Stories. Ed. Brian Finney. Cambridge: Cambridge University Press, 1983.

Sons and Lovers (1913). Ed. and with an introduction and notes by Keith Sagar. Harmondsworth, Middlesex, England: Penguin Books; New York: Viking Penguin, 1981, rpt. 1986.

Sons and Lovers (1992). Eds. Helen Baron and Carl Baron. Cambridge: Cambridge University Press, 1992.

Sons and Lovers: A Facsimile of the Manuscript. Ed. and with an introduction by Mark Schorer. Berkeley: University of California Press, 1977.

"The State of Funk." *Phoenix II: Uncollected, Unpublished, and Other Prose Works by D. H. Lawrence,* eds. Warren Roberts and Harry T. Moore, 565–70. New York: Viking, 1968.

Studies in Classic American Literature. New York: Viking Press, 1961 [1923], rpt. 1966.

Study of Thomas Hardy and Other Essays. Ed. Bruce Steele. Cambridge: Cambridge University Press, 1985.

The White Peacock. Ed. Andrew Robertson. Cambridge: Cambridge University Press, 1983.

The Woman Who Rode Away and Other Stories. London: Martin Secker, 1928, rpt. 1930.

The Woman Who Rode Away and Other Stories. Eds. Dieter Mehl and Christa Jansohn. Cambridge: Cambridge University Press, 1995.

Women in Love. Eds. David Farmer, Lindeth Vasey, and John Worthen. Cambridge: Cambridge University Press, 1987.

Commentaries on D. H. Lawrence and His Work, and Other Secondary Sources

Alcorn, Marshall W., Jr. *Narcissism and the Literary Libido: Rhetoric, Text and Subjectivity.* New York: New York University Press, 1993.

Aldington, Richard. *Portrait of a Genius, But . . . (The Life of D. H. Lawrence, 1885–1930).* London: William Heinemann, 1950.

Apter, T. E. "Let's Hear What the Male Chauvinist is Saying: *The Plumed Serpent.*" *Lawrence and Women,* ed. Anne Smith, 156–77. London: Vision Press; Totowa, N.J.: Barnes and Noble, 1978.

Balbert, Peter. *D. H. Lawrence and the Phallic Imagination: Essays on Sexual Identity and Feminist Misreading.* New York: St. Martin's Press, 1989.

Berman, Jeffrey. "Echoes of Rejection in *Sons and Lovers.*" *Narcissism and the Novel.* New York: New York University Press, 1990.

Black, Michael. *D. H. Lawrence: The Early Fiction, A Commentary.* Cambridge: Cambridge University Press, 1986.

Blanchard, Lydia. "Women Look at *Lady Chatterley:* Feminine Views of the Novel." *D. H. Lawrence Review* 11 (fall 1978): 246–59.

Boadella, David. *The Spiral Flame: A Study in the Meaning of D. H. Lawrence.* Nottingham: Ritter, 1956. Rpt. in *Paunch,* nos. 50–51 (December 1977): 1–144.

Bragan, Kenneth. "D. H. Lawrence and Self Psychology." *Australian and New Zealand Journal of Psychiatry* 20, no. 1 (1986): 56–62.

Britton, Derek. *Lady Chatterley: The Making of the Novel.* London: Unwin Hyman, 1988.

Burns, Wayne. *Journey Through the Dark Woods.* Seattle: Howe Street Press, 1982.

Caffrey, Raymond T. "D. H. Lawrence's Impotence and Frieda Lawrence's Affair with Angelo Ravagli: Fact and Tradition." *Journal of the D. H. Lawrence Society* (Nottingham), 1998: 96–121.

Chambers, Jessie [pseud. E. T.]. (1935), *D. H. Lawrence: A Personal Record.* New York: Knight Publications, 1936.

————. *The Collected Letters of Jessie Chambers.* Ed. and with an introduction by George J. Zytaruk, with illustrations by Jack Bronson. Pub. as *D. H. Lawrence Review* 12, nos. 1–2 (spring–summer 1979): iii–xxxiii, 1–238.

Clayton, John J. *Gestures of Healing: Anxiety and the Modern Novel.* Amherst: University of Massachusetts Press, 1991.

Daleski, H. M. "Aphrodite of the Foam and *The Ladybird* Tales." *Unities: Studies in the English Novel.* Athens: University of Georgia Press, 1985.

Davidson, James. Review of Simon Goldhill, *Foucault's Virginity. London Review of Books* (October 1995).

Davis, Murray S. *Smut: Erotic Reality/Obscene Ideology.* Chicago: University of Chicago Press, 1983.

Delany, Paul. *D. H. Lawrence's Nightmare: The Writer and His Circle in the Years of the Great War.* New York: Basic Books, 1978.

Delavenay, Emile. *D. H. Lawrence: The Man and His Work, The Formative Years, 1885–1919.* Trans. Katharine M. Delavenay. Carbondale: Southern Illinois University Press, 1972.

Dervin, Daniel. *A "Strange Sapience": The Creative Imagination of D. H. Lawrence.* Amherst: University of Massachusetts Press, 1984.

———. "Michael Balint's Contribution to the Psychoanalysis of Literature." *Psychoanalytic Review* (1979–1980).

Dix, Carol. *D. H. Lawrence and Women.* Totowa, N.J.: Rowman and Littlefield, 1980.

Donaldson, George. "'Men in Love'? D. H. Lawrence, Rupert Birkin, and Gerald Crich." *D. H. Lawrence: Centenary Essays,* ed. Mara Kalnins, 41–67. Bristol, U.K.: Bristol Classical Press, 1986.

Dougherty, Jay. "'Vein of Fire': Relationships among Lawrence's *Pansies.*" *D. H. Lawrence Review* 16 (summer 1983): 165–81.

Eagleton, Sandra. "One Feminist's Approach to Teaching D. H. Lawrence." *D. H. Lawrence Review* 19 (fall 1987): 326.

Efron, Arthur. *Life-Energy Reading: Wilhelm Reich and Literature. Paunch,* nos. 67–68 (1997).

———. "The Mind-Body Problem in Lawrence, Pepper, and Reich." *Journal of Mind and Behavior* 1 (fall 1980): 247–70.

———. *The Sexual Body: An Interdisciplinary Perspective. Journal of Mind and Behavior* 6, nos. 1–2 (winter-spring 1985).

Ellis, David. "D. H. Lawrence and the Female Body." *Essays in Criticism* 46, no. 2 (April 1996): 136–52.

———. *D. H. Lawrence, Dying Game 1922–1930.* Cambridge: Cambridge University Press, 1998.

Gamache, Lawrence B., ed., with Phyllis Sternberg Perrakis, assoc. ed. *D. H. Lawrence: The Cosmic Adventure.* Nepean, Ontario, Canada: Borealis Press, 1996.

Gilbert, Sandra M. *Acts of Attention: The Poems of D. H. Lawrence.* Ithaca, N.Y.: Cornell University Press, 1972.

———. "D. H. Lawrence's Uncommon Prayers." *D. H. Lawrence: The Man Who Lived,* eds. Robert B. Partlow Jr. and Harry T. Moore, 73–93. Carbondale: Southern Illinois University Press, 1980.

Goodheart, Eugene. *Desire and Its Discontents.* New York: Columbia University Press, 1991.

Gray, Cecil. *Musical Chairs, or Between Two Stools.* London: Home and Van Thal, 1948.

Gross, Otto, and Frieda Weekley. *The Otto Gross-Frieda Weekley Correspondence.* Transcribed, translated, and annotated, by John Turner, with Cornelia Rumpf-Worthen and Ruth Jenkins. *D. H. Lawrence Review* 22, no. 2 (summer 1990): 137–227. [Letters are printed in both original German and English translation.]

Guest, Barbara. *Herself Defined: The Poet H.D. and Her World.* New York: Quill, 1984.

Gutierrez, Donald. *Subject-Object Relations in Wordsworth and Lawrence.* Ann Arbor, Mich.: UMI Research Press [Studies in Modern Literature no. 65], 1987.

Harris, Janice Hubbard. *The Short Fiction of D. H. Lawrence.* New Brunswick, N.J.: Rutgers University Press, 1984.

Hemingway, Ernest. *The Sun Also Rises.* New York: Charles Scribner's Sons, 1954.

Hepburn, James G. "Disarming and Uncanny Visions: Freud's 'The Uncanny' with Regard to Form and Content in Stories by Sherwood Anderson and D. H. Lawrence." *Literature and Psychology* 9 (winter 1959): 9–12.

Hochman, Baruch. *Another Ego: The Changing View of the Self and Society in the Work of D. H. Lawrence.* Columbia: University of South Carolina Press, 1970.

Hoffman, Frederic J. "Lawrence's Quarrel with Freud." *Freudianism and the Literary Mind,* 2d ed., 151–176. Baton Rouge: Louisiana State University Press, 1957.

Holbrook, David. "The Fiery Hill—*Lady Chatterley's Lover,*" *The Quest for Love,* 192–333. University: University of Alabama Press, 1965.

————. *Where D. H. Lawrence Was Wrong about Women.* Lewisburg, Pa.: Bucknell University Press, 1992.

Holland, Norman N. *The Dynamics of Literary Response.* New York: Oxford University Press, 1968.

Hollington, Michael. "Simultaneous Orgasm and Other Temporal Aspects of *Lady Chatterley's Lover* and Other Late Writings of D. H. Lawrence." *Études Lawrenciennes* no. 12 (1995): 169–87.

Howe, Marguerite Beede. *The Art of the Self in D. H. Lawrence.* Athens: Ohio University Press, 1977.

Hyde, H. Montgomery, ed. *The "Lady Chatterley's Lover" Trial (Regina v. Penguin Books Limited).* London: Bodley Head, 1990.

Ian, Marcia. *Remembering the Phallic Mother: Psychoanalysis, Modernism and the Fetish.* Ithaca, N.Y.: Cornell University Press, 1993.

Ingersoll, Earl G. *D. H. Lawrence, Desire, and Narrative.* Gainesville: University Press of Florida, 2001.

Isaacs, Neil D. "The Autoerotic Metaphor in Joyce, Sterne, Lawrence, Stevens, and Whitman." *Literature and Psychology* 15 (spring 1965): 92–106.

Jarrett-Kerr, Father Martin [pseud. Father William Tiverton]. *D. H. Lawrence and Human Existence.* London: Rockliff, 1951.

Jewinski, Ed. "The Phallus in D. H. Lawrence and Jacques Lacan." *D. H. Lawrence Review* 21, no. 1 (spring 1989): 7–24.

Jones, James H. *Alfred C. Kinsey: A Public/Private Life.* New York: W. W. Norton, 1997.

Katz-Roy, Ginette. "The Process of Rotary Image-Thought in D. H. Lawrence's *Last Poems.*" *Études Lawrenciennes* no. 7 (1992): 129–38.

Kiell, Norman. "'Ay, there's the Rub': Masturbation in Literature." *Masturbation: From Infancy to Senescence,* eds. Irwin M. Marcus and John J. Francis, 459–91. New York: International Universities Press, 1975.

Kinkead-Weekes, Mark. *D. H. Lawrence: Triumph to Exile 1912–1922.* Cambridge: Cambridge University Press, 1996.

————. "Eros and Metaphor: Sexual Relationship in the Fiction of Lawrence." *Lawrence and Women,* ed. Anne Smith, 101–21. London: Vision Press, 1978.

Knight, Richard Payne. *A Discourse on the Worship of Priapus* (1786); together with Thomas Wright, *The Worship of the Generative Powers during the Middle Ages of Western Europe* (1866); reprinted respectively as vols. 1 and 2 of *Sexual Symbolism: A History of Phallic Worship,* with original plates and with an introduction by Ashley Montagu. New York: Julian Press, 1957.

Kuttner, Alfred Booth. "Report and Letter on 'The Wedding Ring'" (10 November 1914). Appendix III in *The Rainbow,* by D. H. Lawrence, ed. Mark Kinkead-Weekes,

483–85. Cambridge: Cambridge University Press, 1989.

———. "*Sons and Lovers:* A Freudian Appreciation." *Psychoanalytic Review* 3, no. 3 (July 1916): 295–317. Rpt. in *D. H. Lawrence and "Sons and Lovers": Sources and Criticism,* ed. E. W. Tedlock Jr., 76–100. New York: New York University Press, 1965. [Cited in the Tedlock collection.]

Laird, Holly A. *Self and Sequence: The Poetry of D. H. Lawrence.* Charlottesville: University Press of Virginia, 1988.

Lawrence, Frieda. *Frieda Lawrence and Her Circle: Letters from, to and about Frieda Lawrence.* Ed. H. T. Moore and D. B. Montague. Hamden, Conn.: Archon Books, 1981.

———. *Frieda Lawrence: The Memoirs and Correspondence.* Ed. E. W. Tedlock Jr. New York: Alfred A. Knopf, 1964.

———. (1934), *"Not I, But the Wind . . ."* Afterword by Harry T. Moore. Carbondale: Southern Illinois University Press, 1974.

Litvinov, Ivy Low. "A Visit to D. H. Lawrence." *Harper's Bazaar* (October 1946): 411–18. Rpt. in *D. H. Lawrence: A Composite Biography,* vol. 1: *1895–1919,* ed. Edward Nehls, 215–22. Madison: University of Wisconsin Press, 1957. [Cited as Litvinov, in Nehls 1.]

Lucas, Robert. *Frieda Lawrence: The Story of Frieda von Richthofen and D. H. Lawrence.* Trans. Geoffrey Skelton. New York: Viking Press, 1973.

Mackenzie, Compton. *My Life and Times, Octave Five: 1915–1923.* London: Chatto and Windus, 1966.

Mahon, Ellen MacLeod. "Behind the Dancing: D. H. Lawrence's 'Apocalypse' and 'Last Poems." Ph.D. diss., Fordham University, 1998. Abstract in *Dissertation Abstracts International* 49, no. 09A (1988): 2669.

Mandell, Gail Porter. *The Phoenix Paradox: A Study of Renewal through Change in the "Collected Poems" and "Last Poems" of D. H. Lawrence.* Carbondale: Southern Illinois University Press, 1984.

Marcus, Steven. *The Other Victorians: A Study of Sexuality and Pornography in Mid-Nineteenth-Century England.* New York: Basic Books, 1964, rpt. 1966.

Marks, W. S., III. "The Psychology of The Uncanny in Lawrence's 'The Rocking-Horse Winner.'" *Modern Fiction Studies* 11, no. 4 (1965–1966): 381–92.

Marshall, Tom. *The Psychic Mariner: A Reading of the Poems of D. H. Lawrence.* New York: Viking Press, 1970.

Meyers, Jeffrey. *D. H. Lawrence: A Biography.* New York: Alfred A. Knopf, 1990.

———. *Homosexuality and Literature: 1880–1930.* Montreal: McGill-Queen's University Press, 1977.

Millett, Kate. *Sexual Politics.* Garden City, N.Y.: Doubleday and Co., 1970.

Monick, Eugene. *Phallos: Sacred Image of the Masculine.* Toronto: Inner City Books, 1987.

Moore, Harry T. "D. H. Lawrence and the 'Censor-Morons.'" *D. H. Lawrence, Sex, Literature and Censorship,* ed. Harry T. Moore, 9–32. New York: Twayne Publishers, 1953.

———. (1954), *The Priest of Love: A Life of D. H. Lawrence.* Rev. ed. New York: Farrar, Straus, and Giroux, 1974.

Murfin, Ross C. *The Poetry of D. H. Lawrences: Texts and Contexts.* Lincoln: University of Nebraska Press, 1983.

Murry, John Middleton. *Son of Woman: The Story of D. H. Lawrence.* London: Jonathan Cape, 1931.

————. *Reminiscences of D. H. Lawrence*. London: Jonathan Cape, 1933.

My Secret Life. New York: Grove Press, 1966.

Nehls, Edward, ed. *D. H. Lawrence: A Composite Biography,* 3 vols. Madison: University of Wisconsin Press, 1957, 1958, 1959.

Nelson, Jane A. "The Familial Isotopy in The Fox," 129–42. *The Challenge of D. H. Lawrence,* eds. Michael Squires and Keith Cushman. Madison: University of Wisconsin Press, 1990.

Neville, G. H. *A Memoir of D. H. Lawrence (The Betrayal)*. Ed. Carl Baron. Cambridge: Cambridge University Press, 1981.

Nixon, Cornelia. *Lawrence's Leadership Politics and the Turn against Women*. Berkeley: University of California Press, 1986.

Ober, William B. "Lady Chatterley's What?" *Boswell's Clap and Other Essays: Medical Analyses of Literary Men's Afflictions,* 89–117. Carbondale: Southern Illinois University Press, 1979.

Pfeffer, Cynthia R. (1988), "In Remembrance of Things Past: Prospects for the Future." *Understanding and Preventing Suicide: Plenary Papers of the First Combined Meeting of the AAS and IASP,* ed. Ronald Maris, 127–38. New York: Guilford Press, 1988.

Rembar, Charles. *The End of Obscenity: The Trials of "Lady Chatterley," "Tropic of Cancer," and "Fanny Hill."* New York: Random House, 1968.

Rieff, Philip. "Introduction," vii–xxiii. vii–xxiii *Psychoanalysis and the Unconscious* and *Fantasia of the Unconscious,* by D. H. Lawrence. New York: Viking Press.

————. "The Therapeutic as Mythmaker: Lawrence's True Christian Philosophy." *The Triumph of the Therapeutic: Uses of Faith After Freud,* 189–231. New York: Harper and Row, 1966.

Ross, Charles L. (1980), "Homoerotic Feeling in *Women in Love:* Lawrence's 'struggle for verbal consciousness' in the Manuscripts." *D. H. Lawrence: The Man Who Lived,* eds. Robert B. Partlow Jr. and Harry T. Moore, 168–82. Carbondale: Southern Illinois University Press, 1980.

Ross, Michael L. "Lawrence's Second 'Sun,'" *D. H. Lawrence Review* 8, no. 1 (spring 1975): 15–18.

Rossman, Charles. "'You are the call and I am the answer': D. H. Lawrence and Women." *D. H. Lawrence Review* 8 (fall 1975): 255–328.

Ruderman, Judith. *D. H. Lawrence and the Devouring Mother: The Search for a Patriarchal Ideal of Leadership*. Durham, N.C.: Duke University Press, 1984.

Rudnick, Lois Palken. "D. H. Lawrence's New World Heroine, Mabel Dodge Luhan." *D. H. Lawrence Review* 14, no. 1 (spring 1981): 85–111.

————. *Mabel Dodge Luhan: New Woman, New Worlds*. Albuquerque: University of New Mexico Press, 1984.

Sagar, Keith M. *D. H. Lawrence: A Calendar of His Works, with a Checklist of the Manuscripts of D. H. Lawrence by Lindeth Vasey.* Austin: University of Texas Press, 1979.

————. "Which 'Ship of Death'?" *D. H. Lawrence Review* 19, no. 2 (summer 1987): 181–84.

Said, Edward. *Beginnings, Intention and Method*. New York: Basic Books, 1975.

Schapiro, Barbara Ann. *D. H. Lawrence and the Paradoxes of Psychic Life*. Albany: State University of New York Press, 1999.

————. "'The Dread and Repulsiveness of the Wild': D. H. Lawrence and Shame." *Scenes of Shame: Psychoanalysis, Shame, and Writing,* eds. Joseph Adamson and Hilary Clark, 147–66. Albany: State University of New York Press, 1999.

————. *Literature and the Relational Self.* New York: New York University Press, 1993.

Schneider, Daniel J. *D. H. Lawrence: The Artist as Psychologist.* Lawrence: University Press of Kansas, 1984.

Scholes, Robert. "Uncoding Mama: The Female Body as Text." *Semiotics and Interpretation.* New Haven, Conn.: Yale University Press, 1982.

Schorer, Mark. "Technique as Discovery," *Hudson Review* 1 (spring 1948): 67–87. Rpt. in Mark Schorer, *The World We Imagine: Selected Essays,* 3–23. New York: Farrar, Straus, Giroux, 1968. [Cited in the Schorer collection.]

Shakir, Evelyn. "'Secret Sin': Lawrence's Early Verse." *D. H. Lawrence Review* 8, no. 2 (1975): 155–75.

Siegel, Carol. *Lawrence among the Women: Wavering Boundaries in Women's Literary Traditions.* Charlottesville: University Press of Virginia, 1991.

Skinner, B. F. *Particulars of My Life.* New York: Alfred A. Knopf, 1976.

Smith, Anne. "A New Adam and a New Eve—Lawrence and Women: A Biographical Overview." *Lawrence and Women,* ed. Anne Smith, 9–48. London: Vision Press, 1978.

Snodgrass, W. D. "A Rocking-Horse: The Symbol, the Pattern, the Way to Live." *Hudson Review* 11 (summer 1958): 191–200. Rpt. *D. H. Lawrence: A Collection of Critical Essays,* ed. Mark Spilka, 117–26. Englewood Cliffs, N.J.: Prentice-Hall, 1963.

Spilka, Mark. "Lawrence and the Clitoris," in *The Challenge of D. H. Lawrence,* ed. Michael Squires and Keith Cushman, 176–86. Madison: University of Wisconsin Press, 1990), 184.

————. "Lawrence versus Peeperkorn on Abdication, or *What Happens to a Pagan Vitalist When the Juice Runs Out?*" *D. H. Lawrence: The Man Who Lived,* eds. Robert B. Partlow Jr. and Harry T. Moore, 105–20. Carbondale: Southern Illinois University Press, 1980.

————. "On Lawrence's Hostility to Wilful Women: The Chatterley Solution." *Lawrence and Women,* ed. Anne Smith, 189–211. London: Vision Press, 1978.

Squires, Michael. "Dickens, Lawrence, and the English Novel." *The Challenge of D. H. Lawrence,* eds. Michael Squires and Keith Cushman, 42–59. Madison: University of Wisconsin Press, 1990.

————. *The Creation of "Lady Chatterley's Lover."* Baltimore, Md.: Johns Hopkins University Press, 1983.

Stephen, Adrian. "The Science of the Unconscious." *The Nation and the Athenaeum,* 25 August 1923.

Stevens, C. J. *Lawrence at Tregerthen.* Troy, N.Y.: Whitston, 1988.

Stoehr, Taylor. "'Mentalized Sex' in D. H. Lawrence." *Novel: A Forum on Fiction* 8 (1975): 101–22.

Stoltzfus, Ben. "D. H. Lawrence: *The Escaped Cock*" and "D. H. Lawrence: 'The Rocking-Horse Winner.'" *Lacan and Literature: Purloined Pretexts,* 19–31 and 32–49; notes, 171–77, 177–82. Albany: State University of New York Press, 1996.

Storch, Margaret. *Sons and Adversaries: Women in William Blake and D. H. Lawrence.* Knoxville: University of Tennessee Press, 1991.

Swift, John N. "Repetition, Consummation, and This Eternal Unrelief." *The Challenge of D. H. Lawrence,* ed. Michael Squires and Keith Cushman, 121–28. Madison: University of Wisconsin Press, 1990.

Turner, John F. "The Capacity to Be Alone and Its Failure in D. H. Lawrence's 'The Man Who Loved Islands.'" *D. H. Lawrence Review* 16, no. 3 (fall 1983): 259–89.

———. "David Eder: Between Freud and Jung." *D. H. Lawrence Review* 27, nos. 2–3 (1997–98): 289–309.

———. "The Perversion of Play in D. H. Lawrence's 'The Rocking-Horse Winner.'" *D. H. Lawrence Review* 15, no. 3 (fall 1982): 249–70.

Turner, John F., with Rumpf-Worthen, Cornelia, and Jenkins, R., eds. "The Otto Gross-Frieda Weekley correspondence. transcribed, translated, and annotated." *D. H. Lawrence Review* 22, no. 2 (summer 1990): 137–227.

Vasey, Lindeth. "A Checklist of the Manuscripts of D. H. Lawrence." Keith Sagar, *D. H. Lawrence: A Calendar of His Works.* Austin: University of Texas Press, 1979.

Weiss, Daniel A. *Oedipus in Nottingham: D. H. Lawrence.* Seattle: University of Washington Press, 1962.

Worthen, John. *D. H. Lawrence: The Early Years, 1885–1912.* Cambridge: Cambridge University Press, 1991.

Psychoanalysis, Medicine, and Human Sexuality

Arlow, Jacob A. "Unconscious Fantasy," *Psychoanalysis: The Major Concepts,* eds. Burness E. Moore and Bernard D. Fine, 155–62. New Haven, Conn.: Yale University Press, 1995.

Atwood, G., and R. Stolorow. *Structures of Subjectivity: Explorations in Psychoanalytic Phenomenology.* Hillsdale, N.J.: Analytic Press, 1984.

Bacal, H. A., and K. M. Newman. *Theories of Object Relations: Bridges to Self Psychology.* New York: Columbia University Press, 1990.

Balint, Michael. *The Basic Fault: Therapeutic Aspects of Regression.* Evanston, Ill.: Northwestern University Press, 1979.

Benjamin, Jessica. "The Alienation of Desire: Women's Masochism and Ideal Love." *Psychoanalysis and Women,* ed. Judith L. Alpert, 113–37. Hillsdale, N.J.: Analytic Press, 1986.

———. *The Bonds of Love: Psychoanalysis, Feminism, and the Problem of Domination.* New York: Pantheon Books, 1988.

Blos, Peter. "The Second Individuation Process of Adolescence," *The Psychoanalytic Study of the Child* 22 (1967): 162–86.

Brecher, Ruth and Edward, eds. *An Analysis of "Human Sexual Response."* New York: Signet Books, 1966.

Brindley, Giles S. "Pilot Experiments on the Actions of Drugs Injected into the Human Corpus Cavernosum Penis," *British Journal of Pharmacology* 87 (March 1986): 495–500.

———. "Sexual and Reproductive Problems of Paraplegic Men," *Oxford Reviews of Reproductive Biology* 8 (1986): 214–22.

Burrow, Trigant. "The Genesis and Meaning of Homosexuality." *Psychoanalytic Review* (1917).

Carson, Culley C., III, Roger S. Kirby, and Irwin Goldstein, eds. *Textbook of Erectile Dysfunction.* Oxford: Isis Medical Media; Herndon, Va.: Distributed in U.S.A. by Books International, 1999.

Clancier, Anne, and Jeannine Kalmanovitch (1984). *Winnicott and Paradox from Birth to Creation.* Translated from the French by Alan Sheridan. Foreword by Prince Masud Khan. London and New York: Tavistock Publications, 1987.

Clower, Virginia Lawson. "Significance of Masturbation in Female Sexual Development and Function." Marcus and Francis, 107–43.

———. Lecture in *Adult Masturbation: Clinical Perspectives.* American Psychoanalytic Association (1979). Audiotape, cassette no. II, side 3.

Cooper, Arnold M. "On Metapsychology and Termination." *On Freud's "Analysis Terminable and Interminable",* ed. Joseph Sandler. New Haven, Conn.: Yale University Press, 1991.

Dunn, Marian E., and Jan E. Trost. "Male Multiple Orgasms: A Descriptive Study," *Archives of Sexual Behavior* 18 (October 1989): 377–87.

Erikson, Erik H. *Identity and the Life Cycle: Selected Papers. Psychological Issues* 1, no. 1 (1959): 1–171.

Fairbairn, W. Ronald D. *An Object-Relations Theory of the Personality.* New York: Basic Books, 1954.

———. "A Revised Psychopathology of the Psychoses and Psychoneuroses." *International Journal of Psycho-Analysis* 22 (1941): Parts 3–4: 250–79.

Ferber, Leon. "Beating Fantasies." Marcus and Francis, 205–22.

Ferenczi, Sándor. "Psychoanalysis of Sexual Habits" (1925). *The Theory and Technique of Psychoanalysis.* New York: Basic Books, 1926, rpt. 1960.

———. "On Onanism" (1912). *The Selected Papers of Sándor Ferenczi, M.D.,* Vol. I: *Sex in Psychoanalysis.* Trans. Ernest Jones. New York: Basic, 1950. 185–92.

[Fleming, Paul]. "Lack of Sexual Desire in Men." *Sex Over Forty* (newsletter, Carrboro, N.C.) 5, no. 10 (March 1987): 1–4.

Fraiberg, Selma. "Tales of the Discovery of the Secret Treasure." *The Psychoanalytic Study of the Child* 9 (1954): 218–41.

———. "Two Modern Incest Heroes." *Partisan Review* 28 (1961): 646–61.

Francis, John J., and Irwin M. Marcus. "Masturbation: A Developmental View." *Masturbation: From Infancy to Senescence,* 9–51. New York: International University Press, 1975.

Freud, Anna. *The Ego and the Mechanisms of Defence.* Trans. Cecil Baines. 4th impression. London: Hogarth Press and the Institute of Psycho-Analysis, 1954.

Freud, Sigmund. *The Complete Letters of Sigmund Freud to Wilhelm Fliess, 1887 to 1904.* Trans. and ed. Jeffrey Moussaieff Masson. Cambridge, Mass.: Harvard University Press, 1985.

———. "Foreword." *David Eder: Memoirs of a Modern Pioneer,* ed. J. B. Hobman, [9]. London: Victor Gollancz Ltd., 1945.

———. *Gesammelte Werke* (17 vols.). London: Imago Publishing Co., Ltd., 1941; rpt 1955.

———. *The Standard Edition of the Complete Psychological Works of Sigmund Freud* (24 vols.), translated under the general editorship of James Strachey, in collaboration with Anna Freud, assisted by Alix Strachey and Alan Tyson (London: Hogarth Press and the Institute of Psycho-Analysis, 1962, rpt. 1975). [Cited in the text as *SE* followed by volume and page numbers.]

Freud, Sigmund, and C. G. Jung. *The Freud/Jung Letters: The Correspondence between Sigmund Freud and C. G. Jung,* ed. William McGuire, trans. Ralph Manheim and R. F. C. Hull. Princeton, N.J.: Princeton University Press, 1974.

Freud, Sigmund, and Ernest Jones. *The Complete Correspondence of Sigmund Freud and Ernest Jones, 1908–1939,* ed. R. Andrew Paskauskas. Introduction by Riccardo Steiner. Cambridge, Mass.: The Belknap Press of Harvard University Press, 1993.

Giovannetti, Marcio de F. "The Scene and Its Reverse: Considerations on a Chain of Associations in Freud." *On Freud's "A Child Is Being Beaten,"* ed. Ethel Spector Person, 95–111. New Haven, Conn.: Yale University Press, 1997.

Glover, Edward. "Eder as Psychoanalyst." *David Eder: Memoirs of a Modern Pioneer,* ed. J. B. Hobman, 89–116. Foreword by Sigmund Freud. London: Victor Gollancz Ltd., 1945.

Greenacre, Phyllis. "Penis Awe and Its Relation to Penis Envy," *Drives, Affects, Behavior,* ed. R. M. Loewenstein, 176–90. New York: International Universities Press, 1953.

Greenberg, Jay R., and Stephen A. Mitchell. *Object Relations in Psychoanalytic Theory.* Cambridge, Mass.: Harvard University Press, 1983.

Greenfield, Barbara. "In Support of Psychoanalyzing Literary Characters." *Journal of the American Academy of Psychoanalysis* 12, no. 1 (1984): 127–38.

Groenendijk, Leendert F. "Masturbation and Neurasthenia: Freud and Stekel in Debate on the Harmful Effects of Autoerotism." *Journal of Psychology and Human Sexuality* 9, no. 1 (1997): 71–94.

Grosskurth, Phyllis. *Melanie Klein: Her World and Her Work.* New York: Alfred A. Knopf, 1986.

Guntrip, Harry. *Personality Structure and Human Interaction.* New York: International Universities Press, 1961.

Hanly, Charles M. T. "Applied Psychoanalysis." *Psychoanalysis: The Major Concepts,* eds. Burness E. Moore and Bernard D. Fine, 553–62. New Haven, Conn.: Yale University Press, 1995.

Hartmann, Heinz. *Ego Psychology and the Problem of Adaptation.* Trans. David Rapaport. New York: International Universities Press, 1959, 6th printing 1973.

———. *Essays on Ego Psychology.* New York: International Universities Press, 1964.

Hartmann, Heinz, Ernst Kris, and Rudolph Loewenstein. "Comments on the Formation of Ego Structure." *The Psychoanalytic Study of the Child* 2 (1946): 11–38.

Hull, J. W., and Lane, R. C. "Repetitive Dreams and the Central Masturbation Fantasy." *Psychoanalytic Review* 83, no. 5 (October 1996): 673–84.

Jones, Ernest. *Free Associations: Memories of a Psycho-Analyst.* New York: Basic Books, 1959.

———. *Hamlet and Oedipus.* New York: W. W. Norton, 1949; rpt. Garden City, N.Y.: Doubleday Anchor Books, 1955.

———. *Sigmund Freud: Life and Work,* 3 vols., rev. ed. London: Hogarth Press, 1974.

———. "Some Problems of Adolescence" (1922), *Papers on Psycho-Analysis.* 5th ed. London: Baillière, 1948.

Julty, Sam. *Male Sexual Performance.* New York: Grosset and Dunlap, 1975.

Jung, C. G. *Memories, Dreams, Reflections.* Ed. Aniela Jaffé, trans. Richard and Clara Winston. New York: Pantheon Books, 1963.

Kaplan, Helen Singer. *The New Sex Therapy: Active Treatment of Sexual Dysfunctions.* New York: A Brunner/Mazel Publication published in cooperation with Quadrangle/ *The New York Times* Book Co., 1974.

Kinsey, Alfred C., Wardell B. Pomeroy, and Clyde E. Martin. *Sexual Behavior in the Human Female.* Philadelphia: W. B. Saunders Co., 1950.

———. *Sexual Behavior in the Human Male.* Philadelphia: W. B. Saunders, 1948.

Kohut, Heinz. *The Analysis of the Self.* New York: International Universities Press, 1971, rpt. 1987.

———. *The Curve of Life: Correspondence of Heinz Kohut, 1923–1981,* ed. Geoffrey Cocks. Chicago: University of Chicago Press, 1992.

————. *How Does Analysis Cure?* ed. Arnold Goldberg with Paul Stepansky. Chicago: University of Chicago Press, 1984.

————. *The Restoration of the Self.* Madison, Conn.: International Universities Press, 1977, rpt. 1988.

————. "The Two Analyses of Mr. Z." *International Journal of Psychoanalysis* 60 (1979): 3–27.

Kohut, Heinz, and Wolf, Ernest S. (1978) "The Disorders of the Self and Their Treatment: An Outline." *International Journal of Psychoanalysis* 59 (1978): 413–25.

Lacan, Jacques. *Écrits: A Selection.* Trans. from the French by Alan Sheridan. New York: W. W. Norton, 1977.

Laplanche, J., and J. B. Pontalis. *The Language of Psychoanalysis.* Trans. Donald Nicholson-Smith. New York: W. W. Norton, 1973.

Laufer, Moses. "The Central Masturbation Fantasy, the Final Sexual Organization, and Adolescence." *The Psychoanalytic Study of the Child* 31 (1976): 297–316.

Laufer, Moses, and E. Laufer. [The central masturbation fantasy (interview, in French)]. *Psychiatrie de l'Enfant* 35, no. 1 (1992): 7–17.

Lax, R. F. "Some Roots of Persistent Homosexual Fantasy and the Quest for Father's Love: Conflicted Parental Identifications in a Male Patient: Fragment of an Analysis." *Psychoanalytic Review* 84, no. 6 (December 1997): 843–63.

Loewenstein, Rudolph M., Lottie M. Newman, Max Schur, and Albert J. Solnit, eds. *Psychoanalysis—A General Psychology: Essays in Honor of Heinz Hartmann.* New York: International Universities Press, 1966.

Lue, Tom F. "Drug Therapy: Erectile Dysfunction," *New England Journal of Medicine* 342, no. 24 (15 June 2000): 1802–13.

MacDonald, Robert H. "The Frightful Consequences of Onanism: Notes on the History of a Delusion." *Journal of the History of Ideas* 28 (1967): 423–31.

Mahler, Margaret S., Fred Pine, and Anni Bergman. *The Psychological Birth of the Human Infant: Symbiosis and Individuation.* New York: Basic Books, 1975.

Marcus, Irwin M., and John J. Francis, eds. *Masturbation: From Infancy to Senescence.* New York: International University Press, 1975.

Masters, William H., and Virginia E. Johnson. *Human Sexual Inadequacy.* Boston: Little Brown, 1970.

————. *Human Sexual Response.* Boston: Little Brown, 1966.

Meyer, Adolf, Smith Ely Jelliffe, and August Hoch. *Dementia Praecox: A Monograph.* Boston: Richard G. Badger, 1911.

Miller, Alice. "Poisonous Pedagogy." *For Your Own Good: Hidden Cruelty in Child-Rearing and the Roots of Violence.* Trans. Hildegarde and Hunter Hannum, 3–91. New York: Farrar, Straus, Giroux, 1984.

Mitchell, Stephen A. *Relational Concepts in Psychoanalysis: An Integration.* Cambridge, Mass.: Harvard University Press, 1988.

Moore, Burness E. "Narcissism," *Psychoanalysis: The Major Concepts,* eds. Burness E. Moore and Bernard D. Fine, 229–51. New Haven, Conn.: Yale University Press, 1995.

Moore, Burness E., and Bernard D. Fine, eds. *Psychoanalytic Terms and Concepts.* New Haven, Conn.: The American Psychoanalytic Association and Yale University Press, 1990.

————, eds. *Psycho-Analysis: The Major Concepts.* New Haven, Conn.: The American Psychoanalytic Association and Yale University Press, 1995.

Morales, A., J. P. Heaton, and Culley C. Carson III. "Andropause, A Misnomer for a True Clinical Entity." *Journal of Urology* 163, no. 3 (March 2000): 705–12. [See also comment in letter by R. Tan, "Re: Andropause: A Misnomer for a True clinical Entity," *Journal of Urology* 164, no. 4 (October 2000): 1319.]

Nagera, Humberto, and S. Baker, R. Edgcumbe, A. Holder, M. Laufer, D. Meers, K. Rees. *Basic Psychoanalytic Concepts on the Theory of Instincts.* New York: Basic Books, 1970.

Ovesey, Lionel. *Homosexuality and Pseudohomosexuality.* New York: Science House, 1969.

Pine, Fred. *Drive, Ego, Object, and Self: A Synthesis for Clinical Work.* New York: Basic Books, 1990.

———. "The Four Psychologies of Psychoanalysis and Their Place in Clinical Work." *Journal of the American Psychoanalytic Association* 36, no. 3 (1988): 571–96.

Psychoanalysis in English. John Gach Books, Catalog 164. Columbia, Md.: 1998.

Roazen, Paul. *Brother Animal: The Story of Freud and Tausk.* New York: Alfred A. Knopf, 1969.

Sandler, Joseph. "The Concept of the Representational World." *Psychoanalytic Study of the Child* 17 (1962): 128–45.

Sandler, Joseph, Ethel Spector Person, Peter Fonagy. "Introduction," ix–xx. *Freud's "On Narcissism: An Introduction".* New Haven, Conn.: Yale University Press, 1991, xi, xii–xiii.

Schonfeld, W. A., and G. W. Beebe. "Normal Growth and Variation in the Male Genitalia from Birth to Maturity." *Journal of Urology* 48 (1942): 759–77.

Silber, Sherman J. *The Male: From Infancy to Old Age.* New York: Charles Scribner's Sons, 1981.

Sklansky, Morris A. "The Pubescent Years: Eleven to Fourteen." *Latency, Adolescence, and Youth,* vol. 2 of *The Course of Life: Psychoanalytic Contributions Toward Understanding Personality Development,* eds. S. J. Greenspan and G. H. Pollock. Adelphi, Md.: National Institute of Mental Health, 1980.

Sparling, Joseph. "Penile Erections: Shape, Angle, and Length." *Journal of Sex and Marital Therapy* 23, no. 3 (fall 1997): 195–207.

Sternbach, H. "Age-associated Testosterone Decline in Men: Clinical Issues for Psychiatry." *American Journal of Psychiatry* 155, no. 10 (October 1998): 1310–18. [See also comments in *American Journal of Psychiatry* 157, no. 2 (February 2000): 307–8.]

Stock, Robert. "How One Man Confronted and Conquered Impotence." *New York Times,* 6 February 1997.

Tausk, Victor. "On Masturbation." Trans. William G. Niederland. *The Psychoanalytic Study of the Child* 6 (1951): 61–79.

Tyson, Phyllis, and Robert L. Tyson. *Psychoanalytic Theories of Development: An Integration.* New Haven, Conn.: Yale University Press, 1990.

Wanderer Z., and D. Radell. *How Big is Big? The Book of Sexual Measurements.* New York: Bell, 1982.

Wessells, Hunter, Tom F. Lue, and Jack W. McAninch, "Penile Length in the Flaccid and Erect States: Guidelines for Penile Augmentation." *Journal of Urology* 156, no. 3 (September 1996): 995–97.

Whipple, Beverly, Brent R. Myers, and Barry Komisaruk, "Male Multiple Ejaculatory Orgasms: A Case Study," *Journal of Sex Education and Therapy* 23, no. 2 (1998): 157–74.

Whybrow, Peter C., Hagop S. Akiskal, and William T. McKinney Jr. *Mood Disorders: Toward a New Psychobiology.* New York: Plenum Press, 1984.

Wiedeman, George H. "Sexuality." *Psychoanalysis: The Major Concepts,* eds. Burness E. Moore and Bernard Fine, 334–45. New Haven, Conn.: Yale University Press, 1995.

Winnicott, D. W. "The Capacity to Be Alone." *International Journal of Psychoanalysis* 39 (1957): 416–20.

———. *Collected Papers: Through Paediatrics to Psycho-Analysis.* London: Tavistock Publications, 1958.

———. *Home Is Where We Start From: Essays by a Psychoanalyst.* Compiled by Clare Winnicott, David Shepherd, Madeleine Davis. New York: W. W. Norton, 1986.

———. *Human Nature.* New York: Schocken Books, 1988.

———. "Ego Distortion in Terms of True and False Self" (1960). *The Maturational Processes and the Facilitating Environment.* New York: International Universities Press; London: Hogarth Press and the Institute of Psycho-Analysis, 1965, 140–52.

———. *Playing and Reality.* London and New York: Tavistock Publications, 1971, rpt. 1986.

Winter, Harold Charles. "An Examination of the Relationships between Penis Size and Body Image, Genital Image, and Perception of Sexual Competence in the Male." Ph.D. diss., New York University, 1989. Abstract in *Dissertation Abstracts International,* 50, no. 5A (1989): 1225.

Wittkower, Eric. *A Psychiatrist Looks at Tuberculosis.* London: National Association for the Prevention of Tuberculosis, Tavistock House North, 1949.

Wolf, Ernest. *Treating the Self: Elements of Clinical Self Psychology.* New York: Guilford Press, 1988.

Yavascaoglu, I, B. Oktay, U. Simsek, and M. Ozyurt. "Role of Ejaculation in the Treatment of Chronic Non-Bacterial Prostatitis." *International Journal of Urology* 6, no. 3 (March 1999): 130–34.

Zilbergeld, Bernie. *Male Sexuality: A Guide to Sexual Fulfillment.* Boston: Little, Brown, 1978.

———. *The New Male Sexuality.* New York: Bantam Books, 1992.

Index